Gesture Generation by Imitation:
From Human Behavior to Computer Character Animation

by

Michael Kipp

ISBN: 1-58112-255-1

DISSERTATION.COM

Boca Raton, Florida
USA • 2004

Gesture Generation by Imitation:
From Human Behavior to Computer Character Animation

Dissertation.com
Boca Raton, Florida
USA • 2004

ISBN: 1-58112-255-1

Gesture Generation by Imitation

From Human Behavior
to Computer Character Animation

by
Michael Kipp

Dissertation

Faculties of Natural Sciences and Technology
Saarland University

Saarbrucken 2003

To my parents

Abstract

In an effort to extend traditional human-computer interfaces research has introduced embodied agents to utilize the modalities of everyday human-human communication, like facial expression, gestures and body postures. However, giving computer agents a human-like body introduces new challenges. Since human users are very sensitive and critical concerning bodily behavior the agents must act naturally and individually in order to be believable.

This dissertation focuses on conversational gestures. It shows how to generate conversational gestures for an animated embodied agent based on annotated text input. The central idea is to *imitate* the gestural behavior of a human individual. Using TV show recordings as empirical data, gestural key parameters are extracted for the generation of natural and individual gestures. The gesture generation task is solved in three stages: observation, modeling and generation. For each stage, a software module was developed.

For observation, the video annotation research tool ANVIL was created. It allows the efficient transcription of gesture, speech and other modalities on multiple layers. ANVIL is application-independent by allowing users to define their own annotation schemes, it provides various import/export facilities and it is extensible via its plug-in interface. Therefore, the tool is suitable for a wide variety of research fields. For this work, selected clips of the TV talk show "Das Literarische Quartett" were transcribed and analyzed, arriving at a total of 1,056 gestures. For the modeling stage, the NOVALIS module was created to compute individual gesture profiles from these transcriptions with statistical methods. A gesture profile models the aspects handedness, timing and function of gestures for a single human individual using estimated conditional probabilities. The profiles are based on a shared lexicon of 68 gestures, assembled from the data. Finally, for generation, the NOVA generator was devised to create gestures based on gesture profiles in an overgenerate-and-filter approach. Annotated text input is processed in a graph-based representation in multiple stages where semantic data is added, the location of potential gestures is determined by heuristic rules, and gestures are added and filtered based on a gesture profile. NOVA outputs a linear, player-independent action script in XML.

Acknowledgements

I want to thank the DFG (German Research Foundation) for the two-year full scholarship that made this research possible, and also the associated "Graduate College for Cognitive Science".

Most of all, I thank Prof. Wolfgang Wahlster for his continual support during my time at Saarland University and at the DFKI (German Research Center for Artificial Intelligence), for accepting and encouraging this project, and for his intense supervision in the final stages of this work. I also want to thank Prof. Elisabeth André for helping me getting this project off the ground in the first year and for joining the doctoral committee.

I would also like to thank the DFKI for providing office, equipment and a creative research environment. Special thanks to the CrossTalk project team for the great spirit, inspiration and motivation. I am especially indebted to Dr. Norbert Reithinger and Prof. Thomas Rist for inviting me to work on various DFKI projects in my post-scholarship days.

Thanks to Prof. Marcel Reich-Ranicki, Prof. Hellmuth Karasek, and the ZDF broadcast company for giving their permission to publish the video stills used in this dissertation which were all taken from the TV show "Das Literarische Quartett".

Some individuals deserve special mention. Thanks to Martin Klesen and Ralf Engel for patiently annotating gestures, to Dr. Christian König and Dr. Kerstin Seiler for a decisive mid-thesis discussion, to Stefan Baumann and Dr. Jürgen Trouvain for personalized advise on Phonetics and to Patrick Gebhard for nerve-wrecking debates and continual life-saving technical support. I would also like to thank all ANVIL users who provided bug reports, suggestions and encouragement. Special thanks to Cornelia Messing for lightning speed proofreading.

Contents

Chapter 1

Introduction

> For some presumptuous reason, man feels the need to create something
> of his own that appears to be living, that has inner strength, a vitality,
> a separate identity – something that speaks out with authority – a cre-
> ation that gives the illusion of life.
>
> — Thomas and Johnston (1981: 13)

1.1   Computer Animated Characters

A new star has stepped onto the computer screen: the human body. Computer
animated characters have always populated computer games before establishing
themselves firmly in the movie industry in 1995 with *Toy Story*, the first completely computer animated feature film. Progress in computer graphics and character animation[1] refueled the ideas of early Artificial Intelligence (AI) to create
artificial humans. However, not as physically present robots but as virtual beings
living in a computer-generated graphical environment. While traditional AI research focused on the thought processes of human beings, now that virtual bodies
are possible another issue is coming to the foreground: communication. In terms
of communication, the human body has much more to offer than text or spoken
language. The research area of human-computer interaction (HCI) is concerned
with applying AI methods to make the complex software and hardware systems
of today more accessible to human users by offering interfaces that go beyond the
customary keyboard/mouse input and windows/text output[2]. The human body is
considered a potentially powerful interface where the hidden and overt channels of
everyday human-human communication can be exploited, such as gestures, facial

---

[1]cf. Witkin and Kass (1988), Badler et al. (1993) and Magnenat-Thalmann and Moccozet
(1998)

[2]The traditional computer interface is sometimes referred to as WIMP: windows, icons, mouse,
and pointer.

expression, gaze, posture and posture change. Such an interface consists of one or many human faces or bodies that interact with the human user. These computer animated characters are called anthropomorphic agents, embodied agents or life-like characters (Prendinger and Ishizuka, 2003, Cassell et al., 2000b). The term *avatar* refers to a special kind of embodied agents. An avatar is a puppet that is fully or partially controlled by the human user. It is meant to represent the user in a virtual space. Notwithstanding this specific meaning, the notion of avatar is sometimes used synonymously with embodied agent (Lindner 2003).

1.1.1   Embodied Agents Systems

Embodied agents are the focus of several research projects. The famous simulations of Marilyn Monroe and Humphrey Bogart in the short film *Rendez-vous in Montreal* by MIRALab in 1987 anticipated the task-oriented systems of today. Monroe was later put into an application for virtual tennis matches as a referee and to announce game results (Molet et al. 1999). This kind of task, information presentation, appears to be a natural application for embodied agents. For instance, in the PPP[3] system an anthropomorphic agent called *Persona* uses speech and gesture to explain technical devices (André et al. 1996). Pointing gestures are used to disambiguate references in speech and to focus user attention (see Figure 1.1). The Persona agent is animated by keyframe-based animation (Müller 2000). It relies on a library of animations in the form of keyframe sequences. The keyframes can be concatenated or merged to a single frame to give the illusion of continuous movement. The more sophisticated approach, called model-based animation, is based on an internal 3D bone model that is used to compute the animation's frames at runtime. Gestures are produced with the help of a library of pre-fabricated motion patterns that is accessed at runtime to animate the 3D model. An internal 3D model offers much more flexibility in animation. Pointing gestures and manipulative actions can be adapted to arbitrary situations, i.e. varying locations, shapes, dimensions of objects, people and places. Movements can be modified along various dimensions such as abruptness, smoothness, force etc. (Chi et al. 2000). Also, parallel motions can be merged in a single motion (e.g., a smile and a gesture) and sequential motions can be connected by smooth transitions (Perlin and Goldberg 1996). The *Virtual Human Presenter* (Noma and Badler 1997) is such a model-based system based on the *Jack* engine, a 3D character animation software that is controlled by a script of text and commands. Beyond libraries of predefined gestures, the feature-based animation approach aims at creating each new gesture on the fly from single form or motion features (Kopp and Wachsmuth 2000).

Presentation agents like Jack and PPP Persona can be used in arbitrary information systems, for instance to read the news, present tourist information or

---

[3]**P**ersonalized **P**lan-Based **P**resenter

report book reviews. They can also be used in e-commerce applications to advertise and sell products, or in e-learning environments to teach and supervise. Cassell et al. (2000a) developed REA[4], a 3D agent who presents houses to potential buyers. The agent coordinates gesture and speech with respect to both semantics and pragmatics. For instance, REA makes a circular gesture to semantically express "surrounding", and in terms of pragmatics she places gestures on *new* items in the speech stream. For another pragmatic function, signalling beginning and end of discourse segments, REA has been extended to utilize posture shifts (Cassell et al. 2001a).

 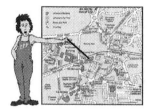

Figure 1.1: *Two applications of the PPP Persona system which automatically generates presentations, coordinating gesture and speech. On the left, Persona explains technical details of a modem. To the right, Persona acts as a city guide using a map of Portsmouth. Pointing gestures are used for focusing user attention on regions and for referencing concrete objects. (Taken from Müller, 2000.)*

While most presentation systems consists of a single embodied agent, André and Rist (2000) argued for a *team* of presentation agents to exploit the benefits of dialogue (see also Rist et al., 2003). Dialogue is livelier and easier to follow than monologue. Different agents can represent different viewpoints or degrees of expertise. This can even be used to manipulate the opinion of the listener. André et al. (2000) implemented this vision in a scenario called the Inhabited Marketplace where embodied customer and sales agents engage in an automatically generated dialogue about a product. The viewer is thus informed about the product's various properties. Selectable agent profiles of personality and interest guide the dialogue generation. Gaze behavior is used to focus the viewer's attention on the current speaker. The CrossTalk project is based on the same paradigm of team presentation (Gebhard et al. 2003). It is a self-explaining interactive system where a separate agent welcomes the user, explains the system and starts the actual presentation: a car sales dialogue. The agents use conversational gestures to make their interactions more life-like. Even if no user actively interacts with the systems the agents give

---

[4]**R**eal **E**state **A**gent

the impression of "living on" by engaging in smalltalk amongst themselves. This is to show that the system is permanently on stand-by, never to be turned off, never "freezing" or becoming inactive as electronic devices usually do. In the nonverbal behavior of the agents this is reflected in idle-time actions like scratching the forehead or blinking and breathing (Müller 2000). A similar idea is followed in the PEACH[5] project where continuous assistence is to be guaranteed in the form of a museum guide that jumps to different end devices, e.g., from a projected painting to a mobile palm top (Kruppa et al. 2003). The illusion of a continuous life is central to these systems and must be backed by believable nonverbal behavior by the agents.

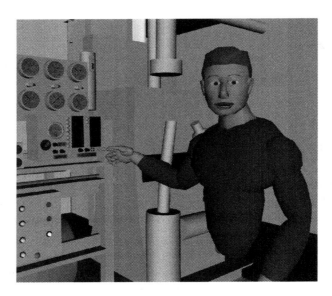

Figure 1.2: *The Steve agent describing an indicator light (figure taken from Rickel and Johnson, 1999). His pointing gestures help to resolve speech references to the currently explained object. Steve uses gaze behavior for pointing (looking at objects) and regulating the interaction with the user (looking at the user when expecting input).*

Besides the presentation of facts and products, agents can be employed in educational and training systems to convey knowledge and skills. Examples are Cosmo, who teaches how the Internet works (Lester et al. 1997c), and Herman the Bug,

---

[5]**P**ersonal **E**xperience with **A**ctive **C**ultural **H**eritage

a system to explain plants (Lester et al. 1999). The Steve[6] system was developed to accompany a human trainee in his/her hands-on experience of operating complex machinery in a virtual reality environment (Rickel and Johnson 1999). It interacts with the user by answering questions and demonstrating procedures. Steve uses pointing gestures to indicate the explained object and gaze behavior to show that Steve is listening to the user (Figure 1.2)[7]. Based on the Steve agent technology (Rickel et al. 2002), the Mission Rehearsal Exercise (MRE) project creates training simulations for a whole *team* of soldiers in a virtual reality theater with projections of 3D life-size embodied agents on a large curved screen with a 150 degree field of view (Swartout et al. 2001). MRE is supposed to prepare soldiers for critical situations on peacekeeping missions. For instance, faced with a wounded local inhabitant lying in the street next to his crying mother and with an urgent mission waiting somewhere else what decision must the platoon leader take? The system allows to realistically act out possible alternatives. Appropriate nonverbal behavior must be generated to recreate the social factors that lead to the above described stress situation. In a similarly immersive 3D environment, the VirtualHuman[8] project provides both a virtual teacher and a virtual student to give astronomy lessons to a human user (Figure 1.3). The teacher follows different paedagogical paradigms and behaves according to parametrized personality settings. The co-student extends the usual one-to-one (computer-human) setting to a classroom situation where students can help each other and compete with each other. Conversational gestures and facial expressions must be generated to make the experience as authentic as possible.

Complex applications like MRE and VirtualHuman demonstrate that embodied agents can inspire wholly new forms of interaction. Gottlieb (2002), co-creator of the highly popular computer game *You don't know Jack*, sees the potential of embodied agents in acting as guides, thus offering a new interaction style. It lies between a navigation-style communication (web-browser, newspaper) and a continually running show (TV, movie, lecture). The user can set his/her own *pacing* but the system controls the structure of the information which is important in educational scenarios. Pacing can be influenced by the agent's nonverbal behavior, for instance by yawning or tapping with one foot when the user pauses for too long.

To support the development of embodied agents applications, toolkits have been created that provide high-level scripting languages to control the agents. Examples are: Jack (Badler et al. 1993), IMPROV (Perlin and Goldberg 1996), Microsoft

---

[6]Steve is an acronym for **S**oar **T**raining **E**xpert for **V**irtual **E**nvironments. Soar is a general cognitive architecture for developing systems that exhibit intelligent behavior (Laird et al. 1987) and has been in use since 1983. For further information visit http://www.eecs.umich.edu/~soar/main.html

[7]Copyright by the University of Southern California

[8]http://www.virtual-human.org

Figure 1.3: *Screenshot detail of the 3D VirtualHuman system. The virtual student (left) listens to the virtual teacher (right). The teacher formulates a question that must be answered by virtual student or human user in direct competition.*

Agents and CharActor[9]. All tools are based on pre-fabricated motion patterns, some offering motion blending and online motion modifications with respect to form and tempo.

In summary, embodied agents are being developed for many application areas, including presentation/information, sales, assistance, education, training, and entertainment. They make possible new forms of interaction by bringing a new realism and social factors into computer applications.

1.1.2 Why Use a Body?

Using a body opens up new possibilities: broader and more efficient communication, expression of personality and emotion and the motivation resulting from the social presence of a life-like entity.

In terms of communication, hand and arm gestures play a major role in the body's communicative capabilities. Gestures can be used for pointing in order to resolve references to world objects, e.g. when asking "what's that?" while pointing to an expresso machine. The listener can resolve the anaphor "that" by following the pointing gesture. Gestures can also visually illustrate aspects of the message that are difficult to express verbally, e.g. by drawing the shape of an object into the air, by demonstrating a manual action or by recreating complex spatial arrangements with hands, fingers, arms. Consider the complex arrangements one would have to describe when retelling scenes from a Sylvester & Tweetie animation movie

---

[9]http://www.charamel.de

(see Figure 1.4 for examples from McNeill, 1992). With gestures both dynamic (speed, trajectory) and static (direction, distance, size) aspects can be expressed in a way that is simple to perform and quick to comprehend. In contrast to these highly context-dependent gestures that must be invented anew for each new situation there are gestures with standardized form and conventionalized meaning like the thumbs-up gesture, meaning "OK" or "good!", that can be used instead of speech where speaking is restricted by noise (construction site), convention (library) or taboo. Gesture can also be used to regulate a conversation, i.e. to assign, yield or claim the speaking turn using e.g. pointing or conventionalized signs like waving (Duncan and Fiske 1977). This is especially important since embodied agents systems strive to become more interactive and thus need to implement behavior that regulates agent-user as well as agent-agent dialogues. On the discourse level, gestures are used to segment the speech stream, to "highlight" parts of particular interest and to signify rhetorical relations (McNeill 1992). Politicians exploit such gestural devices to increase the intelligibility of their public speeches and even to control audience reactions like applause and laughter (Atkinson 1984). A major advantage of communication by gesture is that the signals are well-known to human users from everyday usage so that, when used in a computer interface, users do not have to learn new signs and behaviors.

Embodied agents have advantages beyond communication issues. With their social presence they can act as a guide, giving orientation, or as a trainer, demonstrating physical actions, but most importantly, they can motivate human users (Lester et al. 1997a). This motivation may stem from pure curiosity in the virtual "personality" or from the lowered technological barrier since human-agent interaction requires less expertise than interaction with traditional WIMP interfaces (McBreen 2001). For pedagogical applications, Lester et al. (1997a) conducted a formal empirical study suggesting that embodied agents can be pedagogically effective. Lester et al. (1997b) found that the students perceived the agent as being helpful, credible, and entertaining. McBreen (2001) and van Mulken et al. (1998) both found that an embodied agent makes an application more enjoyable and engaging but that user trust in the system is not necessarily enhanced. Reeves and Nass (1996) show how easily human users take technical equipment as living beings with a personality. They conducted two series of social-psychological experiments on social interaction, one with a human partner and one where this partner was substituted with a computer. Various aspects of human interaction were paralleled in human-computer interaction. For example, humans behaved politely when interacting with computers, they liked to be flattered by computers, and they judged computers that praised themselves lower than computers that praised other computers. Systems that aim at producing personality thus reinforce a natural tendency. However, while human users easily ascribe a personality to technical gadgets, they are at the same time highly sensitive to inconsistencies and

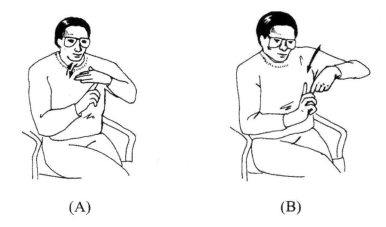

(A)   (B)

Figure 1.4: *Gestures of subjects retelling scenes from a Sylvester and Tweetie animation movie (drawings taken from McNeill, 1992). In (A) the speaker says: "he steps on the part where the street car's connecting". The gesture complements this by expressing aspects of direction and trajectory (lower hand) and shape (upper hand). In (B) the speaker says: "he swallows it". The gesture expresses relative locations, direction of movement and aspects of shape.*

mistakes in the agent's behavior (Nass et al., 2000, Paiva et al., 1999). A human body must always display a consistent picture of human behavior. The resulting challenge is to create *believability*.

1.1.3 Believability

Letting agents create an "illusion of life", making them *believable* and *like-life*, is a major goal of embodied agents research. Since DePaulo (1992: 234) found that it is impossible to regulate nonverbal behavior in such a way that no impression at all is conveyed, the agents' behavior must be carefully controlled to convey the intended impression. Speakers who actively suppress movement are perceived as being unexpressive, inhibited, withdrawn and uptight (DePaulo and Kirkendol 1989). Schaumburg (2001) found that designing an interface that takes advantage of the social bias of the user is difficult because users are easily annoyed by unsocial conduct.

Personality and emotions have been found to be key concepts to make an agent believable and can be used to guide speech and gesture generation. In speech, emotion was shown to correlate with intonation, tempo, intensity and voice quality (Schröder et al. 2001), and also personality has been shown to be marked in speech

(Scherer 1979). As far as the body is concerned, Ekman and Friesen (1975) claim that emotion is mainly expressed by the face[10]. However, other researchers found that gestures as well as postures say something about the speaker's emotional state, about his or her personality and status (Collier, 1985, Scheflen, 1964, Scherer et al., 1979). A number of popular science books exploit these insights to advise people on how to interpret and control "body language" (Fast, 1970, Molcho, 1983). As concerns posture, McGinley et al. (1975) showed that a speaker can achieve a higher degree of *opinion change* in his/her addressee when assuming an open posture as opposed to a closed one. In terms of status and liking, Mehrabian (1972) found evidence for two correlations: a more relaxed posture is perceived as low status, and a more *immediate* posture (forward lean, eye contact, body orientation) increases liking. In contrast to posture findings, the relation between gestures and emotion is still quite unexplored.

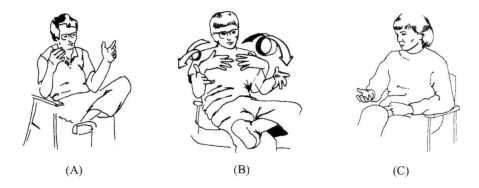

(A)   (B)   (C)

Figure 1.5: *Three instances of metaphoric gestures that frequently occur in normal conversation (drawings taken from McNeill, 1992). In (A) the speaker says: "it was a Sylvester and Tweety cartoon". The gesture indicates a substance held between the hands. The substance is taken as a metaphor for "cartoon". In (B) a circular gesture metaphorically illustrates a process or transition while the speaker says: "and now we get into the story proper". In (C) the speaker a variant of the gesture in (A). A virtual substance is presented on the open palm as a metaphor for something also expressed in speech.*

Most scenarios of embodied agents systems involve normal conversation with the user. Conversational gestures must not necessarily have an explicit function. McNeill (1992) explored a class of gestures he called *metaphorics* that illustrate the

---

[10]In fact, the correlation between emotions and facial expression is so strong that it works in both directions, that is not only does emotion affect the face but changing the facial expression affects the emotions, a phenomenon called *facial feedback* (Tomkins, 1962, Izard, 1990).

spoken content only via a metaphor as shown in Figure 1.5. According to Webb (1997), such gestures dominate most conversations, so automatically generating conversational gestures should become a research focus to let embodied agents act more life-like. Cassell and Thórisson (1999) show that users are more likely to consider agents life-like when they display *appropriate* nonverbal behavior. A small number of such gestures were integrated in a system by Cassell et al. (1994), using a functional approach (Figure 1.6)[11]. However, since these gestures' function is difficult to unearth and their benefits in terms of communication unclear, there should be an effort to implement a broad spectrum of conversational gestures in a shallow approach. Then, the generated gestures can not only be used to make a single agent believable but also, to make each agent acting in a team stand out as a distinct individual.

Figure 1.6: *In a functional approach the* Animated Conversation *system annotates utterances with how the content can be expressed in gesture, in this case: metaphorically. The agent says: "Will you help me get fifty dollars?". The open palms illustrate the readiness to receive a substance. This substance acts as a metaphor for the answer. (Figure taken from Cassell et al., 1994.)*

Making embodied agents believable still needs much interdisciplinary research (cf. Gratch et al., 2002). The research by Lee et al. (2002) shows how specialized yet important research topics for embodied agents have become. The authors implemented the simulation of saccadic eye movement based on empirical measure-

---

[11]Copyright by Justine Cassell, Northwestern University

ment with human subjects. An evaluation study showed that this added movement made the face look more natural, friendly and outgoing. In contrast, switching off eye movement led to attributions of lifelessness while random movement led to attributions of unstability. This demonstrates the task complexity of simulating humans: the blink of an eye may count as much as moving the whole body.

1.1.4 Multimodal Interfaces

In the past, research in HCI has primarily been concerned with understanding *input* from different modalities like keyboard, mouse, speech, gesture, touch or facial expression. Gestures were seen as a powerful modality to complement speech input for a more efficient human-computer communication. The Put-That-There system was one of the first systems that understood both speech and (pointing) gestures (Bolt 1980). The system used speech recognition and a 3D space sensing device to let the user manipulate virtual objects on a wall-sized display. The XTRA[12] system, designed as an interface to expert systems, allowed input by gesture and speech using empirical results from experiments on the functions of deixis (Wahlster 1991). The projects ICONIC (Koons et al. 1993), SGIM[13] (Latoschik et al. 1998) and IFP-GS[14] (Hofmann et al. 1998) added data gloves to recognize gestures. SignRec (Hienz et al. 1999), like IFP-GS a system for sign language recognition, relies on a video-based approach: subjects are fitted with colored marks that can be reliably located in image processing. Most of these approaches to gesture recognition[15] consist of three steps. First, the gesture must be segmented, i.e. it must be established where a single gesture starts and where it ends. Second, the gesture must be classified, i.e. in a list of predefined classes the current gesture must be assigned to one class. Third, the recognized gesture must be understood in conjunction with co-occurring speech input.

Whereas early multimodality research focused on *understanding* only, current research is pushing toward *symmetric* multimodality (Wahlster 2003). This means that not only input should be multimodal but that also output should be generated in multiple modalities (text, sound, diagrams, gesture, posture, facial expression). As part of the multimodal output, embodied conversational agents (ECA) are integrated in multimodality projects like SmartKom (Wahlster 2003). SmartKom is a mixed-initiative multimodal dialogue system with three applications as a communication, infotainment and mobile travel companion. The integrated embodied agent Smartakus uses speech, facial expression and gestures coordinated with graphical output to communicate with the user. How to coordinate speech and gesture thus

---

[12]e**X**pert **TRA**nslator

[13]**S**peech and **G**esture **I**nterfaces for **M**ultimedia

[14]Interdisziplinäres Forschungsprojekt "Gebärdenerkennung mit Sensorhandschuhen", German for: interdisciplinary research project "gestural sign recognition with sensory gloves"

[15]See Wachsmuth and Fröhlich (1998) for representative papers on gesture recognition.

becomes part of the more general question of how to coordinate different modalities. Since fully symmetric multimodal applications must process input as well as output representations, research strives for a single working representation that contains complex multimodal content as well as information about segmentation, synchronization and other processing data. In SmartKom this is called M3L[16] and can be thought of an interlingua for semantic and pragmatic aspects of a message.

A major and often neglected prerequisite for symmetric multimodal interfaces are empirical studies based on annotated corpora (Bunt et al. 2003). However, much is lacking in terms of software to aquire and manage the data as well as exchange of existing corpora. For the systematic study of nonverbal communication, body movements (arms, face, posture) must be recorded in actual communicative situations. While Efron (1941) had to rely on sketches and photographs, researchers have moved to VCRs and now, to digital video for their analysis (Loehr and Harper 2003). However, the move to digital video and computerized transcriptions is still in progress. Generic tools and standards of transcription are a matter of current research.

When human coders transcribe observed movements from video, they necessarily reduce the primary information in an interpretative process. For certain purposes more objective and exact methods are required. Therefore, some researchers work on the automated capturing of movement using image processing. Quek and McNeill (2000) developed a tool that computes hand position and head orientation from video frames. Grammer et al. (1997) point out the neglect of motion quality (speed, acceleration, spatial extension etc.) in behavior research and ascribe this deficit to the methods used. They developed a system of automatic movie analysis (AMA) where digitized video is analyzed using image filters. The motion energy detection (MED) works by computing the difference of a gray-scale video frame from the previous frame pixel by pixel. Alternatively, one could obtain exact data by using data gloves or other methods from motion capturing and gesture recognition.

1.2 Research Aims

The previous sections introduced embodied agents as a potentially beneficial interface between human and computer. However, to make these agents work the human user must perceive them as living beings without being distracted by unnatural gestural behavior. When a team of agents works together an additional requirement arises: that the agents display individual differences. Otherwise, the human user would perceive them as clones with identical gestural behavior. This is potentially distracting even if each single agent has believable behavior.

---

[16]**M**ulti**m**odal **M**arkup **L**anguage

1.2.1   Generation by Imitation

This dissertation deals with the problem of generating gestures for a team of computer-animated agents. The gestures must be believable, entertaining and individual. To generate gestures means to simulate an aspect of human behavior. The Oxford English Dictionary (OED) defines *to simulate* in the narrow sense as to "produce a computer model of (a process)" (Brown 1993). In Cognitive Science, simulations refer to *functional* simulations of cognitive processes that are created to test hypotheses on the original human processes. Other simulations recreate, according to the OED, "the conditions of (a situation or process), esp. for the purpose of training". For the gesture generation approach of this dissertation this definition of simulation appears to be too broad. Neither is the creation of a functional model of human gesture production nor that of a training environment simulation intended. Therefore, the more specific notion of *imitation* will be used here. The Chambers Science and Technology Dictionary gives the following definition (Walker 1991):

> **imitate** *(Behav.)*. Learning through the observation of another individual (model) which is accomplished without practice or direct experience.

This definition contains some important concepts. It emphasizes that imitation usually refers to human individuals. One *imitates* a specific person, whereas one *simulates* more generally a human being. For three reasons it makes sense to take a single, especially selected individual as the basis for modeling as opposed to relying on a population of subjects. First, in a team of agents each agent must display individual behavior to avoid creating behavioral clones which degrades the believability of the team. Second, for the target applications of presentation, sales, education etc. the agents should be more regarded like actors on a stage instead of simulated humans (André and Rist 2000), actors who perform for an audience: the user(s). Consequently, the agents should display a certain proficiency with gestures or, in other words, they must not display monotonous or distracting gestures. Such a proficiency can be ascertained by selecting experienced public performers. Third, instead of focusing on a few specimen that are functionally modeled, the aim is to arrive at a broad range of output gestures. The focus lies on creating a rich gestural base behavior that can be complemented by functionally modeled gestures where necessary.

The dictionary description of imitation also states that the method of imitation is pure observation without "direct experience". Technically, this can be translated to a corpus-based approach to generation in three phases. First, the behavior of the target must be observed. The observed behavior is strongly context-dependent and has many degrees of freedom. Therefore, in the second phase, the observed behavior must be generalized from its specific context and those parameters must be selected that are most significant for the behavior. The result of the second phase is a model of behavior, represented in individual *gesture profiles*. Finally, in order to reproduce the observed behavior the model must be applied in a generation algorithm to compute new behavior for a given text input. To sum up, the three phases of imitation are: observation, modeling and generation.

The natural final phase would be gesture rendering which is not realized in this work. Instead, rendering by concatenating pre-fabricated motion patterns is *assumed* as the targeted output. This means that the hypothetical rendering device would concatenate either prerecorded video clips or prefabricated model-based movement patterns. For model-based movement patterns that are rendered with a real-time player, some smoothing and contextual adaptations like motion blending can be performed. This approach is comparable to the *unit selection* approach in speech synthesis where pre-recorded speech segments are concatenated to generate utterances (Campbell 1996). Such systems currently dominate the speech synthesis market and the same can be said about gesture synthesis. Many agent systems, like the *Jack* agent (Noma and Badler 1997) or *REA* (Cassell 2000), rely on this approach. Such approaches make sense as gesture researchers have found conversational gestures, which are the gestures of primary interest here, to comply to standards of form (Webb, 1997). Other contexts generate more idiosyncratic gestures that can only be generated by triggering certain features that are synthesized online to form a gestural movement. Therefore, there are researchers specifically concerned with making gesture synthesis parametrizable, generating gesture from abstractly defined form features (Kopp and Wachsmuth 2000).

This work is primarily concerned with providing a work pipeline through the three phases. For each step in the pipeline one approach had to be found, not necessarily the optimal one, but one that offers plausible solutions for this particular step. Because of the many interdisciplinary influences in this research area, often only a *shallow* approach could be taken in order not to get stuck halfway through the pipeline. Finding optimal solutions for each step of the pipeline is an issue for future research.

1.2.2 Limitations

To define the objectives of one's work one also has to say what it is *not* about. The work stops short at the end of the gesture generation pipeline. It provides an output script but leaves open the graphical realization where new technical problems arise in the field of computer graphics and animation, e.g. the problem of modulation or co-articulation. Modulation relates to shortening or stretching movement phases in order to make them comply to synchronization constraints. Co-articulation refers to the problem of how to blend subsequent or overlapping gestures while preserving human movement characteristics. Model-based approaches have solved part of these problems already (Perlin and Goldberg, 1996, Badler et al., 1993).

Moreover, this work excludes emotions and movement qualities. Considering emotions would open up a whole new research field. The corpus-based approach would require decoding emotions from video using the time-consuming[17] FACS[18] annotation. This work focuses on how to identify and implement determinants that drive gesture generation. Emotions are taken to be orthogonal to most problems in this field and can be added later on. For the same reason, motion qualities are left aside. Since they appear to be closely related with emotions they should be studied in close connection with them. Also, this dissertation does not examine the cognitive processes underlying human gesturing, it does not provide a functional simulation of gesture production. Finally, although the results of the empirical investigation may turn out to be useful for gesture recognition, it is neither intended for this purpose nor does the resulting annotated corpus make any claim to be suitable for training automatic classifiers or other recognition devices.

1.2.3 Applications

The targeted application is a team of presentation agents that interact with each other and with a human user. This approach should ensure that gestures are automatically generated that are both natural and individual. While many systems have implemented gestures, they are usually generated to fulfill a function (pointing, illustration etc.). The conversational gestures used in this work are less intended to fulfill communicative functions but rather, to give the agent the rich gestural base behavior of the imitated human speaker. This could be used to complement existing systems that focus on functions to provide a certain gestural default behavior that is overridden for cases when actual communication must be performed by gesture. The large gesture lexicon assembled in this research has already been used in the projects CrossTalk and VirtualHuman. The European NECA[19] project is also relying on a subset of this repertoire.

Another area that has already profited from this work is video-based empirical behavior analysis and video corpus annotation. The video annotation tool ANVIL has been developed for gesture annotation and will be presented in Chapter 6. Its distribution as freeware has started in the year 2000 and it is used at research institutes around the world, in research fields of Computer Science, Linguistics, Gesture Research, Ethology, HCI, Psycholinguistics etc. Especially in the field of multimodal HCI much empirical groundwork remains to be done and standard corpora must be created. Applications like video browsing[20] will offer summarization,

---

[17]According to Ekman et al. (1988) it takes 100 min to encode 1 min of facial behavior.

[18]**F**acial **A**ction **C**oding **S**ystem (Ekman and Friesen 1978)

[19]**N**et **E**nvironment for Embodied Emotional **C**onversational **A**gents; see http://www.ai.univie.ac.at/NECA

[20]The AMI project will build on the well-known, speech-only ICSI Meeting Recorder Corpus (Janin et al. 2003) but will be video-based.

browsing and retrieval of information for a large corpus of videos. Such systems need training material to detect interesting regions in the video, e.g. *hot spots* where participants are highly involved in the discussion. Nonverbal cues like gestures and posture shifts can indicate the beginning or end of such regions of interest. Certain gestures used to emphasize words could be used for a guided search on the speech stream.

As mentioned in the previous section, gesture recognition is not a target application of this work. However, gesture recognition may benefit from the empirical research conducted here. The developed gesture annotation scheme and the annotated corpus may help in recognizing gestures on a high level, using this as a top-down input for segmentation, for instance. Vice versa, video-based gesture recognition could be integrated in the ANVIL video annotation tool to bootstrap manual annotation. Bootstrapping means that manually annotated data is used to train a recognizer which then automatically annotates another portion of the corpus. The automatically annotated part is corrected and then used to train the recognizer again and let it annotate yet another part of the corpus that must be corrected and so forth. ANVIL offers a plug-in interface that allows external developers to integrate bootstrapping modules.

Another area that might profit from this work is Robotics. The virtual realities where embodied agents reside may act as a testbed for the move back into the real world. Robots have gained new popularity with consumer electronics products like Sony's *Aibo*, a four-legged robot dog, and, more recently, with Honda's *Asimo*[21], a 1.20 meter sized humanoid machine that can walk on two legs. The robot Kismet, developed at MIT, was built to mimic the facial expressions of humans (Breazeal and Scassellati 1999) showing that Robotics has entered the arena of multimodal communication already. The Aibo robot dog is programmed to assume postures and perform gestures that express emotions like joy and sadness. For producing coordinated articulation through speech and gesture in robots, the results on gesture generation found for virtual agents will prove a useful resource.

To sum up, the research of this dissertation aims at providing agents with a rich gestural base behavior taken from an imitated human subject. The resulting generation system should be usable in many applications including other (functional) gesture generation systems that could complement this system. The empirical research tool ANVIL can be of use for empirical sciences studying behavior by video. The annotation scheme and annotated corpus could be interesting for theoretical and applied behavioral sciences as well as multimodality HCI studies including gesture recognition. The gesture repertoire collected from analyzing the corpus has already been used in various projects.

---

[21] **A**dvanced **S**tep in **I**nnovative **Mo**bility

1.3   Research Questions

In the following sections, for each of the three research phases of observation, modeling and generation the major research questions will be asked and appropriate methods will be proposed. Since each phase must be implemented the implementational issues have been generalized and are treated in a separate section.

1.3.1   Observation

When observing gestures one needs categories and methods to classify and transcribe nonverbal behavior. These methods must be collected from the literature. Then, in an approach to generate gestures by imitation it is vital to decide on *who* to imitate. This means finding suitable primary material to begin with. This will be tackled by devising a number of selection criteria and measuring them against potential data. For finding and testing these criteria methods from conversation analysis (CA) are borrowed (Weinrich 1992). Once the primary data is selected it must be transformed to digital video. Then, the next research objective is to transcribe speech and gesture. This actually translates to three subtasks. First, a suitable transcription software must either be found or developed if no such tool exists. Second, a coding scheme for speech and gesture must be devised and technically specified for the annotation tool. Finally, the video data must be transcribed according to the scheme. To assess the quality of the scheme as well as the transcription coding, coding reliability tests have to be made.

The transcription will be based on a lexicon of gestural lemmas which is part of the coding scheme. The creation of this lexicon must be supported by the research literature, i.e. existing gesture inventories and classifications. In summary, the following research questions must be answered:

- What primary data is suitable for generating gestures by imitation?

- What transcription methods exist in the field of gesture research?

- Does a video annotation tool suitable for this project exist? If not, how must a tool be designed to satisfy the requirements of this project?

- How must speech, gesture and posture shifts be transcribed to create an annotated corpus?

- Which gesture lemmas can be identified to build a gesture lexicon?

1.3.2   Modeling

A measure for the suitability of the lexicon from the previous phase is again a coding reliability test. To make the lexicon usable for a rendering using pre-fabricated motion patterns, the size has to be controlled. This can be done by selecting only the lemmas most frequently occurring in the original data. However, a coverage test must ensure that the selected lemmas still cover a sufficiently large part of the original data.

Based on the analysis results, individual models of nonverbal behavior, called *gesture profiles*, must be created that reflect the speaker's individual style. The methods used are the statistical linguistic methods of n-grams and maximum likelihood (Jelinek, 1990, Reithinger and Klesen, 1997). Similar concepts have been developed in Ethology under the name of *sequential analysis* (Bakeman and Gottman, 1986, Gottman and Roy, 1990). Moreover, transition matrices known from Psychology are used (van Hooff 1982). To sum up, the following research questions must be dealt with:

- Is there an upper bound to the size of the gesture lexicon?
- Which aspects of the transcribed information can be used to model individual gestural behavior?
- Which methods are appropriate for modeling individual gesture profiles?
- How does the final gesture profile look like?

1.3.3 Generation

First of all, existing gesture generation systems must be surveyed to extract current approaches to gesture generation. Then, an algorithm must be devised that generates gestures from annotated speech input. The algorithm must decide where to place which gesture and must fix parameters like handedness. It must do so using the data contained in the gesture profiles in conjunction with heuristic knowledge taken from the research literature. It should recreate the key parameters of the models, i.e. frequencies and probabilities. Finally, output must be produced that is readable by an agent animation engine, also called a *player*. In short, the following questions must be treated:

- What are the principal approaches to gesture generation in existing systems?
- What input structures are required for the generation process?
- Which gesture(s) can be selected for a given word or semantic concept?
- During which parts of the utterance can a gesture occur?
- How are parameters determined (e.g., handedness)?
- How are all aspects of the gesture profile considered (transition probabilities, frequencies), both local and global factors?
- How must the output be translated to a player-independent script?

1.3.4   Implementation

The main implementation objective is to build a single software platform that meets all annotation requirements, allows the computation of gesture models and implements the generation algorithm.

The central method is the layered-architecture approach from database technology which distinguishes the physical, logical and application levels of a system (Bird and Liberman 2001). Together with the object-oriented programming paradigm, these concepts make the system modular, thus reusable and extensible. The implementation language used should be Java to make the software platform-independent. To allow seamless integration of external programs a plug-in interface must be offered. For external representation of data XML should be used to make the system transparent and the stored data accessible to existing XML tools, e.g. for converting it to other formats.

To sum up, the research questions that guide the implementation are the following four:

- How can the architecture be organized in physical, logical and application layers?

- How can multi-layered annotations be visualized and accessed in an intuitive and effective graphical interface?

- How can the software guarantee extensibility?

- Which data exchange format should be used?

The evaluation of the software must first assess whether all tasks can successfully be performed with the tool: annotation, modeling (including analysis) and generation. The task of annotation is of general interest in the research community. Here a comparison with existing tools is a first step towards an evaluation. Also, standardization of data representation must be considered. Finally, the most essential aspect of annotation is the genericness of the tool. It guarantees that the tool can be used with various annotation schemes.

1.4   Dissertation Structure

The dissertation is organized in three parts. The first part, consisting of the next three chapters, establishes the necessary background knowledge for gesture generation. Chapter 2 starts with explaining fundamental gesture concepts and brings together relevant results from the gesture research literature. This is complemented by a chapter on methods, Chapter 3, where approaches to gesture transcription are investigated and appropriate software tools for video annotation are surveyed. Having thus covered the empirical side, Chapter 4 shifts to implemented embodied agents systems. Existing gesture generation approaches are analyzed and their underlying principles are presented.

The second part of the dissertation deals with the empirical phase of this work. It starts with Chapter 5, describing the criteria for selection the primary video material and how to technically prepare it for later annotation and analysis. The selected TV show *The Literary Quartet* (LQ) is introduced together with the two selected speakers Marcel Reich-Ranicki (MRR) and Hellmuth Karasek (HK). What follows is a treatment on the development of the ANVIL[22] system in Chapter 6. ANVIL is a generic video annotation tool, allowing the empirical investigation of video-recorded nonverbal behavior with an intuitive graphical interface. It also functions as an extensible research platform that integrates annotation, analysis and generation of gestures in a single software. The next chapter, Chapter 7, defines the first part of the task-specific coding scheme NOVACO[23], dealing with the annotation of speech. This scheme consists of words, parts-of-speech, theme/rheme and three discourse relations. The second part of the NOVACO scheme, dealing with how gestures are transcribed for the purpose of generation, is defined in Chapter 8. This part of the transcription is organized in terms of gesture structure (movement phases), classes, lemmas and the gestures' relation to speech. The application of the speech and gesture annotation schemes to transcribe the LQ corpus is described in Chapter 9. The annotated corpus is analyzed to reduce the number of gestures for generation and to find suitable concepts for the extraction of gesture profiles.

The third part of this work is concerned with generation. Chapter 10 shows how the NOVALIS[24] module extracts individual gesture profiles, one for each speaker, from the annotated corpus. These profiles contain a concept-to-gesture mapping and statistical models for timing, handedness, transitions and frequencies of gestures. The application of these profiles in the NOVA[25] generator, an implemented generation-by-imitation system, is then presented in Chapter 11. Input and working representations are described as well as the output action script CAML. Finally, the approach is compared with other generation systems.

The concluding Chapter 12 summarizes the major achievements of this work, reports on the impact of the findings and tools presented here and points to both open issues and future directions.

---

[22]**An**notation of **Vi**deo and Spoken **L**anguage
[23]**No**nverbal and **V**erbal **A**ction **Co**ding Scheme
[24]**No**nverbal **A**ction Analy**sis**
[25]**No**nverbal **A**ction Generator

Chapter 2

Conversational Gestures

The previous chapter introduced the motivation, aims and structure of this work, the major objective being the generation of conversational gestures. In preparation of this task, this chapter first clarifies the notion of *gesture*, relying on existing work in gesture research, before focusing on gestures in a conversational context. Various results from the research literature are reviewed and their implications for gesture generation examined.

Gesture research is a wide and multidisciplinary area so the material presented here follows a strict selection. The research field can be differentiated by research aim (analysis, recognition, generation), method (linguistic, psychological, engineering), examined conversational domain (storytelling, psychotherapy, talk-show) and observational conditions (laboratory, field data, TV recordings). The relevance of research results must be measured against these four aspects. In this work, the research aim is generation, the domain is conversation, the conditions are those of a recorded TV show, the methods come from multiple disciplines. All of the following treatments, apart from the most fundamental ideas presented in the first section, will have a close relation to this work in one of the four respects.

2.1 Kinds of Gesture

Although the term *gesture* can be used to refer to any kind of bodily movement, many researchers take it to denote non-manipulative hand/arm movements that occur during speech (McNeill, 1992: 1, Tuite, 1993: 84, Kendon, 1983: 13). This definition will be the one used throughout this work unless otherwise signified. Gestures are closely linked with the accompanying speech in terms of timing, meaning and communicative function. They can be grouped into six major categories or classes based on their principal functions. This classification is a useful tool when investigating gestures.

2.1.1 Gesture Classes

Gesture classifications have been proposed by various researchers. The six gesture classes used in this work go back to work by Efron (1941), Ekman and Friesen (1969), and McNeill (1992: 12–18, 75–77). The classes are: adaptors, emblems, deictics, iconics, metaphorics, and beats. In the following sections each class is described in detail. Figure 2.1 gives a concise overview of all six classes.

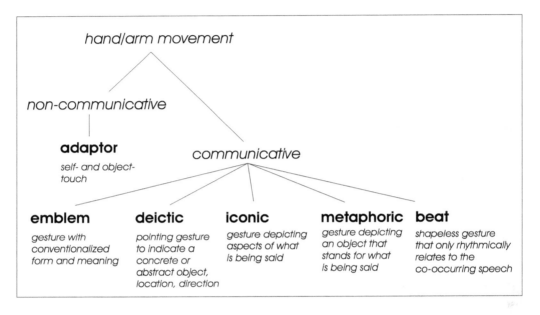

Figure 2.1: *The six gesture classes and their defining properties.*

Adaptors

Adaptors are non-communicative self- and object touches, like scratching one's ear lobe or fiddling with a pen, that are usually not considered part of the communication (Figure 2.2).

The introduction of adaptors goes back to Ekman and Friesen (1969) who believe that these movements "were first learned as part of adaptive efforts to satisfy self or bodily needs [...] or to develop or maintain prototypic interpersonal contacts". Then, during adulthood "only a fragment of the original adaptive behavior is seen" and only "reductions of previously learned adaptive acts are maintained by habit".

Adaptors are usually not considered gestures. Kendon (1983: 13), McNeill (1992: 78), Duncan (1983: 151) and Webb (1997: 17) exclude them from their def-

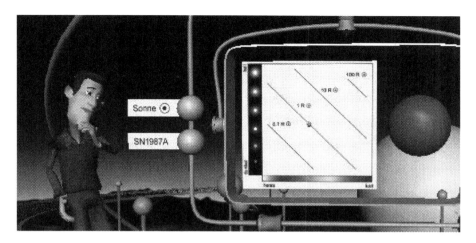

Figure 2.2: *A self-adaptor performed by the virtual student Ritchie in the Virtual-Human system. It expresses the need to concentrate while trying to find an answer to the teacher's question.*

inition of gestures[1]. They do this because the relation to speech is very loose and they are not intentionally communicative. However, adaptors can be considered signs that give away information about the speaker's state, like being nervous, uncomfortable, bored. For instance, Freedman (1977) claims that self-touches signal the speaker's need to focus and concentrate. According to Freedman and Hoffman (1967), they occur most frequently during pauses in the speech stream. With this theory in mind, adaptors become an important means to characterize an individual in his/her need to concentrate. Moreover, adaptors help recipients segmenting the speech stream by providing segment boundary signals. Therefore, adaptors are considered gestures in this work.

Emblems

Emblems are gestures with conventionalized form and meaning that can be used independent of speech. The gesture's meaning can be directly translated to words that are sometimes uttered in conjunction with the emblem. One example is the *thumbs-up* gesture where the thumb sticks out from an otherwise closed hand, pointing up (Figure 2.3 A). The gesture's meaning can be expressed by utterances like "yes", "good" or "great". Since they can be used in the absence of speech they are often employed when the verbal channel is somehow restricted, by noise, by distance, by library rules, by an interlocutor being busy on the phone etc. Many emblems are culture-specific (Efron, 1941, Axtell, 1998).

---

[1]McNeill and Webb do not use the term adaptors but speak of self-touching and object manipulations that they both declare non-gestures.

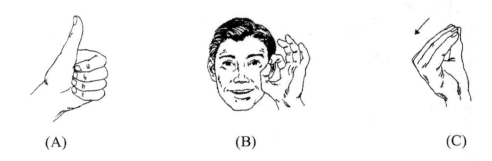

(A)   (B)   (C)

Figure 2.3: *Three emblems called (A) the thumbs-up gesture, (B) the finger-ring, and (C) the purse hand (drawings taken from Morris, 1994).*

Emblems were introduced by Efron (1941) and taken up by Ekman and Friesen (1969: 63ff.) and Johnson et al. (1975). For the creation/emergence of emblems see Posner (1993) and Calbris (1990: 198 ff.). Kendon (1983) calls them *autonomous gestures* and *quotables* in later work, Barakat (1973) *semiotic gestures*, Bitti and Poggi (1991) *symbolic gestures.*

Emblems used in conversation are often not called emblems at all for two reasons: either because they do not function as signs for conventionalized content or because the variation in form is higher than usual. So Bitti and Poggi (1991) insist that emblems must have an autonomous meaning, replacing either a whole sentence (holophrastic use) or a phrase/word (articulated use). They reject conversational gestures' emblematic status even if they resemble emblems in form. Webb (1997: 70) rejects many conversational gestures their emblematic status, classifying them as *metaphorics* instead "since they have more variation in their forms than typically expected of emblems" but adds that there is no sharp boundary between emblems and metaphorics. However, emblems like the *finger-ring* (Figure 2.3 B) or the *purse hand* (Figure 2.3 C) do occur in normal conversation but may serve a function different from conveying a conventionalized semantic content. Kendon (1995) analyzed videotaped conversations of Southern Italians who used four gesture types widely understood to be emblems. He found that these gestures had pragmatic functions: indicating speech act type and aspects of discourse structure. It can be concluded that emblem-like gestures are used in conversations but possibly serve pragmatic functions apart from the semantic function they have by definition. Gestures with emblematic form used in conversations will retain their classification as emblems in this work, although they may be otherwise classified by other researchers.

Deictics

Deictic gestures are pointing movements whose function is to indicate a concrete person, object, location, direction but also to point to unseen, abstract or imaginary things (Krauss et al. 2000). Deictic gestures occur in most treatments on gestures (cf. McNeill, 1992: 18) and belong to the best examined gestures, especially in a human-computer interaction context (cf. Schmauks, 1991). Wahlster (1991) found that deictics can also be used to shift focus[2] and that focus can be used to disambiguate gestures. If, for instance, a lecturer moves to another part of the blackboard she can shift the focus by pointing with one hand to a region on the blackboard while using the other hand to point to an exact word or line.

Sometimes deictics are subsumed under emblems because the meaning is conventionalized (Johnson et al., 1975, Saitz and Cervenka, 1972, Morris, 1994), Webb (1997) classifies them as metaphorics. Ekman and Friesen (1969: 68) take them to be illustrators because they are directly tied to speech and serve to illustrate what is being said. For similar reasons, Schegloff (1984: 282), who calls them *locationals*, places a subset of them in the category of iconic gestures.

Since deictics are easy to tell apart from other gesture classes there is no reason to merge them with one of them. So deictics will remain a class here.

Iconics

Iconics are gestures that illustrate what is being said by depicting some property of the speech referent (McNeill, 1992: 12-14). For instance, when talking about a gallery picture and drawing a rectangle in the air the gesture iconically illustrates the rectangularity of the picture and is therefore an iconic (see Figure 1.4 on p. 18 for two other examples). McNeill's definition that is used here goes back to Ekman and Friesen (1969: 68ff.) who introduced the class of *illustrators*, subdividing it into six sub-categories: batons, ideographs, deictics, spatial movements, kinetographs and pictographs. Iconics can be seen as the union of the last three categories. These categories are described as follows: spatial movements depict a spatial relationship, kinetographs depict a bodily action and pictographs draw a picture of their referent.

Iconics usually do not comply to standards of form, they are often made up on the fly. The most arbitrary iconics are probably spatial movements, for instance when describing the spatial constellation of a car accident. Kinetographs, e.g. depicting sleeping, sawing, shooting, are relatively standardized as well as pictographs (the gallery picture example of above) which are the most frequent iconics in the data of this work.

---

[2]Focus is used in the sense of *discourse focus* as used, for instance, by Grosz (1981).

Metaphorics

Metaphoric gestures are similar to iconics in that they illustrate the speech content. However, a metaphoric does not illustrate the content directly but via a third element that acts as a metaphor. The gesture illustrates this third element which in turn refers to the speech content. For instance, a speaker says "this is a good story" while holding some imaginary object with her two hands. The imaginary object acts as a metaphor for the concept "story" (see Figure 1.5 on p. 19). McNeill (1992: 146) calls the gesture a *sign*, the imaginary object the *base* and the concept of "story" the *referent*.

Metaphorics were introduced by McNeill (1985: 356) as gestures that exhibit images of abstract concepts by depicting the vehicles of metaphors. The class of metaphorics is also used by Calbris (1990: 194-196, 198) and Webb (1997). The latter finds them to be the "most frequent gestures produced in everyday speech" (p. 15). The boundary between metaphorics and iconics, both called *illustrators* by McNeill, cannot be sharply drawn. Krauss et al. (2000) attack the concept of *metaphorics* on the grounds that according to their observations "iconicity (or *apparent* iconicity) is a matter of degree rather than kind" so that "it makes more sense to think of gestures as being more or less iconic rather than either iconic or metaphoric (or non-iconic)". McNeill (1992: 145) concedes that there is a "continuum between iconic and metaphoric gestures".

Two gestural categories defined by Ekman and Friesen (1969) can be considered metaphorics. First, *ideographs* were defined as "movements which sketch a path or direction of thought" (p. 68). Second, *alter-adaptors* are hypothesized to be learned in early interpersonal contacts (pp. 88–90). They include movements for giving/taking, for attacking/protecting, for establishing affection/intimacy or withdrawal/flight, for establishing sexual contact (invitation, flirtation, courtship) and a sexual relationship.

In this work, metaphorics will be used non-withstanding the critique by Krauss and colleagues because many of the metaphorics described by McNeill (1992) and Webb (1997) will be shown to be contained in the LQ corpus (Appendix B).

Beats

Beats are rhythmic movements that accompany speech but where the hand shape bears no relation to the speech content. Beats are also called *batons* by Efron (1941) and Ekman and Friesen (1972). Krauss et al. (2000) calls them *motor gestures* and describes them as "simple, repetitive, rhythmic movements that bear no obvious relation to the semantic content of the accompanying speech. Typically the gesturer's hand shape remains fixed, and the movement may be repeated several times." Webb (1997: 5) agrees on beats having no semantics, that they are non-referential and that their forms do not correspond to a meaning.

2.1.2 Why These Classes?

The selection of classes was governed by three criteria. First, the classes had to be well-documented and recognizable. Second, the classes had to be a disjoint decomposition of all possible gestures. Third, the classes should cover all possible gestures.

The first criterium is fulfilled by the extensive research literature[3]. Recognizability is trivially fulfilled for adaptors and deictics. For emblems there are a number of dictionaries, they are easy to recognize by definition since otherwise they would not be emblems. Metaphorics are harder to detect but are clearly documented by the works of McNeill (1992) and Webb (1997). Lastly, iconics act as a rest class for idiosyncratic complex gestures. They demarcate the line where the approach taken in this work must fail since many truly iconic gestures must be generated on the fly according to various features of the underlying mental representation. So this class is good as a detector for gestures that are hard to integrate.

The second criterium, that the classes disjointly decompose the set of all gestures, is not fulfilled without an auxiliary construct. Since the criteria for classifying a gesture a member of a class lie on different dimensions for each class the gesture classes actually overlap. For instance, a gesture is classified an emblem according to its degree of conventionalization, whereas an iconic is found by examining the illustrative relation between gesture form and speech content. These two criteria do not exclude each other so an emblem can be an iconic and vice versa. Consequently, the classes do not disjointly decompose the set of all gestures. However, this can be fixed by imposing priorities on the classes. If emblems are given a higher priority then in a case of doubt between emblem and iconic, a gesture is classified an emblem.

Finally, the last criterium, that the classes should cover all possible gestures is fulfilled. A gesture is either communicative or not. In the latter case it is an adaptor. In the former case the communication is either transported by form or not. If it is transported by form, the gesture is either an emblem, a deictic, a metaphoric or an iconic. Iconics act as a rest class in this sub-category. If form is not of importance the gesture is a beat. In this decision tree-like view all possible gestures are covered since there is a rest class in each branch (see also Figure 8.1 on p. 142).

2.1.3 Conversational Gestures

In this work a special subset of gestures is considered. Two gesture sets are excluded. These are sign language gestures and true emblems. The notion *true*

---

[3]The six categories used here have been criticized, remolded and renamed by various researchers, for instance, by Weinrich (1992), Bitti and Poggi (1991), Müller (1998), and Rimé and Schiaratura (1991).

emblems refers to emblems made in the absence of speech. The reason is that these gesture types rarely occur at all in conversations between hearing people. Kendon (1983) suggested a classification of all gestures according to their degree of lexicalization. This classification was not discrete but on a continuum where fully lexicalized gestures (emblems and sign-language) were located on the one extreme and gestures without meaning (adaptors) were located on the other extreme. Krauss et al. (1996) localize *conversational gestures* between the extremes and attribute three properties to them: (1) they do not occur in the absence of speech, (2) they are temporally coordinated with speech and (3) they seem related in form to the semantic content of the speech they accompany. In this work, a similar stance is assumed although adaptors are included simply because they often occur during conversations, whereas sign language and true emblems rarely occur.

According to Webb (1997), metaphorics are expected to be the predominate class in the data. Conversely, it can be assumed that iconics will occur only rarely. These two properties of conversational gesture make a generation approach with pre-fabricated motion patterns attractive because a reasonable degree of standardization in form can be assumed (see Section 2.2.4 below for more discussion on this).

2.2 Results from Gesture Research

2.2.1 Gesture Function

That gesture is strongly related to speech can be made plausible by the observation that only speakers perform gestures, excluding adaptors, whereas listeners only gesture under certain circumstances, for instance, if they want to claim the next turn (Schegloff, 1984: 273). However, how important the function of gesture in speech is remains unclear.

Cassell (1998) argues that hand gestures serve a communicative function in face-to-face communication basing her view on various results from the research literature. So there is proof that when speech is ambiguous or when there is noise that listeners rely on gestural cues. Also, people exposed to gesture and speech where each expresses a slightly different information treat gestural information equally to that of speech (Cassell et al. 1999). Finally, gestures co-occur with semantically parallel linguistic units (McNeill 1992). All seems to indicate that gesture performs some communicative function in speech. Kendon (1996) lists the different communicative functions gestures can serve. In the absense of speech, the conventionalized emblem gestures have a lexicalized meaning that can be decoded using a dictionary. Iconic gestures depict some semantic content: a path of movement, a mode of action, relations in space between objects and entities. Pointing gestures can serve the function of referent resolution but, according to Wahlster

(1991), can also serve to shift focus as explained in Section 2.1.1. Another important function is discourse related: The information-theoretic status, topic vs. comment, of parts of utterances seems to be related to where a gesture is placed (Kendon 1996). Also, certain gestures appear to function as speech act markers that signify an utterance to be appeal or a question (Kendon 1995). Finally, gestures are used to regulate an interaction, i.e. managing the turn-taking in a dyadic or group discussion.

Krauss et al. (1991) investigated the communicative value of spontaneous conversational hand gestures in five experiments. The first two experiments dealt with the recognition of *lexical affiliates* (Section 8.4.2) which are words that correspond in meaning to the gesture. Recognition was better than chance. In experiments three and four recall tasks were performed where different modality combinations were used (speech-only, gesture-and-speech, gesture-only). Recognition results for speech-only were equal to the gesture-and-speech results. In the last experiment it was shown that judgement of a gesture's semantic category is determined principally by the accompanying speech. The authors conclude that although gestures can convey some information, they are not richly informative and the information they convey is largely redundant with speech. In a similar vein, Krauss et al. (1995) conducted three experiments where subjects described a stimulus to a partner who then tried to select it from a set of similar stimuli. The experiments differed in the type of stimulus described: abstract graphic designs, novel synthesized sounds and samples of tea. In none of the experiments was accuracy enhanced by allowing the listener to see the speaker's gestures. The authors conclude that semantic information is not the primary function of conversational hand gestures.

Rimé and Schiaratura (1991: 240) agree that the function of gesture must be other than communicative on the grounds that human speakers use nonverbal behavior to an equal degree when not seeing each other. However, they reject the theory that it is the increase of a speaker's general arousal level that causes nonverbal behavior. They let subjects hold conversations with different heart rates induced by physical exercise but found no significant correlation between arousal and and speech-accompanying nonverbal behavior. However, nonverbal behavior does seem to have an effect on speech production because Rimé and Schiaratura (1991) found that restricting subjects in their gesticulation caused a significant decrease in the vividness of imagery in the speech channel.

These results, although partly contradicting, are relevant to gesture generation insofar as they call into question *deep* or functional approaches to gesture generation where semantic content and communicative function are logically modeled and translated to gestural correlates. Most research results seem to indicate that in terms of semantics in the linguistic sense, gestures contribute little in conversations. So does Calbris (1990: 171) who says that "nonverbal expression is probabilistic and secondary with respect to the linguistic textual information". Therefore, in generation one can hardly make any "mistakes", that is, one can hardly create misunderstandings or even handicap the conversation by producing the "wrong" gestures. This may seem counterintuitive when considering spoken language where the choice of a single word can make a big difference. Research indicates that gestures are rather a tool for the *speaker*, be it for thinking, for planning speech or for lexical retrieval. The listener, however, perceives gestures less as a communicative device that is indispensable for understanding what the other says but rather as part of the speaker's personality. With regard to gesture generation, this calls for a *shallow* approach where one tries to recreate surface patterns of a speaker's gestural behavior instead of trying to figure out the exact communicative functions. Interesting surface patterns could be gesture frequency, types of gestures used, timing patterns, and handedness.

2.2.2 Models of Gesture Production

Gesture production can be explained in three ways. Gestures are either a by-product of speech, i.e. gesture is secondary to speech. Or speech is a manifestation of imaginistic concepts that are more immediately expressed by gesture, i.e. speech is secondary to gesture. Finally, gesture and speech could be two manifestations of the same underlying concept. Most researchers tend toward the last hypothesis.

In Psycholinguistics, McNeill (1992) explains gestures as the manifestation of an underlying *idea unit* that also causes speech production. McNeill and Duncan (2000) describe the so-called *growth point*[4] (GP) as such an idea unit. A GP is neither word nor image but "thinking in global imagery and linguistic categories simultaneously". The GP causes speech as well as gesture production and can be indirectly inferred by the speech-gesture synchronization. Apart from the conviction that gesture and speech originate from the same underlying idea unit, McNeill and Duncan (2000) claim that gestures are externalized means of the thinking process itself. That means that gestures, like words, do not only *express* thinking but are are *thought*, i.e. cognitive being, themselves.

McNeill's work is centered around proving his contention that gesture and speech originate from a single underlying concept. However, he has not put forward a concrete model of how such an underlying concept could be represented and how gesture and speech could be generated from it. Krauss et al. (1996) devised such a model of gesture production, based on the speech production model by Levelt (1989). Like McNeill they assume a common underlying concept called the *source concept* that is multiply encoded in propositional and non-propositional form. While the propositional form is used for speech production, parts of the non-propositional form (spatial and dynamic aspects) are selected by a module called *feature selector* for gesture generation. The module outputs specifications that are

---

[4]The notion of growth points was first introduced by McNeill (1992: 219ff.).

translated by a motor planner to a motor program that provides the motor system with a set of instructions for executing the lexical movement. The motor planner receives input from the *phonological encoder*, a module in the speech production pipeline, to translate the cadence of stressed syllables in terms of the periodicity of strokes of the gesture, and the loudness of the stressed syllables in terms of the gesture's amplitude.

In a shallow approach to gesture generation both models prove useful in the way they predict surface behavior. McNeill's model predicts that speech and gesture cohere since they originate from the same idea unit. The units in speech where this cohesion becomes manifest are called *lexical affiliates* (this concept will be elaborated in Section 8.4.2). Schegloff (1984) calls the outer temporal limits of speech and gesture signs that belong to the same underlying idea unit *projection space*. The model by Krauss et al. gives a more concrete picture of the generation process but only for iconic gestures. On the surface, however, their model also comes down to a lexical affiliation relationship between gesture and speech. The McNeill model has the additional benefit of not only explaining speech-gesture but also gesture-gesture relationships through the notion of *catchments* that will be explained in Section 2.2.6 below. Note that for a deep generation approach a modality-free representation language would become necessary where abstract messages and functions are encoded that have not yet been assigned a modality or surface form. The "short-cut" of the shallow approach is exactly to omit this modality-free representation.

2.2.3   Gesture-Speech Synchronization

Gesture and speech are two parallel output streams that are semantically interrelated, no matter which gesture production model one assumes. How gesture and speech are *temporally* coordinated is still a matter of research. There seem to be two levels of interest concerning the "granularity" of investigation. On the more abstract level, looking at a whole (speech) utterance, one may ask on which speech segments to place the gesture, i.e. one is concerned with gesture *placement*. On the more fine-grained level, looking at syllables, one may ask how the single movement phases of the gesture are synchronized with syllables, i.e. one is concerned with gesture-speech *synchronization*.

In this work, only gesture *placement* is considered because it is more primary in the process of gesture generation, it is an earlier task in the generation pipeline. Fine-grained synchronization would be more relevant for actual gesture rendering, the last step in the pipeline, which will not be treated here (cf. McClave, 1994, for an investigation of gesture-speech synchronization on the phase/syllable level). For the rest of this dissertation, the term gesture placement will used synonymously with the notions *timing*, *coordination* and *synchronization*.

Most researchers agree that a gesture occurs at around the same time as its co-expressive speech correlate. Schegloff (1984: 285) points out that specific distances in terms of time cannot be predicted but only "a weak ordering principle of acme/thrust" can be given. This ordering principle is: the stroke of the gesture (called acme by Schegloff) must precede or co-occur with the corresponding speech segment (see also McNeill, 1992: 25–29). Although Krauss et al. (1996) agree on the ordering principle they found that gesture can precede the co-expressive speech segment by considerable length. In one experiment they measured temporal distances from zero seconds, i.e. co-occurring with speech, up to 3.75 seconds. Moreover, van Meel (1984) found differing ways of gesture-speech coordination at different developmental stages. He observed four- to six-year old children making gestures before the beginning of their verbal answer. Eight- to ten-year-olds tended to gesture at the beginning of their speech and continue it throughout their utterance. Finally, twelf- to fourteen-year-olds displayed their gestures in temporal correspondence with the part of the sentence comprising the symbolized element. Although the latter coordination pattern seems to predominate in adults it remains unclear whether the other two patterns vanish in adulthood.

It can be concluded that the question of how to place a gesture within a speech utterance cannot be resolved by consulting the literature alone. Although most researchers agree that the gesture must precede the corresponding speech segment, this statement leaves open the exact place of the gesture and gives no prediction about its *duration*.

2.2.4   Standards of Form

An important question in gesture generation is: How many different gestures exist? Are there recurring patterns across speakers, i.e. standards of form that would make all gestures elements of a finite repertoire? Or are gestures individual creations of the moment, independent of other people's behavior, making the amount of different gestures infinite?

Only in the first case, assembling a *lexicon* of gestures would be possible where each entry has a number of meanings and a relatively stable form. The question of stable form can only be answered with regard to the type of gesture. So emblematic gestures have stable forms together with associated meanings *by definition* (Section 2.1.1). A number of emblem lexicons and inventories have already been assembled, form and meaning being culture-specific, for Colombian/US gestures (Saitz and Cervenka 1972), for Arabic gestures (Barakat 1973), for Israel emblems (Broide 1977), for American emblems (Efron, 1972, and Johnson et al., 1975) and many more.

While most researchers agree on the form/meaning stability of emblems, opinions are divided over other gesture types. For iconic and metaphoric gestures the content of the conversation seems to play an important role in this question. So Kendon (1996) presumed that "the more abstract and metaphorical the content the gesture pertains to, the more likely we are to observe consistencies in the gestural forms employed". For metaphoric gestures, Webb (1997) presents evidence for the existence of a finite repertoire. By investigating the gestural repertoire of three speakers she presents evidence for the existence of "a single community lexicon, with each speaker producing only a subset of all the lexical items, as well as having some idiosyncratic variations on some of the forms" (Webb, 1997: 52). Investigating conversational gestures used in Southern Italy, Kendon (1995: 248) also comes to the conclusion that "speakers frequently make use of gestural patterns taken from a repertoire that is widely shared".

This view is supported by a combination of work by McNeill (1992) and Webb (1997). McNeill hypothesized that more abstract talk fosters the use of metaphoric gestures. Webb found evidence that metaphoric gestures are characterized by relatively stable forms that correspond to certain meanings. Taken together one can conclude that abstract talk produces gestures of stable form.

In contrast, Calbris (1990: 196) claims that "many [metaphorical] expressions are personal creations". This can be countered by making these "personal creations" be subsumed under the notion of individual *variation* of a lexicon entry as suggested by Webb (1997).

Deictic gestures are sometimes considered emblems Johnson et al. (1975), sometimes *creative* gestures, i.e. gestures created on the spot (Poggi and Magno Caldognetto 1999). The latter view stems from the impression that deictic gestures are adapted on demand in terms of angle and hand shape. However, the same can be said for regular emblems that have to be adapted to guarantee visibility (in angle but also in size and duration). So, although the variation of deictics is indeed high, since a speaker can point with such different means as chin, gaze, elbow, various objects in his/her hand, one can safely assume for this work a number of stable gestural forms that are recognizable as deictics.

However, standards of form seem to disappear the more one moves towards iconic gestures. McNeill (1992: 41) claims that gestures inherently have no standards of form. However, in his research there is a strong focus on iconics and in the same book he describes various recurring forms of metaphoric gestures (pp. 147–163). Also, his remark seems rather to refer to the fact that individual speakers utilize different gestures in the same context instead of gestures being arbitrary in form. Saitz and Cervenka (1972: 8) exclude "heavily iconic gestures (a child's imitation of driving a car, a finger rubbing teeth to denote brushing teeth, fingers closing to depict a scissors, etc.)" from their gesture lexicon because they are too arbitrary. Their talking of "*heavily* iconic gestures", however, indicates that there is "less heavy" iconicity. There seems to be a fuzzy boundary between some iconic gestures and emblems which was also found by Webb (1997)[5]. Indeed, Kendon (1981: 151–156) hypothesized emblems to origin from iconics.

To conclude, all but iconic gestures comply to standards of form. Even for iconics, some can be seen to be similar to emblems, thus having standards of form, too. Most researchers agree that more abstract topics lead to more consistency in form. Since the LQ data, book reviews, is of an abstract nature one can expect that only a little percentage of occurring gestures in the LQ data are of the idiosyncratic iconic type.

Having established that many researchers found standards of form for gestures in conversation the question arises how gestures interact with one another. Do they syntactically and semantically build up hierarchical structures where the parts combine to a *composed* meaning like spoken language does? The next section treats this question of compositionality.

2.2.5 Compositionality and Componentiality

Are gestures compositional? Compositionality means that the meaning of a composite expression is built up from the meanings of its basic expressions. In short: the whole is the sum of its parts. McNeill (1992: 41) characterizes gestures as being *global and synthetic*, i.e. the meanings of the parts of gestures are determined by the meaning of the whole, so that the meaning determination is whole-to-part. McNeill and Duncan (2000) see this property in direct opposition to the compositional property of speech where the semiotic direction is part-to-whole. Moreover, McNeill (1992: 41) calls gestures *non-combinatoric*, i.e. they do not combine with one another in a hierarchical fashion, the way words do, to produce gestural phrases or sentences. However, there are examples of gestures that defy these claims. For instance, if a person makes a gesture for "mad" by circling his forefinger somewhere near his temple while pointing at another person at the same time, the two meanings of the two gestures combine to the meaning "this person is mad", a simple predicative relationship. This is clearly a compositional construct. Kendon (1995) gives another example with two pointing gestures. Nevertheless, the claims by McNeill and colleagues may be interpreted in the sense that gestures only rarely combine in a compositional fashion.

While Webb (1997: 71) agrees with McNeill that metaphoric gestures are non-combinatoric, she presents evidence that metaphoric gestures are *componential*. She shows that gestural form features have a meaning independent of the whole gesture and that these features, comparable to morphemes, are themselves members of a lexicon. Thus, they can be combined in a single gesture to express two meanings

---

[5]Webb (1997: 70) found it "difficult to determine whether certain gesture types should be classified as metaphorics or as emblems". Since she has a very wide definition of metaphoric this statement can be generalized to metaphorics and iconics that are both difficult to sharply separate from emblems.

at the same time. This is in accord with McNeill's definition of *synthetic*, meaning that "different meaning segments are synthesized into a single gesture" (McNeill, 1992: 41). Similar results on componentiality have been reported by Kendon (1995) and Calbris (1990) for Italian and French gestures. However, Webb (1997: 61) found that most of the gestures, 88%, contained only a single feature component so that componentiality does exist but seems to be rarely exploited in single gestures.

It can be concluded that gestures are both compositional and componential. Compositionality seems to occur only rarely and is possibly restricted to certain gesture classes, so it seems to be negligible for generation purposes. Componentiality means that gestures are built from certain basic components that can be compared to morphemes. However, Webb (1997) found that 88% of her examined gestures contained only one single component, using empirical material similar to the one in this work. Therefore, neglecting componentiality and identifying only gestures with a single component seems to be tolerable. Moreover, gestures being componential does not mean that *arbitrary* combinations of components can make up new and valid gestures. In fact, Webb's few examples suggest that only very particular combinations are possible. Since these combinations can be treated as gestures themselves they can modeled with pre-fabricated motion patterns as well. "Factoring out" these combinations seems to be possible without running the risk of exponential growth.

2.2.6   Gestures and Discourse

The relationship between gesture and discourse has been investigated by various researchers. From the point of view of gesture generation, two results seem of special relevance because of their practical application value.

Lists and Contrastive Pairs

In his treatment of nonverbal actions in political speeches Atkinson (1984) presents a number of devices to catch applause from the audience, so-called *clap traps*. To make these clap traps work the speaker must generate attention and facilitate audience reactions, usually applause.

The *list of three* device, an enumeration of three items, is a frequently used rhetorical device. The author observed that enumerations often have exactly three items which seems to be a strong bias when generating such lists. In fact, the bias is so strong that in cases where speakers only have two items, fillers like "and so forth" or "things like that" etc. are used to make the list of three complete. The bias toward three items helps the audience anticipate the *completion point* of the enumeration, thus facilitating applauding. The recognition of the completion is often supported by gesture. If, for instance, the first two items are accompanied by the same gesture each while the third item is accompanied by a different gesture, the change of gesture signals the approaching completion point. Atkinson calls the list of three an *applause-eliciting sequence*.

Another clap trap device are *contrastive pairs*, also called *antithesis*, where two contrastive concepts, words or phrases, are juxtaposed. Atkinson argues that the first item generates attention for the second item. The second item is marked as the completion point and thus, facilitates applauding. Again, gestures can help recognize the completion point simply by emphasizing the contrastive items. This is achieved by either accompanying both items with gestures or by accompanying only the first and leaving the second without gesture, together with a more relaxed intonation. The third possibility is to only accompany the second item by a gesture and thus marking the completion point.

Atkinson takes these two devices as general mechanisms that are used to make discourse successful, also used in commercials and newspaper writing. In his work, these phenomena are taken to be tools intentionally used by speakers to catch attention and provoke reactions. Gestures are used to make discourse items cohere or to set them apart. *Catchments*, the topic of the next section, mark similar phenomena but are, in contrast, not interpreted as a consciously used tool but rather as an emergent effect of the underlying representations of the discourse items.

Catchments

The term *catchment* denotes the phenomenon of one or more gesture features recurring in at least two (not necessarily consecutive) gestures (McNeill et al. 2001). Catchments are a means to infer textual cohesion in speech by looking at a speaker's gesture stream. The idea is that the recurrence of an image of the speaker's thinking generates recurrent gesture features.

McNeill et al. (2001) present a detailed analysis of 32 seconds of discourse where a speaker describes a house. They observed that when talking about the back of the house the speaker used right hand gestures (RH) only whereas she shifted to two-handed gestures (2H) when moving thematically to the front of the house. The right handedness of the gestures are recognized as a catchment caused by the imagery of the back of the house.

Catchments can be manifest in handedness, in the gesture itself or more componential aspects of the gesture. Apart from the last point this can be modeled in generation with pre-fabricated motion patterns.

2.2.7 Individuality

The claim that people differ in the way they use gestures needs no proof, one can observe it every day. But *in what respect* does their gesturing differ? One obvious factor is frequency: some people gesture all the time, some almost never.

Krauss et al. (1996) found substantial individual differences in gesture rate in all of their studies, in one experiment it ranged from 1.0 to 28.1 gestures per minute. Other obvious factors are movement parameters like expansiveness, abruptness, force etc., also called movement *qualities* (Section 4.2.3). If gestures are taken as entries in one large, shared lexicon of gestures one may wonder whether all people use the same gestures or only a subset of this lexicon. Webb (1997: 49+) found indeed that her four examined subjects used different subsets of a single, shared lexicon of metaphoric gestures with stable form-meaning pairs. McNeill (1992: 41) claims that different speakers display the same meaning in idiosyncratic ways, even when it occurs in the same context. This means that some gestures can be used synonymously. On the other hand, Bitti (1992) proved for two manual gestures that each can express at least two different meanings, revealed only by differing facial expressions. So that the lexicon must also incorporate polysemy. Polysemy can be modeled in two ways. Either the lexicon contains multiple meaning entries for a polysemous gesture or the meanings are factored out so that a gesture with N meanings occurs with N lexicon entries. Only in the latter case it suffices to say that individuals differ with respect to their gesture subset. In the former case, individuals must differ in the way they use a single gesture's meaning or function.

According to McNeill et al. (2001: 10), individuality also shows up in the occurrence of catchments (Section 2.2.6) since "individuals differ in how they link up the world into related and unrelated components". Since catchments become manifest most prominently in handedness, it implies that handedness contributes to individuality. One remaining factor is gesture timing. Do different speakers prefer different patterns of timing? The literature usually relies on the simple proposition that gesture and speech segments with equal meanings co-occur (Section 2.2.3). The data that will be used in this work draws a more detailed picture of timing possibilities, discussed in Section 8.4.3. Without advancing on the subject it is a hypothesis that people differ in the way they time gestures with co-expressive speech. This is somewhat supported by data by Krauss et al. (1996) who found in their studies considerable differences in the temporal distance between gesture and corresponding speech segment (0 to 3.75 seconds) as well as in gesture duration (0.54 to 7.71 seconds).

To sum up, individuality is potentially achieved by individual gesture frequency, movement qualities, subset of the shared gesture lexicon, gesture function usage, handedness, and timing patterns.

2.3   Summary

Gestures are defined to be non-manipulative hand and arm movements that occur during speech. They can be classified into six functional classes: adaptors, emblems, deictics, iconics, metaphorics, and beats. Adaptors are pseudo-manipulative movements like scratching one's cheek or tapping with a finger on the table. Emblems are gesture with a conventionalized meaning (within a limited community), like the "thumbs-up" gesture that means "OK!" or "good!". Deictics are pointing gestures to indicate locations, directions and concrete objects but also abstract concepts and absent objects. Iconics are gestures that relate in shape or movement to the object or process being talked about, e.g. drawing a round shape in the air when talking about a ball. Metaphorics are gestures that model a concrete shape, e.g. a box, and where this shape metaphorically refers to the concept being talked about. The modeled shape can refer to a bank account, the contents of the last sentence or an abstract concept like "freedom" or "luck". Finally, beats are small, rhythmic, shapeless motions.

Psycholinguistic research indicates that gestures emerge in parallel to speech from a single underlying concept called an *idea unit*. Those speech units that correspond to the gestural movement are called *lexical affiliates*, a notion usually applied to iconic gestures only. Since most research focused on the question what function gesture has, conversational gestures are relatively unexplored. Webb (1997) considers almost all gestures in conversations metaphorics, whereas Kendon (1995) showed that some emblems occur in conversations as well.

While many researchers find gestures to not possess linguistic properties, some degree of compositionality as well as componentiality seems to exist. However, both properties seem to come to effect only in a negligible amount of cases. Many researchers assembled lexicons of meaning-form pairs, mainly for emblems but also for other gesture classes. This justifies an approach to generation based on a lexicon of gesture prototypes.

Gestures can be used to support discourse relations. Atkinson (1984) analyzed the *list of three* and *antithesis* in-depth, finding important correlations with gesture. McNeill et al. (2001) postulate the existence of *catchments*, a device where recurring gestural features correlate with recurring aspects in the speech stream.

Individuality is hypothesized to be achievable using gestures, to be precise: using individual gesture frequency, movement qualities, gesture function usage, handedness, timing patterns, and an individual subset of the shared gesture lexicon.

Chapter 3

Transcription Approaches

After the previous chapter has defined the subject of this work to be conversational gestures, this chapter presents existing methods of analyzing them. First, methods for gesture transcription will be described. Second, software tools to support the transcription process will be surveyed.

Although gesture research has been conducted in a wide variety of disciplines, mainly Psychology, Anthropology, Linguistics, Conversation Analysis (CA) and Ethology, the methods used in each field for the transcription of gestures are similar. A gesture can be captured with respect to its structure in time, its structure in space, and its function. The analysis of the temporal structure has resulted in the concept of movement phases that is centered around the stroke as the most energetic and meaning-carrying phase of the gesture. For the transcription of a gesture's structure in space, i.e. its form, various degrees of descriptive exactness have been applied, from more Gestalt-oriented approaches to the reductionist approach of specifying all possible degrees of freedom. The transcription of function involves interpretative processes of the coder on the premise that all coders are competent members of their respective communicative community. Interpretative coding is widely applied in Linguistics and used for gesture transcription by researchers influenced by Linguistics, most notably by conversation analysts.

Given that many researchers from different disciplines examine gestures, one would expect many existing tools that make use of modern technology to analyze video recordings. Surprisingly, only few such programs existed in the year 2000 when this research began. Since then, three factors have caused rising interest in video annotation tools that led to the initiation of new projects like NITE[1], AT-

---

[1] **N**atural **I**nteractivity **T**ools **E**ngineering, http://nite.nis.sdu.dk

LAS[2] and EUDICO[3]. First, a recent surge of interest in multimodality for human-computer interfaces, including both gestural input and output, created a need for empirical research material for domain explorations and systems development. Second, research in embodied conversational agents has reached a point where more empirical research is needed to make the agents' behaviour more believable. Third, researchers from various disciplines concerned with the analysis of nonverbal behaviour have started to communicate over sharing data and tools which will also foster the development of standards for transcription, data formats and tools engineering.

This chapter presents a survey of existing annotation tools, focusing on advantages, disadvantages and lessons to be learned for designing such a tool. The chapter concludes that no suitable tool for the task of this work exists and that therefore, a new tool had to be created.

3.1 Transcription of Nonverbal Behavior

This section shows how researchers approached the problem of bringing the complex shapes and meanings of nonverbal behavior to paper, or rather: into a data file, for further analysis, be it qualitative or quantitative. The process of recording certain aspects of nonverbal behavior using letters and symbols is called *transcription*.

3.1.1 Structural Transcription

When trying to transcribe gestures a number of questions arise. First of all, one needs to distinguish movements that are gestures from movements that are not gestures. Once this is clarified, one must identify the exact beginning and end of a gesture. Finally, one may ask if there is a segment of the gesture that is more important or significant than the rest. Kendon (1978) found that people seem to know very well what movements to classify as "significant gestures" and which not. Moreover, in his experiments all subjects agreed that there were certain segments which they regarded as standing out as being the "main point" of the gesture. Driven by such questions and insights various researchers arrived at the idea to decompose movements into *phases*. Efron (1941) introduced the classical partition of a gesture into three phases: preparation, stroke and retraction. This was extended and operationalized by McNeill (1992). Based on his system, Kita et al. (1998) developed criteria for movement segmentation and phase identification using objective, non-interpretative measures only. For the transcription of movement

---

[2]**A**rchitecture and **T**ools for **L**inguistic **A**nalysis **S**ystems,
http://www.nist.gov/speech/atlas
[3]**Eu**ropean **D**istributed **Co**rpora Project,
http://www.mpi.nl/world/tg/lapp/eudico/eudico.html

structure it is widely used and can be regarded as a quasi-standard. Therefore, it will also be used in this work and described in detail in this section (see also Figure 3.1).

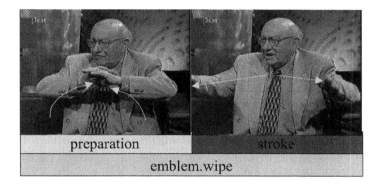

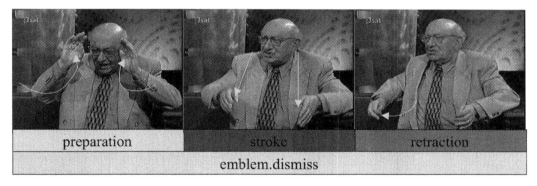

Figure 3.1: *A sample transcription of movement phases and gestures performed by speaker MRR. Each frame represents a movement phase. A sequence of movement phases constitutes a gesture as also encoded in this sample.*

A *gestural excursion* begins with the hands departing from a resting position and ends with the hands' arriving at a resting position. The *resting position* is part of the body or furniture where the hands can be supported. The gestural excursion can be a single gesture or a sequence of several gestures. The next step is to identify phase boundaries and then, to classify these phases. A phase boundary is a time point where two conditions hold:

1. abrupt change of direction in the hand movement
2. discontinuity in velocity before or after the direction change

If only the first condition holds there is no boundary. Instead, the whole unit is a so-called *multi-segment phase*. If the same movement is repeated without holds the entire movement is a single *repetitive phase*.

Having segmented a gesture into phases the phases are classified. Figure 3.1 shows the different phases of two gestures performed by speaker MRR. Each gesture develops in time from left to right, the first consisting of two, the second of three phases. The *stroke* phase is a phase where more force is exerted than in neighboring phases. Also, multi-segment and repetitive phases are always stroke phases. McNeill (1992: 82-84) defined the stroke as the "most energetic" or "meaning-carrying" part (cf. Kendon, 1983: 19). Other names for this concept are *apex* (Efron 1941) or *acme* (Schegloff, 1984: 294). The *hold* phase is a phase where the hand is held still. If the gesture does not contain a stroke phase the hold is termed an *independent hold*. A non-stroke phase that departs from the resting position is a *preparation*, one that arrives at a resting position is a *retraction*. A single phase between two strokes is also a preparation. After a stroke, if the hand approaches a resting position but shifts to a preparation before reaching it, the interrupted retraction phase is called a *partial retraction*.

This approach subsumes the concepts from Conversational Analysis as defined by Schegloff (1984: 294). In his transcription method he makes use of phases like acme (corresponding to *stroke*), cocked position (corresponding to *hold*) and retraction.

3.1.2 Descriptive Transcription

One approach to gesture transcription is to describe its form. Form can be encoded by specifying the positions of all joints at a time point and proceeding thus for regular time intervals. In the Berne system (Frey and Pool 1976) joint positions are encoded for all relevant body parts such as head, face, shoulder, torso, upper arm, lower arm etc. (see also Frey et al., 1983). Each body part has a number of dimensions reflecting the degrees of freedom in the respective joints. The head, for instance, has three dimensions: sagittal, rotational, lateral – where each dimension is a continuum of possible positions, e.g. the rotational dimension of the head is a continuum from "head rotated to far right side" to "head rotated to far left side". The authors discretize this continuum into five steps (1 = far right, 5 = far left) so that, combining all possible values in each dimension for the head, one can discriminate between 5 x 5 x 5 = 125 different head positions. In total, excluding facial expression, the Berne System considers 8 body parts and 55 dimensions. A recent successor to this purely descriptive approach is the FORM gesture annotation scheme (Martell 2002). In FORM, however, descriptions are not encoded at regular time points but for time spans. First of all, gestural excursions are identified and within these excursions, static and dynamic phases are encoded using degrees of freedom like in the Berne system. Static phases are encoded with a single description, dynamic phases with a start and end position description.

Both approaches share the advantage to be methodically uncritical since no subjective judgements have to be made. Problems arise in the capability of the human coder to precisely detect movement boundaries and to work on the prescribed "resolution" of the discretized continuum of positions in a particular joint. Moreover, such purely descriptive approaches are only useful for particular research aims because the analytic interpretation of such large amounts of reductionist data is difficult (Weinrich, 1992: 18–21). Global properties get lost in a heap of position data. Even simple pointing gestures are hard to reconstruct in analysis from the highly resolved data. Frey (1999) used such data to animate a synthetic computer agent in a process called *re-animation* and conducted experiments that observed gesture perception by changing the re-animation along certain degrees of freedom. On this low level of abstraction, purely descriptive methods yield good and solid results. However, if one considers gestures to be discrete and categorizable elements in conversations that can be recreated using prefabricated movement patterns these approaches are too reductionistic to be useful.

The Berne system and FORM are two extreme examples of descriptive transcription. The following section which deals with functional transcriptions will also introduce some less detailed descriptive methods from Psycholinguistics that are the basis for a functional transcription.

3.1.3 Functional Transcription

As soon as a researcher ascribes meaning or function to gestures in a transcription, one speaks of a functional transcription. Meaning and function can be inferred by carefully observing the gestures and their accompanying speech. Such an approach can be called *interpretative* or *hermeneutic* (Krauss et al. 1996).

Weinrich (1992) calls her investigation of nonverbal communication in TV shows *ethnomethodological conversation analysis*. According to Bergmann (1994) ethnomethodologists assume that every utterance is a solution to an interactional problem. They first strive to find this problem before reconstructing the methods that the speaker used to solve it and that became manifest in the verbal or nonverbal utterances. These so-called *ethnomethods* are considered institutionalized solutions for the problems. Having analyzed the singular case, one moves to collecting a corpus of cases where the identified object recurs with certain variations. The validity of the interpretation that builds on the analyst's intuition and competence as a member of the language community can be made plausible by three means:

1. finding **co-occurring, functionally equivalent phenomena**, assuming that an interactant has a whole arsenal of means at his/her disposal for the solution of structural problems in interaction

2. finding **counter cases** and proving their status as trespasses against conventions

3. analyzing the subsequent utterance(s) as **reactions of a third party** to the object in question, using it as support for the own interpretation.

McNeill (1992) uses *psycholinguistic* methods to investigate gestures. In comparison with Ethnomethodology and CA, Psycholinguistics focus on cognitive processes of a single person and approach the problem of interpreting gestures from the producer's perspective. In their transcription of gestures they therefore use a number of descriptive dimensions before ascribing meaning that is inferred from these descriptive features in conjunction with the accompanying speech. The gestures' description is done linguistically, i.e. with discrete descriptive units and based on a classification similar to the one presented in Section 2.1.1. The transcription is performed in the following steps (McNeill, 1992: 78–88, 375–387):

1. Identify gestures: All hand/arm movements except self- and object-adaptors.

2. Identify gesture phases: Using the procedure outlined in Section 3.1.1.

3. Code gesture type: Iconic, metaphoric, deictic, or beats (together with a confidence score from 1 to 5, a higher number reflecting higher certainty). See Section 2.1.1 for a description of these types.

4. Code gesture form (if gesture is not a beat):
   - handedness: right hand, left hand, two hands with same shape or two hands with different shapes
   - hand shape: specified with the American Sign Language (ASL) hand form encoding system
   - palm/finger orientation: pointing up, down, toward center, outward, inward etc.
   - location: specified as a section of gesture space
   - movement trajectory: toward the body, away from the body, parallel to front of body, parallel to side of body
   - movement location: specified as sections of gesture space
   - movement direction: unidirectional, bidirectional, both hands move in same way, each hand moves in its own way

5. Code gesture meaning:
   - hand meaning: which character or object does the hand represent?
   - movement meaning: which action does the motion represent?

In this annotation scheme, *gesture space* refers to a decomposition of the space around a seated person into sections, for instance "center", "upper periphery" or "extreme upper periphery" (see Figure 3.2). The scheme is tailored to the investigated material that consisted of retellings of TV cartoons. Most of the time the speakers talk about the two protagonists acting and interacting so that encoding of the gesture's meaning in terms of characters and character actions appears plausible and appropriate for the task. In the examples McNeill presents in his book sometimes the *lexical affiliate* is also encoded in the meaning section, e.g. when the action represented by the gesture is also mentioned during speech. This is an important piece of information for gesture generation that is meant to be based on speech input because only thus can the relationship between gesture and speech be established.

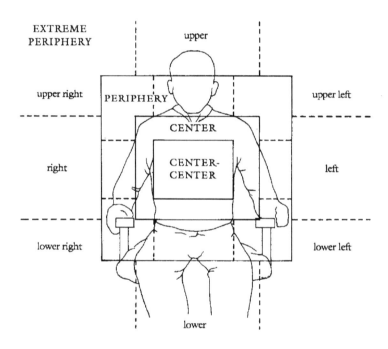

Figure 3.2: *Division of the gesture space for McNeill's (1992: 378) gesture coding scheme. (Taken from Pedelty, 1987.)*

Functional transcriptions are well suited for empirical studies in the development of multimodal natural interaction systems. The encoded functions can be used as training or test material for automated processes in such systems. The SmartKom project relies on an annotated video corpus of human users performing gestures (pointing, circling etc.) on a flat graphical tablet (Schiel et al. 2002). The 2D gestures are described in three functional categories: interactive, supporting and other (Steininger et al. 2001). Interactive gestures are task-oriented movements like pointing or encircling, supporting gestures are movements that help the user reading (e.g. following words with a finger) or orienting him-/herself on the screen. The third category is a rest category for all other gestures. For transcription, the logged gesture coordinates from the tablet and two video views are utilized: one showing the user's face, another showing user and graphical tablet from the side. Both video views are necessary for the human coders to identify the gestures's function.

Krauss et al. (1996) criticize all interpretative approaches for the absence of independent corroboration. In establishing a relation between a feature of the gesture to the meaning of the speech it accompanies the investigator ignores all other features of the gesture. The established relation could be merely a construction based on the accompanying speech. Therefore, the authors regard such interpretations as a source of hypotheses to be tested rather than usable data.

Although this argument is plausible, a system for gesture generation needs to learn from the communicative competence of a coder. It can only do so if the coder applies his/her interpretations in the coding. A compromise between a full-fledged interpretation of nonverbal behavior and purely non-semantic transcriptions are limited interpretative codings. Coding only lexical affiliates while letting automatic routines infer quantitative relationships between gestures and lexical entries would be such a limited interpretative coding approach.

3.1.4 Categorial Transcription

Many researchers agree on a classification of gestures in a few major categories such as the six classes described in Section 2.1.1. Categorial transcription means to assemble a such a categorization, formalize the category descriptions and to systematically annotate the corpus using these descriptions. A categorization can be done in the form of a gesture lexicon obtained in a pre-analysis of video data. Weinrich (1992), in her exploration of three TV conversations, devised a lexicon of 27 gestures that are described by form only. Similarly, Webb (1997) identified three lexicons of metaphoric gestures with 29, 32 and 14 entries each in her investigation of three conversational settings, one of them a TV talk show, also described by form only. For her formalization of lexicon entry description, Webb (1997: 93–106) uses the following features:

- handedness: one hand (1H), two hands (2H)
- hand shape: all fingers extended, index finger extended etc.
- hand shape/flexion: flat, relaxed, curved, claw
- location: whole gesture space, head, chest, shoulder etc.
- orientation: away from body, toward body up, down etc.

- movement: no movement, lateral, up, down, etc.

- movement/manner: arc-shaped, linear, repeated etc.

Lexicon entries are defined via *formational features* (see Table 3.1). A feature being formational means that it is a necessary condition to identify the gesture. For instance, the gesture PRECISE has only one formational feature: a hand shape where thumb and index finger form a ring. Along all other dimensions (handedness, location, movement etc.) the gesture can vary and still realize the PRECISE gesture. Thus, it is possible for two gestures to be performed at the same time if the formational features are located on different dimensions. Webb (1997: 56) treats an example where the two gestures PRECISE and MENTAL are performed simultaneously. Table 3.1 shows the different formational features of the two gestures, called *lexemes* by Webb, making clear their compatibility.

	MENTAL	PRECISE
hand	—	—
hand shape	—	ring
location	head/ point to head	—
orientation	—	—
movement	—	—

Table 3.1: *Specification of two lexemes from the lexicon of metaphoric gestures assembled by Webb (1997).*

Webb's descriptive dimensions are a subset of the ones introduced by McNeill (1992) whose transcription system was described in Section 3.1.3 as being functional but not categorial. However, for the gesture class of metaphorics he devised a number of sub-categories that he identified as recurring patterns in conversations (McNeill, 1992: 147–163). These sub-categories can be understood as lexicon entries in the sense of Webb and Weinrich, and several of McNeill's metaphorics occur in the video corpus of this work that will be introduced in Chapter 5 (see Appendix B for the gesture lexicon). Figure 3.1 shows how categorial transcription can be applied to empirical material on video with an existing structural transcription layer (gesture phases).

Identifying lexicon entries goes well together with the generation approach pursued here because they can be stored as prefabricated movement patterns which only need slight variation when put into context. The approach of identifying formational features is not only helpful in transcribing the gestures from empirical material but can also be used in generation approaches that are more flexible than an approach with fixed motion patterns, e.g. systems that can blend two motions (i.e. gestures) thus creating two superimposed gestures.

3.1.5 Conclusions

This section presented a number of approaches to the transcription of nonverbal behavior. The approaches were distinguished into structural, descriptive, functional and categorial. Structural transcription deals with identifying boundaries and internal phases of a gesture, the stroke being the central concept referring to the meaning-carrying phase of the gesture. Descriptive transcription serves to transcribe gestures with objective, strictly non-semantic means. In its most consequent form, all degrees of freedom of skeletal joints are specified in regular time intervals. Functional transcription relies on the coder's communicative competence to ascribe meaning to gestures. This is critical insofar as it is an act of interpretation. Finding a gesture's lexical affiliate is one such interpretative task. Finally, in categorial transcription a lexicon of gestures is devised, each entry being described by a number of descriptive and/or functional features. Transcription consists of assigning to each occurring gesture one lexicon entry.

These four principal approaches of structural, descriptive, functional and categorial transcription are not mutually exclusive but, on the contrary, complement each other. They can be seen as building blocks serving the single purpose of categorizing gestures in a lexicon, i.e. categorial transcription. Categorial transcription appears best suited for the purpose of generation, more specifically the following methods appear to be most appropriate. On the structural level, the transcription by Kita et al. (1998) offers a quasi-standardized and reliable method. For devising a gesture lexicon the concept of characterizing gestures with formational features seems most appropriate (Webb 1997). The formational features which reflect the descriptive level go back to concepts by McNeill (1992) who also devised some important categories for metaphoric gestures. On the functional level, lexical affiliates are a concept rather vaguely defined by Schegloff (1984) but widely used in gesture research. This concept needs some further specification to be useful in annotation. In research this relationship is often not coded at all. Instead, co-occurrence of gesture and speech is taken as an indicator of this speech-gesture relation. However, there are many cases where gesture and lexical affiliate do not co-occur. For instance, Krauss et al. (1996) found that there can be a distance of up to 3.75 seconds between gesture and lexical affiliate. Therefore, although human coders quickly identify a gesture's corresponding lexical affiliate, for automatic generation this relationship must be explicitly coded.

3.2   Transcription Software Tools

Gesture research usually relies on videotaped material as the primary data for analysis. However, in some research areas like gesture recognition more sophisticated media are explored as well, like data gloves where the exact spatio-temporal coordinates of extremities and joints are recorded while the action takes place. However, such special hardware requires the human subjects to be "wired up" which has an impact on the naturalness and spontaneity of their movements. Also, this purely descriptive data may be irrelevant for the specific research aims. Exact descriptive data may also be retrieved using image processing where hands and fingers are identified and automatically tracked using only the video frames. So, while other media exist, video is still an important if not the predominant medium for gesture analysis. The first step in an analysis by a human researcher is the transcription of the various speech and bodily events according to a coding scheme like the ones described above in Section 3.1.

An obvious technology for transcribing such data is a software that allows the annotation of digital video. Early systems of a time where digital video was not easily available used the interaction's speech transcript instead of the video as the basis for further annotation. The following example shows a speaker's speech transcript in one line and his gesture transcribed in the next line, the temporal duration being indicated with special signs:

```
So here you see our new HIAT-DOS system
    o------- pointing to screen -------o
```

In this approach, the detailed temporal information of the original speech stream is lost and temporal relationships between speech and nonverbal behavior can only be described on the word or syllable level. Therefore, modern systems use speech transcriptions where words are anchored in time. Nonverbal behaviors are transcribed on other layers that are also anchored in time so that the exact temporal relationship between speech and behavior is preserved. This concept of *multiple layers* where each type of information (speech, gesture, gaze etc.) is transcribed on a single layer is the basis of practically every annotation tool. A strong visual metaphor for this layered approach is that of a musical score. In a musical score each instrument has a track for its notes and all tracks run in parallel from left to right in perfect time-alignment. Thus, a reader can easily and exactly see the temporal relationships between the instruments' notes. Analogously, behavioral events can be transcribed like notes on different tracks that model the layers, the only difference being that behaviors have a duration, usually indicated by denoting them as bars or boxes where the length of the box reflects the duration (see Figure 3.3).

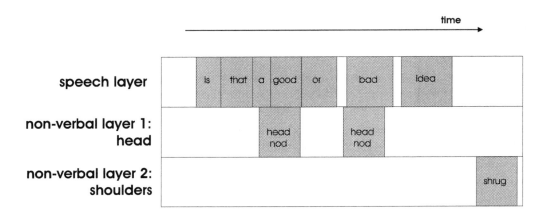

Figure 3.3: *Example for an annotation on three layers. The layers run from left to right with time and contain information about words (top layer), head movement (middle layer) and shoulder movement (bottom layer).*

This section will first review early tools that had not yet integrated digital video but introduced important concepts like multiple layers, the musical score metaphor and the separation of annotation data from annotation scheme. It will then present modern tools that seamlessly integrate digital video players.

3.2.1   Annotation on Multiple Layers

This section will present four early tools that have been used for transcription of speech and behavioral data. The first one, PRAAT, is of peripheral importance since it is a pure audio tool created for phonetic analysis. However, it offers multiple layers and has a good graphical user interface. Moreover, it can be used for speech transcription, thus producing data that can be further processed by a video annotation tool.

The other three tools are presented in chronological order of their creation. HIAT-DOS is a classical tool used in CA and probably the oldest software using multiple layers. The CLAN tool introduced a separation of annotation scheme and annotation data which makes it both generic by opening it to arbitrary research fields and robust by introducing a controlled vocabulary. Finally, the more recent BAS Partitur format, although not a tool but only a file format, shows nicely how the layers can be interrelated and how these relations must be reflected in the definition of annotation schemes.

PRAAT

PRAAT[4] is a tool for speech analysis developed by Paul Boersma and David Weenik (Boersma 2002). Apart from its powerful phonetic analysis features it can be used as a multi-layered audio transcription tool. There are two types of layers: layers that contain intervals and layers that contain time points. In interval layers each new element is specified by marking a beginning and end, whereas in point layers a single time point is specified. For both layer types, the annotation consists of free-form text can be attached to the elements.

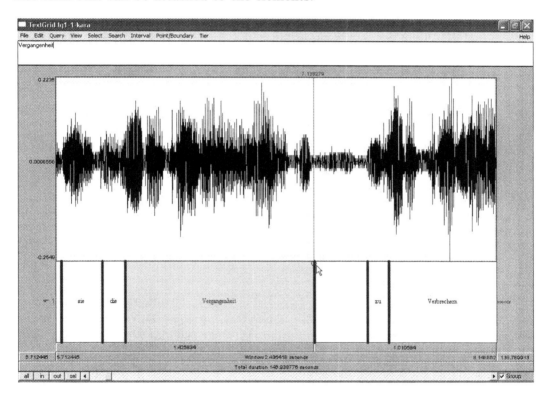

Figure 3.4: *Screenshot of PRAAT's edit window. In this example, PRAAT is used to transcribe words on a single layer below the audio waveform.*

Speech transcription can be performed using a single interval layer by marking beginning and end of each word and inserting the word's transcription (see Figure 3.4). Users can create an arbitrary number of layers on the fly and then add elements in the coding process. The finished annotation is called a textgrid that can be written to an ASCII file.

---

[4]http://www.praat.org

PRAAT runs on Windows, Unix, Macintosh platforms and can be obtained for free by mailing the author[5].

HIAT-DOS

HIAT-DOS[6] is a multi-layer annotation tool that was developed for the HIAT[7] coding scheme (cf. Ehlich, 1992, and Ehlich and Rehbein, 1976). HIAT is an early effort to transcribe conversations on multiple layers and is widely used for conversation analysis (CA). The scheme work with three layers, one for orthographic transcription, one intonation and one for nonverbal communication. The corresponding coding tool HIAT-DOS models these layers as lines in an ASCII file. The basis for the annotation is the orthographic speech transcription that is input like in a word processor. Likewise, nonverbal events are inserted, their temporal extension, beginning and end, are marked with special signs. The lines of the transcript are regarded like tracks in a musical score so that events are seen as being simultaneous if they are vertically aligned. So a word and a nonverbal event are simultaneous if they begin in the same column in the transcript. HIAT-DOS allows the parallel transcription of up to nine speakers.

HIAT-DOS, version 2.2, runs on MS-DOS and Windows platforms. The temporal granularity of the tool is rather crude (word level). Hence, fine-grained temporal relationships cannot be explored. Moreover, it is tailored to the specific HIAT annotation scheme.

CLAN

CLAN[8] is a tool for annotations in the CHAT coding scheme and statistical analysis. It was developed as part of the CHILDES[9] project started in 1984 as an effort to standardize transcription of verbal interactions (MacWhinney 1995). The CHAT[10] coding scheme and file format uses multiple layers (called *tiers*), represented as lines in the file format, and distinguishes between *main* and *secondary* layers. The main layer contains the transcription of one speech utterance including special symbols for interjections, pauses, intonation, stress etc. The secondary layers serve to specify linguistic information like morphosyntax and speech acts or events like actions, facial expressions or gestures. Using the CLAN tool, events can be added using *codes*, a sequence of colon-separated tags. For instance, the code `$MOT:POS:Que` on the speech act tier stands for "mother:positive:question". Each

---

[5]Paul Boersma's e-mail address is `paul.boersma@hum.uva.nl`

[6]`http://www.daf.uni-muenchen.de/HIAT/HIAT.HTM`

[7]**H**alb**i**nterpretative **A**rbeits**t**ranskriptionen

[8]**C**omputerized **L**anguage **An**alysis, `http://childes.psy.cmu.edu/clan`

[9]**C**hild **L**anguage **D**ata **E**xchange **S**ystem, `http://childes.psy.cmu.edu`

[10]**C**odes for the **H**uman **A**nalysis of **T**ranscripts

component is taken from user-defined tag sets that are specified in a separate file: the coding scheme. Events specified on a secondary layer temporally refer to the *whole duration* of the respective main line but can also be marked to refer to a span of words in the main line. In a special movie layer the position of the utterances in the original video can be specified using time-stamps.

CLAN's analysis facilities include reliability analyses where two annotations of the same interaction can be checked for matches and mismatches.

BAS Partitur Format

The BAS[11] Partitur[12] Format (BPF) was inspired by the SAM Label Format and was used to collect large speech corpora of segmental information like transliteration, pronunciation, prosodic information and dialogue acts (Schiel et al. 1998). These different information types are stored on different *tracks*. It has been used to collect data for the development of the translation system VerbMobil (Wahlster 2000) and is currently being used for the SmartKom project (Wahlster 2002) to represent multimodal video annotations of human-computer interactions (Schiel et al., 2002, Steininger, 2001).

The BPF is used to represent dialogues. Each turn is contained in a single file and the whole dialogue is represented by all turn files in a single directory. Within one turn file, there is one reference track which all other tracks refer to, the so-called canonical track which contains words in a phonological transcription. The elements of other tracks (lexical entries, dialogue acts, part-of-speech etc.) can point to an arbitrary collection of elements of the canonical track. Track can also point to non-canonical tracks enabling the user to define dependency hierarchies. For instance, in VerbMobil *dialogue phases* contained multiple *dialogue acts* which contained multiple *words*. These relationships were modeled using three BPF tracks where one track points to the next until the canonical track with *words* is reached.

The description of an annotation element consists of arbitrary strings. There is no in-built facility to define a coding scheme. BPF is merely a file format, meant for centralized data collection and distribution, there are no generic tools for coding. Instead, multiple tools are used to perform annotations, the different output formats are transformed to BPF using Perl scripts (Schiel et al. 2002).

---

[11]**B**avarian **A**rchive for **S**peech Signals,
http://www.phonetik.uni-muenchen.de/Bas/BasHomeeng.html
[12]The word "Partitur" is German for "musical score", a standard metaphor for displaying events that are parallel in time. As early as 1979, Scherer et al. (1979) speak of a "Verhaltenspartitur" (musical score of behavior) when referring to their transcription method of nonverbal behavior.

3.2.2 Annotation of Digital Video

The tools of the previous section either had a strong linguistic/phonetic focus or were rather old. In the transcription of gestures it is important to have close control of digital video during coding. The following tools have all a digital video player as integral part of their coding facilities.

Akira

The video annotation tool Akira[13] was created to support the analysis of movies. Apart from a video player it provides a coding window with time-aligned tracks. The tracks can be structured in hierarchies (sub-tracks) like file directories for organizational purposes. Coding is performed by adding *parts* to a track. These parts are represented as rectangles in the coding window and can contain a single *label* that is displayed in the rectangle. Additionally, parts can be colored and filled with textual comment and symbols. Complete annotations are stored as binaries but can also be exported MS Word files. Akira runs on Windows platforms.

Akira lacks a definition of a coding scheme that is separate from the actual annotation. Tracks are created on-the-fly during coding and the coding elements (parts) contain labels that are not pre-defined. This approach reflects Akira's purpose as a tool for film studies where for each film a separate coding scheme must be created to fit the needs of the specific film. It is therefore more suited for exploratory research and less for the systematic annotation with a pre-defined coding scheme.

MacSHAPA

MacSHAPA[14] is a multi-layered video annotation tool for the analysis of observational data created by Penelope Sanderson (Sanderson et al. 1994). It supports coding with typed elements and pre-defined vocabularies (tag sets), has both a time-aligned and spreadsheet view on the data, and comes with search routines and statistical processing functions.

The basic metaphor for data storage is the spreadsheet. Thus, the coding takes place in spreadsheet columns, also called *variables*, which can be regarded as what is usually called layers. Within each column *cells* can be added, the elements of annotation. The annotation elements must assume one of the following types: text, nominal, matrix, predicate, float or integer. Nominal, matrix and predicate data need further explanation. Nominal typed data consists of a single label. Matrix data is a comma-separated list of labels. MacSHAPA allows the user to pre-define

---

[13]http://www.split.uni-mannheim.de/R3/index.htm

[14]http://www.aviation.uiuc.edu/institute/acadprog/epjp/macshapa.html

matrix templates that dictate what kind of data must be inserted where like in the following template:

(<speaker>, <recipient>, <topic>, <tone>)

During annotation the user is guided through the structure letting him/her only insert values from the pre-defined vocabularies. Predicate data is the most powerful data type consisting of a main descriptive term, the predicate, followed by arguments specific to the predicate. For instance,

GOAL (<who>, <variable>, <value>)
COMMAND (<from>, <to>, <topic>, <tone>)

The time-aligned view is a *passive* view, i.e. it is generated from the spreadsheet and cannot be edited directly. The statistical functions include transition and lag sequential analyses as well as reliability analyses. Annotated data can be exported to spreadsheets or SPSS for further quantitative analyses.

MacSHAPA only runs on Macintosh platforms. More importantly, development and support stopped in 1997.

MediaTagger

CAVA[15] is a project started in 1994 at the MPI for Psycholinguistics in Nijmegen dealing with the linguistic analysis of multimedia data. CAVA's *MediaTagger* component allows multi-layered annotation of digital videos. In MediaTagger, layers are called *tiers* and come in three types: no dependency, temporal inclusion (all tags are included in one tag of the parent tier), and simultaneity (all tags correspond to tags in the parent tier). A tier can hold elements that are inserted by the coder. Elements can contain either a string or a tag from a pre-defined vocabulary. For the latter case, during coding the interface offers all possible values in a graphical menu. MediaTagger also provides string search over annotated tags. Moreover, it offers multiple viewers for the same video.

MediaTagger runs on Macintosh platforms. It offers a dependency relationship between layers (temporal inclusion) and two basic element types (string and tag set). The coding scheme can be specified in a separate file. It does *not* provide a time-aligned view on the annotation in the musical score metaphor.

The Observer

The Observer[16] is a commercial annotation, analysis and management tool for observational data. The system consists of four modules: Project Manager, Configuration Designer, Event Recorder, and Data Analysis.

---

[15]**C**omputer **A**ssisted **V**ideo **A**nalysis, http://www.mpi.nl/world/tg/CAVA/CAVA.html
[16]http://www.noldus.com

The *Project Manager* is used for configuration and for managing the annotation data files. In the *Configuration Designer* module the user specifies the coding scheme in terms of classes, behavioral elements and modifiers. Classes are what is usually called a layer and are used to store behavioral elements. These behavioral elements represent activities, postures, movements, positions, facial expressions etc. They can be defined to be either events without duration or states with start and end time. For specification of variable features of a behavioral element, up to two modifiers can be added to hold further information. For a modifier class, a range of values can be pre-defined in the coding scheme. Elements can also be defined as being reciprocal. During coding, the user has to code only one direction (Alpha plays with Beta) after which the program automatically inserts the reciprocal event (Beta plays with Alpha). Multiple subjects can be analyzed with the help of channels. A channel is the combination of one subject and one class. In the *Event Recorder* module the actual coding takes place by adding elements and time-stamps. The *Checksheet* view displays a chronological log of all events plus time-stamps, the *Channels* window indicates the current state of each channel, and a *Notepad* allows taking time-stamped user notes.

In the *Data Analysis* module data can be searched, the results can be saved. Searching can be based on independent variables (e.g. Sex=Male), time windows (e.g., from time=30 to event="John looks"), co-occurrence (to extract events of different classes with AND/OR operators) and search masks like "actor-behavior-modifier1-modifier2" where each component can be wildcarded. The search results can be analyzed using three procedures. The *Reliability Analysis* computes the agreement between pairs of observational data files. The user can specify tolerance level (time window) and get percentage of agreement, an index of concordance and a detailed report. The *Elementary Statistics* procedure computes simple descriptive measures like frequency, duration, latency, proportion of time spent for single events or combinations of concurrent events/states. *Lag Sequential Analysis* analyzes the temporal relationships between preceding and following events. The program counts the transitions between pairs of events, the separating interval is called *lag*.

The tool was conceived for psychological and anthropological work. It runs on Windows platforms. It has no time-aligned view during annotation. The definition of behavioral elements is restricted in various ways: only two modifiers, no links/dependencies between elements, restricted number of classes and elements. The system is neither platform-independent nor XML-based. The statistical analysis capabilities include reliability, descriptive statistics and lag sequential analysis. However, the data can also be exported for external analysis. In comparison with other tools, The Observer sticks out by having a project manager and allowing reciprocal behavior.

SignStream

SignStream[17] is a multi-layer annotation tool for research in sign languages. Layers are called *fields*. The tool provides a set of predefined layers specifically designed for representing sign language data but also allows the user to define new layers and new layer values. The so-called *gloss window* displays the annotated elements in time-alignment during coding (Figure 3.5). The gloss window can be partitioned according to the number of transcribed subjects. For each subject the whole range of layers is replicated in a separate pane.

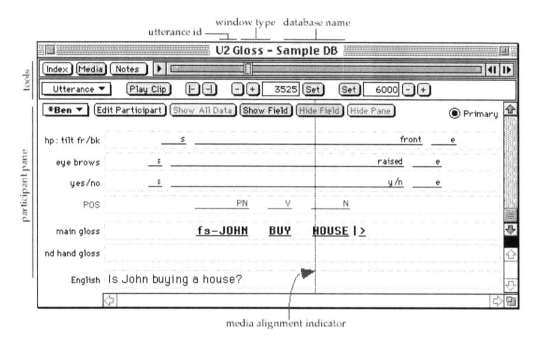

Figure 3.5: *SignStream's gloss window where the annotation takes place. It provides a set of predefined fields specifically designed for representing sign language data. However, the program also allows the user to define new fields and new field values.*

SignStream allows the user to conduct sophisticated searches of SignStream databases. A search query can be formulated by combining search operators with data specifications. In addition to standard Boolean combinatorial operations (AND, OR, and NOT), SignStream provides a number of operators that are relevant to the particular type of data represented in the databases. For example,

---

[17]http://www.bu.edu/asllrp/SignStream

the WITH operator can be used to search for combinations of data that are co-extensive, permitting a user to search for utterances containing, e.g., an index sign co-occurring with eye gaze. Searches can be conducted in a number of sequential stages, where subsequent stages search over the results found in a previous stage. This allows the user to narrow in on the data of interest.

SignStream runs on Macintosh platforms. It offers a timeline view and powerful search facilities. However, it includes potentially unnecessary layers specific to the domain of sign languages. Also, it does not allow to define tag sets separately in an annotation scheme. Moreover, although it allows the transcription of multiple subjects it does not generalize this concept to allow arbitrary *groupings* of layers. It also lacks the temporal inclusion relationship between layers.

syncWRITER

syncWRITER, version 2.0, is a commercial transcription tool for Macintosh platforms in conjunction with Quicktime videos (Hanke and Prillwitz 1995). It allows video transcription on multiple layers. Synchronicity is achieved by using special *syncTabs* that are visualized as small rectangles in the header of the layer window. The transcription input is text that can be aligned to any of the syncTabs. The input need not be pre-specified nor conform to any scheme.

syncWRITER does not offer to define an annotation scheme with pre-defined tag sets. The annotation elements can only be synchronized with time points using syncTabs but they do not have a *duration*.

TASX-annotator

The TASX[18]-annotator[19] tool allows video transcription on multiple layers (Milde 2002). It offers three annotation views: the time-aligned view, the text view and the HTML view. The time-aligned view implements the music score metaphor. The text view displays each track on an editable page, each element taking up one line. The HTML view is a non-editable view as a HTML page that can also be loaded to normal browsers.

The tool uses an internal text representation of the annotation data. For storing and loading this data, XML style sheets (XSL) are used to transform the data to XML documents. The advantage of this approach is the simple and quick integration of new formats that can be done by writing two style sheets, one for writing, one for reading.

The TASX-annotator does not allow to define an annotation scheme. Also, it offers no facilities to establish temporal or other relationships *across* layers.

---

[18]**T**ime **A**ligned **S**ignal data e**X**change format
[19]http://tasxforce.lili.uni-bielefeld.de

Elan

The EUDICO[20] project, started in 1997, is an effort to re-implement the CAVA system in a Java-based environment where users can annotate corpora via the Internet in a client-server scenario (Brugman et al. 2000). ELAN[21] is the corresponding video annotation tool and the Java-based successor to the MediaTagger tool (Figure 3.6). It offers multi-layered annotation and search options. There are two types of layers: independent and referring. In independent layers elements are anchored in time, having a beginning and end. In referring layers each element points to an element of the respective *parent* layer. The relation between an element E in a referring layer and an element P in the parent layer can be of the following types: time subdivision, symbolic subdivision and symbolic association. Time subdivision means that E decomposes P into smaller time intervals. For instance, if P defines a sentence, E could decompose P into words specifying internal temporal boundaries while inheriting beginning and end times. Symbolic subdivision is similar in that E decomposes P into smaller units but differs in that there are no temporal boundaries are specified. For instance, a word can be decomposed into morphemes that have no temporal boundaries. Finally, symbolic association means that E as a whole refers to P. It is a one-to-one mapping.

ELAN is superior to the MediaTagger because it provides a timeline view during coding, it is platform-independent and uses XML for data files. However, unlike MediaTagger it does not offer to define an annotation scheme. Also, ELAN is still under development.

3.2.3 Conclusions

All reviewed annotation tools are based on the concept of multi-layered annotation. However, not all tools allow working with digital video during coding. The classical tool for conversation analysis, HIAT-DOS, rather relies on the transcribed speech in conjunction with analogue video. The BAS Partitur Format does not provide an annotation tool for video annotation at all.

Most digital video annotation tools run on specific platforms which restricts their use. MacSHAPA and the MediaTagger only function on Macintosh computers. Moreover, MacSHAPA is neither supported nor updated anymore. Almost all of the tools offer a timeline view that most closely approximates the metaphor of a musical score and facilitates reading the annotation by the human coder. However, The Observer only offers this view in a separate analysis step, meaning that during coding the timeline view is not available. The storage format for annotation files is not standardized yet. Only the most recent tools, Elan and TASX, make use of the

---

[20]**Eu**ropean **Di**stributed **Co**rpora,
http://www.mpi.nl/world/tg/lapp/eudico/eudico.html
[21]**E**UDICO **L**inguistic **A**nnotator, http://www.mpi.nl/tools

Figure 3.6: *Elan's graphical user interface offers a video viewer (top), a waveform viewer (below video), a subtitle viewer (below waveform) and a time-aligned annotation board (bottom).*

quasi-standard XML, Akira even produces binaries as output. Most importantly, many tools incorporate some degree of genericness for defining the properties of the annotation, the so-called annotation scheme. However, they differ in how powerful the concepts are that can be defined by the user. CLAN offers hierarchical values for each layer but does not have any form of interrelatedness between layers.

MediaTagger offers three types of layers that allows elements of one layer to temporally subsume a number of subsequent elements in another layer. Only a single tool, The Observer, incorporates a project manager that allows to handle multiple annotations for searching and browsing.

With regard to the insights gained in Section 3.1 on transcription methods, the following list features can be assembled that are necessary for the transcription of gestures:

- Video player: a video player is integrated

- Timeline view: during coding the annotation is displayed in time-alignment

- Coding scheme definition: coding scheme (tag set) and data are separated; the coding scheme can be specified electronically

- Layer dependencies: there is a temporal inclusion relationship between layers

- Cross-level coding: elements in one layer (level) can be related to elements in another layer

- Analysis functions: e.g., search facilities

- XML output: an accessible file representation is used for data storage and exchange

- Platform independence: the software runs on many platforms

Although some of the reviewed tools are quite powerful, no single tool incorporates all listed features. The feature of cross-layer coding is not offered by any of the tools although it is necessary to connect gestural and speech annotations as argued in Section 3.1.5. It must be concluded that no tool exists suitable for the annotation of gesture in the context of gesture generation as approached in this work. Therefore, a new tool had to be developed that will be described in Chapter 6. The same chapter will also present a more detailed comparison and evaluation of all tools, including the newly developed one.

Chapter 4

Generation Approaches

Chapter 2 gave an overview of the classes of conversational gestures and their properties. This chapter shows how computer scientists exploit this knowledge to build systems that generate nonverbal behavior for embodied synthetic agents. In the first part of this chapter, nine existing generation systems are described, their advantages and disadvantages identified. The second part reviews the major principles of generation, exemplifying them with the presented systems.

The survey will show that existing generation systems lack in two respects. First, almost all systems rely on the gesture research literature for their gesture generations rules. Only for one system own empirical research was conducted. Second, none of the systems tries to model *individual* behavior. Instead, the systems make use of general rules that were proved or hypothesized to apply to *most* speakers. For instance, one general rule claims that iconic gestures are triggered by shape parameters of the object being talked about. Another rule claims that the "give-take" gesture (open palm upwards, hand halfway outstretched) is used when asking a question or giving an answer (Noma et al. 2000). However, individual speakers differ in which gestures they use and in what context they use them. Some people may not use iconics at all in conversations, others may not use the "give-take" gesture when asking questions. None of the surveyed systems takes such individual gesture habits into account.

The chapter is organized as follows. Existing generation systems are surveyed in Section 4.1, and key principles are identified and compared in Section 4.2. Finally, the essential features of all systems are summarized in Section 4.3.

4.1 Generation Systems

Nine existing systems for generating nonverbal actions are now surveyed. Although this work is concerned with gesture generation, three systems dealing with facial expression, posture shifts and gaze are included here because they deal with issues relevant to gesture generation. To better refer to all systems, those without a system name are given an explicit name in the following sections.

4.1.1 PPP: Plan-based Generation

André et al. (1996) developed an agent called PPP[1] persona which uses gesture and speech to explain technical devices (see Figure 1.1 on p. 13). The input consists of high-level instructions like "explain modem". These so-called *goals* are automatically decomposed by a planner into lower-level communicative strategies, e.g. "describe object". These are in turn translated to elementary actions like speaking, gesturing or showing images (see Figure 4.1). The actions are brought into a temporal sequence using time constraints that are resolved by a scheduler.

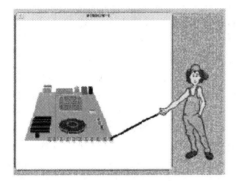 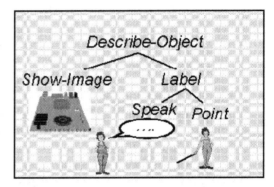

Figure 4.1: *The PPP persona agent explaining a modem using pointing gestures (left). Speech and gesture of the agent are generated in a process called planning (right). Speech and gesture are elementary actions represented as leaves in a plan tree and triggered by higher-level communicative strategies. (Pictures taken from Rist et al., 2003)*

The selection of gestures and their coordination with speech is encoded in *plans*, also called communicative strategies. The system can therefore be considered a concept-to-gesture generation system. PPP is specialized in pointing gestures (deictics) that are created at runtime depending on the position and dimensions of the object to be pointed at. Complex pointing gestures can be generated by concatenating basic pointing gestures (e.g., letting the pointing gesture run along the lines of a diagram). Besides deictics, the PPP persona is one of the first agents to perform *idle-time* gestures: it keeps moving even when "off-duty" (Müller, 2000: 135–136).

---

[1]**P**ersonalized **P**lan-Based **P**resenter

Such gestures include blinking, breathing or scratching a body part. Since part of these gestures can be considered adaptors, the gestural repertoire of PPP persona comprises deictics and adaptors.

The PPP agent is animated in a keyframe-based approach, i.e. keyframes are concatenated at runtime according to the generated plan tree. Transitions between gestures are handled by inserting suitable intermediate keyframes. In the plan-based approach, this is solved by assigning IDs to all "resting" body positions. The IDs are then inserted in the pre- and post-conditions of a gesture's plan depending on the begin and end position of the body when performing the gesture (Müller, 2000: 106–109).

The PPP persona was extended with facial expressions in the AiA[2] project (André et al. 1999). Two recent successor agents were provided with an extended gestural repertoire, including conversational gestures. The agents are called Cyberella (Gebhard 2001), a virtual receptionist, and Smartakus, the digital assistant in the SmartKom system (Wahlster 2002). However, even in these recent systems the rules governing gesture selection are still hand-crafted.

PPP is an early agent concept-to-gesture system that relies on hand-crafted gesture generation rules encoded in plans while details of the generated pointing gestures are computed at runtime (type, location, duration of the gesture). Gesture-speech synchronization is handled by letting (pointing) gesture and concept in speech co-occur. Adaptors are generated randomly during "resting" times.

4.1.2 VHP: Text to Gesture

Noma et al. (2000) designed a *Virtual Human Presenter* (VHP), a system that takes text plus commands as input and generates a speaking and moving agent (Noma and Badler 1997). The commands can be used to let the agent perform one of the following gestures:

1. Giving and taking: hand out with palm up

2. Rejecting: sweeping hand, palm down

3. Warning: hand out, palm to addressee like stop sign

4. Move in palm direction: show a flow (on map/chart)

5. Pointing, index finger: basic pointing gesture

6. Pointing, palm back: covering larger area

7. Pointing, palm down: emphasize phrase or list item

The input text is considered the "temporal axis" for the presentation. A more abstract and semantically annotated input was rejected by the authors in order to

---

[2]**A**daptive Communication Assistant for Effective **I**nfobahn **A**ccess

keep the system application-independent. Commands are executed simultaneous with the following word. Gesture selection is performed using heuristics: Certain words in the text stream automatically trigger gesture commands. These selection rules were taken from (1) the psychological literature and (2) popular books on presentation and public speaking. Apart from gesture, the system supports the generation of posture, gaze behavior and walking. The scheduling of the input is handled using PaT-Nets[3], an extended and parallelized form of finite state machines. For rendering, VHP uses the *Jack* system which computes agent animations at runtime based on a 3D model (Badler et al. 1993).

VHP is a text-to-gesture system with a small gesture repertoire of seven gestures. Generation is driven by rules taken from the literature, gestures are timed to coincide with their related concepts in speech. The project stands out from other approaches by attempting to generate "good gestures" by consulting the literature on presentation and public speaking.

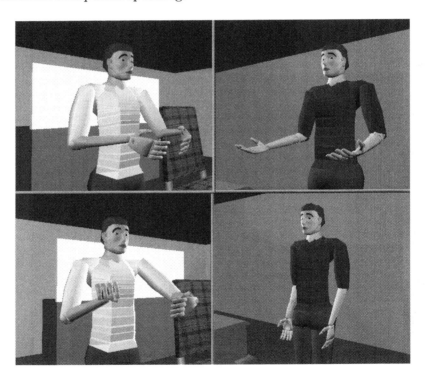

Figure 4.2: *In the Animated Conversation (AC) system, two agents engage in a money exchange dialogue using iconic, metaphoric, deictic and beat gestures. (Taken from Cassell et al., 1994.)*

---

[3]Parallel Transition Networks (Badler et al. 1995)

4.1.3   AC: Rule-based Generation

In the Animated Conversation (AC) system, Cassell et al. (1994) automatically generate a money exchange dialogue with two agents (Figure 4.2)[4]. *Representational* gestures (iconics, metaphorics, deictics) are generated by look-up in a dictionary using semantic representations of form features. Gesture selection relies on rules triggered by words:

- *Iconics* are triggered by words with literally spatial or concrete content (example: "check")

- *Metaphorics* are triggered by words with metaphorically spatial or abstract content get metaphorics (example: "account")

- *Deictics* are triggered by words with physically spatializable content (example: "this bank")

- *Beats* are generated when semantic content cannot be represented spatially (example: "fifty dollars").

Gestures selection is also driven by information structure. Representational gestures are selected for (1) rhematic elements[5] or (2) hearer new references (excluding deictics). They are mapped from semantic representations to motion prototypes, and are timed so that preparation starts before the intonational phrase and the stroke coincides with nuclear stress. Beats are selected for discourse new definite references, e.g. "fifty dollars", and are timed to coincide with the stressed syllable. The selected gestures, together with gaze actions, are realized using PaT-Nets that produce an action script to be executed by the *Jack* character animation system.

AC is a concept-to-gesture system with a lexicon of prefabricated movement patterns. The authors argue that such an approach can be justified by the observation that gestures are more standardized in terms of form than previously assumed (Kendon 1980). The implemented gestures encompass members of four different gesture classes: iconics, metaphorics, deictics and beats. The rules governing gesture selection were taken from the literature. The gestures are timed that the stroke coincides with the stressed syllable of the co-occurring concept in speech, a rule introduced by McNeill (1992) and henceforth called the *stroke-stress rule*.

4.1.4   REA: Grammar-based Generation

Cassell et al. (2000a) developed a system that generates gestures in a grammar-based approach: an embodied agent called REA (Real Estate Agent) presents houses to potential buyers using speech, gestures and facial expressions (Figure 4.3)[6].

---

[4]Copyright by Justine Cassell, Northwestern University
[5]See Section 7.3 for details on the terms *theme* and *rheme*.
[6]Copyright by Justine Cassell, Northwestern University

Figure 4.3: *In the REA system, a virtual real-estate agent interacts with the user using conversational gestures.*

For the gesture generation task, an empirical study was conducted. Human subjects had to study a video and floor plan of a particular house and were then asked to describe this house to a second subject. The conversations were transcribed (328 utterances, 134 referential gestures), and the communicative goals and semantic features were encoded. In the analysis, the relationship between content of gesture, content of speech and communicative functions was captured in six rules. According to Yan (2000), these rules account for 60% of the gestures in the transcription (recall), and apply with a precision of 96%.

Speech and gestures are both generated using a single grammar. The entries of this grammar, called lexicalized descriptors, contain syntactic, semantic and pragmatic data. Descriptors can translate to words or (prefabricated) gestures in the surface realization. To reflect gestural polysemy, the same gesture can have multiple descriptors. On the syntactic level, the grammar entries are tree structures where nodes can be replaced by other entries using LTAG[7] operations. A special node allows the coordination of a gesture with a speech utterance: it translates to a synchronization of the gesture's stroke with the speech part's most prominent syllable.

This grammar-based approach can also be regarded a *deep* approach to gesture generation since gestures are generated based on semantic and pragmatic information. The grammar works in a deterministic fashion: The same context will

---

[7]Feature-Based Lexicalized Tree Adjoining Grammar (Joshi et al. 1975)

always generate the same gesture. This contradicts the opinion of Calbris (1990) that gestures are probabilistic. The REA system is exceptional in that it relies on empirical studies specifically designed for the project and utilized to inform the generation grammar. However, the selection of the material can be criticized. The subjects were not real estate agents and the experimental setup was not a sales situation. Thus, it was not ensured that the collected gestures were the ones that should appear in the final application. Moreover, the approach does not aim at individual behavior. In contrast, it tries to achieve a generality by abstracting away from individual subjects.

4.1.5 MAX: Feature-based Generation

Kopp and Wachsmuth (2000) created the MAX agent who can speak and perform deictic and iconic gestures (Figure 4.4). Deictic and iconic gestures cannot be efficiently animated by playing prefabricated clips or movement patterns because their exact form strongly depends on the current situation. Therefore, the authors rely on an approach where single features are triggered and then assembled to a gesture at runtime in a 3D-model-based animation engine.

Figure 4.4: *The MAX agent and its underlying skeleton.*

The system takes speech annotated with communicative intent as input. Generation is based on a lexicon of gestures, a *gestuary* (de Ruiter 1998), where each entry includes the gesture's communicative intent and a feature-based representation of the gesture consisting of spatial constraints. In generation, the communicative intent of speech triggers all possible gestures in the gestuary. The gesture entry which best matches the current movement conditions of the 3D agent is selected. The gesture is then adapted to the current body context and timing constraints are applied to ensure that the stroke shortly precedes or coincides with the stressed syllable of the associated word, called *affiliate*. The stroke is set to span the whole affiliate before retraction starts (Kopp and Wachsmuth 2002).

Feature-based generation is based on the idea that gestures exist as spatio-temporal representations of "shape" somewhere in human memory. Opinions are divided over how these shapes become manifest as gestures and what role the modality of speech plays in the processing. The solution by de Ruiter (1998) has a module called *conceptualizer* to decide which aspects of a pre-verbal message are realized by gesture, which by speech. In contrast, in the *process model* by Krauss et al. (2000) the gestures' features bypass the conceptualizer and become manifest immediately so that the emerging gesture can facilitate the retrieval of lexical items in speech processing.

MAX is a concept-to-gesture system for generating iconics and deictics. It is capable of rendering gestures based on fully parametrizable specifications. It thus rejects using prefabricated movement patterns and allows fine-grained temporal synchronization with speech by stretching and compressing movement phases while preserving human movement qualities. For synchronization with speech the authors rely on the classical stroke-stress rule.

4.1.6   BEAT: Text to Concept to Gesture

Cassell et al. (2001b) developed the *Behavior Expression Animation Toolkit* (BEAT) which generates gestures and other nonverbal output from plain text. It was devised as a tool for professional animators suggesting a "baseline" of gestures that can be manually improved or be used for mass scenes. Processing is conducted in a pipeline of four modules responsible for (1) language tagging, (2) behavior suggestion, (3) behavior selection and (4) scheduling. The architecture is depicted in Figure 4.5.

The language tagging module transforms the text input into a tree structure. An utterance is divided into clauses, a clause is decomposed into theme and rheme[8] using heuristic rules. Single words are tagged with "newness" and "contrast". The latter concept is found with the help of the synonym-antonym relationship in WordNet[9]. The resulting syntax tree is passed on to the behavior suggestion module which produces behavior suggestions using if-then rules. The suggested gestures are added to tree nodes with a priority number. If no rules fire, a beat gesture is added

---

[8]See Section 7.3 for details on the terms *theme* and *rheme*.

[9]WordNet is an electronic lexical reference system where English nouns, verbs and adjectives are organized into synonym sets, each representing one underlying lexical concept (Miller et al. 1990). Different relations link the synonym sets. The approach is inspired by current psycholinguistic theories of human lexical memory.

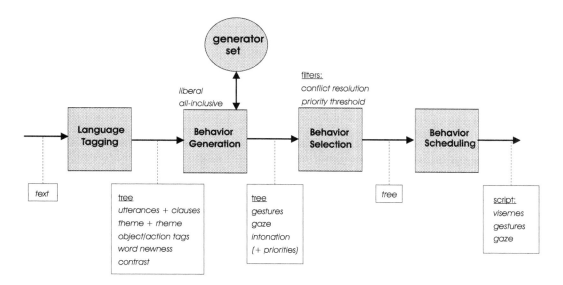

Figure 4.5: *BEAT architecture.*

with low priority. Iconics are generated for "surprising" or "unusual" features in a rheme part. They are also selected for all verbal phrases in a rheme part whose action have an associated gesture in the database. A "contrast" triggers a specific contrast gesture if there are exactly two items, or the beat gesture.

In the behavior selection module, the overgenerated gestures are reduced by a number of consecutive filters. They delete incompatible behaviors and "can reflect the personalities, affective state and energy level of characters by regulating how much nonverbal behavior they exhibit". Two filters are implemented. The *conflict resolution* filter detects mutually incompatible behaviors and deletes the ones with lower priority. The *priority threshold* filter removes behavior with a priority underneath a certain threshold. It can be used to regulate the amount of overall gesturing.

The scheduling module converts the tree structure to linear script. First, text commands are sent to the speech synthesis system to obtain word and phoneme times. Then, these times are used to compute absolute time values for nonverbal behavior. In a last step, the abstract commands are compiled to an application specific format.

BEAT is a text-to-gesture approach that performs syntactic preprocessing on the input text. The system produces beats, some iconic gestures and one metaphoric gesture. Gestures are timed using the stroke-stress rule. To achieve individuality, the authors suggest to implement specific filters but offer no hints as to how these filters could look like.

4.1.7 FACE: Facial Action Generation

Pelachaud et al. (1996) generate facial expressions from annotated speech input using rules. They consider emotions, intonation and information structure to compute facial expressions, head and eye movements, including timing with respect to speech. The output is a script in the universal FACS[10] format that is rendered with the *Jack* software.

The input consists of text, its phonetic representation, emotions with intensity, pauses, syntax tags (function word vs. content word), mood (declarative, interrogative) and intonation markers (pitch accent, phrasal and boundary tones; see Pierrehumbert and Hirschberg, 1990). The rules governing the generation process are grouped according to so-called *determinants*. A determinant is a specific meaning interpretation of a facial expression. It can manifest itself by a combination of different facial action units (AUs). For example, the determinant *highlight word* (a conversational signal) can be realized by raising an eyebrow, by nodding or blinking etc. The following four determinant types are used:

1. **Conversational signals** serve to clarify and support what is being said, occur on accented items or emphatic segments, usually eyebrow movements, e.g. the eyebrow flash.

2. **Punctuators** serve to group sequences of words to phrases. A boundary (comma) is underlined by slow movement, a final pause coincides with stillness. A question is often indicated by raised eyebrows, a period may be marked by a frown.

3. **Regulators** serve to control the speaker-listener interaction, mainly head and eye movements. For a question the head is positioned toward the listener (speaker-turn) and raises up toward the end. For a statement the head looks away from the listener (speaker-state) and looks down at the end. Between two intonational phrases in the same sentence the head turns toward the listener (speaker-within-turn) and turns away (speaker-continuation-turn).

4. **Manipulators** serve to satisfy biological needs such as blinking to wet the eyes. Blinks are added to pauses (punctuators) and accents (conversational signals). Further blinks are added to make them occur periodically.

For generation, the input emotions are mapped to a facial expression as a basis for further manipulation. Then, determinant rules translate the other input annotations to facial actions units (AUs). The AU intensity depends on the speech rate. Empirically found heuristics are used to compute the timing of the facial actions, their onset, apex and offset). The final output consists of a list of AUs for each phoneme and pause.

---

[10]**F**acial **A**ction **C**oding **S**ystem (Ekman and Friesen 1978)

The system, that is called FACE here, is a rule-based text-to-gesture system working on annotated input. The generation rules are derived from the literature and coded by hand. Information structure is derived from intonation, it is not explicitly coded in the rules. The generated output is rendered with a 3D talking head. The integration of emblems is planned for the future with the help of a library.

4.1.8   Greta: Gaze and Facial Expression Generation

Pelachaud et al. (2002) generate facial expressions and gaze behavior for a female 3D talking head called Greta. In an interactive dialogue system, it acts as a medical advisor. During user interactions, the dialogue manager generates abstract dialogue moves which are automatically enriched with semantic and pragmatic information like rhetorical relations, turn-taking acts, certainty values or deictic components. This results in text annotated with *communicative functions* in a format called APML[11] which is passed on to the generator.

The generator produces facial actions by look-up in a lexicon that contains a meaning-signal pair for each communicative function (Poggi et al. 2000). The authors devised five categories of communicative function:

1. Deixis and information on physical or metaphorical properties of referents. For instance, small aperture of the eyes for expressing the property "small" or looking in a certain direction as a deictic act.

2. The degree of certainty with which the agent believes what she is saying. For instance, a frown for "certain".

3. The expression of the agent's goal: the performative of her sentence, the topic-comment distinction, rhetorical relations, the turn-taking act. For instance, flashing the eyebrows on the comment part of an utterance.

4. The expression of emotions. For instance, expressing joy by smiling.

5. The kind of thinking activity in which the agent is currently engaged. For instance, looking up to show that the agent is thinking.

The lexicon was devised based on findings in the literature as well as undocumented empirical research.

Conflicts may arise if a single utterance contains two communicative functions that trigger incompatible facial actions. For instance, the communicative function to convey "satisfaction" generates raised eyebrows, a smile and a head nod. In the same utterance, the function to convey "certainty" triggers a frown. The frown and raised eyebrows are conflicting facial actions. The authors suggest to use a

---

[11]**A**ffective **P**resentation **M**arkup **L**anguage

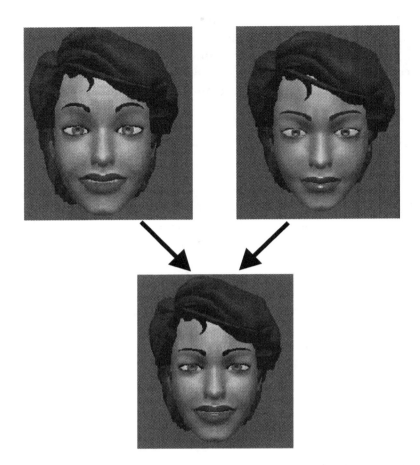

Figure 4.6: *The Greta system resolves generation conflicts by consulting a belief network (BN). Here, the input "satisfaction" (top, left) generates raised eyebrows, a smile and a head nod. For "certain" (top, right) a frown is generated. For the input "satisfaction and certain" (bottom) the conflicting facial actions are resolved to be a frown, a smile and a head nod. (Pictures taken from Pelachaud, 2003.)*

belief network (BN) to resolve such conflicts (Figure 4.6). The BN is a two-layered feed-forward network that has input nodes for communicative functions and output nodes for facial actions. The distribution of weights and an intermediate layer of nodes control the conflict resolution.

Greta is a concept-to-gesture system where the input representation includes the speaker's emotion, beliefs and goals. Generation is based on a lexicon of meaning-to-signal mappings. The generation overgenerates actions and resolves conflicts using a belief network. The output consists of text and MPEG-4 commands rendered by a talking head with a 3D muscle-based facial model. Pelachaud and Poggi

(2002) suggest that individuality is achievable by tuning the BN. By setting individual preferences for what signals to express given an communicative function one creates what they call an *expressive idiolect*.

4.1.9 REA/P: Probabilistic Posture Shift Generation

Based on the empirical analysis of monologues and dialogues, Cassell et al. (2001a) generate posture shifts for the REA agent (see Section 4.1.4). The system generates postures shift from annotated input utterances. For dialogues, the concepts that trigger posture shifts are: utterance boundaries, topic segment, end-of-segment and the turn-taking act (take, continue or give up turn). These factors act as conditions in probabilistic rules that generate different types of posture shift. The posture shift type is determined by energy (low or high), duration (short, default, long) and body part (upper, lower, upper and lower, upper or lower). There are four energy/body part combinations actually used in the generation rules. Thus, the repertoire of nonverbal actions consists of four different movements. For monologues, two rules suffice to model posture shift generation. In case of a *change topic* act a high energy posture shift is generated with 84% probability, whereas a *continuation* act triggers a low energy posture shift with a probability of 4%.

The system, called REA/P here, is a concept-to-gesture system using probabilistic rules derived from empirical data. The results were implemented and rendered using the REA agent.

4.2 Generation Principles

Having described nine generation systems, this section explores the underlying principles that are used in the various architectures.

4.2.1 Input Structures

Generation of gestures consists of scanning the input for data that can trigger specific gestures. This can be words, commands or complex semantic structures. The necessary data may not be directly represented in the input, instead having to be inferred in a linguistic preprocessing step like in the BEAT system.

The input must allow the reconstruction of gestural determinants. Some systems, like the VHP and BEAT, achieve this by working on pure text, whereas the AC, REA/P, FACE systems require additional input information concerning meaning, intention or emotion. What all five systems share is that processing of the two modalities, speech and gesture, is performed separately. Generation can proceed in two sequential steps. In contrast, the systems PPP, REA, MAX and Greta create multimodal output from pure meaning representations in an integrated approach. Processing in the two modalities runs in parallel. The problem of resolving conflicts, i.e. which modality to prefer to communicate a meaning aspect, can either be part of the generation engine (PPP, REA) or handled in a separate module. Thus, MAX has the *conceptualizer* module and Greta uses a belief network for conflict resolution, also called *goal-media prioritizing* by Poggi et al. (2000) or *multimodal fission* by Wahlster (2002).

The kind of input structure not only depends on theory but also on the integration of the generation system in a greater context. Working with text allows the generation system to be connected to any other system that produces text output, making it very flexible. If concepts beyond plain text are required, like syntax, information structure, semantic, systems like BEAT resort to *internal* preprocessing of the input to find these concepts. Internal parsing is not necessary, however, if gesture generation is embedded in a automatic discourse generation system where abstract linguistic concepts emerge as a by-product of discourse planning. PPP and Greta exploit this by reusing the internal concepts for generation. This principle is known from *speech* generation. So-called text-to-speech (TTS) systems take text input and are therefore easy to use and application-independent, whereas so-called concept-to-speech (CTS) systems achieve potentially better results but must be provided with complex input structures. In analogy, gesture generation based on plain text input can be called *text-to-gesture* (TTG) systems, whereas systems requiring semantic input structures can be called *concept-to gesture* (CTG) systems. The term *gesture* in TTG and CTG are taken to include posture shifts, gaze behavior and facial expressions, using the term in the broadest sense possible.

4.2.2 Generation

The task of gesture generation can be decomposed into three subtasks:

1. gesture selection
2. gesture-speech coordination
3. gesture parametrization (handedness, motion qualities)

Gesture selection answers the question what triggers a gesture (e.g. communicative intent) and whether a gesture is triggered in a particular context. If a gesture is triggered in a particular situation, its timing with respect to speech must be determined. This is called gesture-speech coordination. Finally, the gesture may have several degrees of freedom (which hand, which force, which extension) that have to be fixed. This is meant by parametrization.

Gesture selection is usually based on rules obtained from the literature on gesture research. All systems, except for REA/P, use rules in the form of word-to-gesture or concept-to-gesture mappings to generate gestures from the input. But whereas VHP and FACE always generate gestures, AC produces gestures only for rhematic elements and hearer new references. MAX lets a separate component, the conceptualizer, integrate speech and gesture output. All these approaches are *local* in their consideration of context. More global aspects like the overall frequency of gesturing or even whether a gesture is more probable to be used in conjunction with a particular other gesture are not captured thus. However, the BEAT and Greta systems both filter all the generated gestures in a separate step, allowing for the implementation of global rules. This can be called an *overgenerate and filter* approach. Another solution to implement global control is to work with probabilistic rules like the REA/P system.

Phenomena like catchments that link gestures through time are not treated at all. Neither is the problem of compositionality that two gestures can be performed at the same time. Conflict resolution is done in BEAT by excluding all colliding gestures in the filter module, whereas Greta uses a belief network to resolve conflicts.

For gesture-speech coordination, most systems rely on the rule that the gesture's stroke must coincide with the stressed syllable of the associated word (REA, MAX, AC, VHP). FACE uses heuristics based on observation. REA/P is the only system that explores new timing patterns by empirical analysis (beginning-of-sentence vs. end-of-sentence timing).

Gesture parametrization is performed in different places of the generation process. In MAX, gesture parameters like handedness are encoded in the lexicon entries. The selection algorithm chooses the entry that most closely matches the current body configuration. Hence, parametrization depends on the body context and is performed during selection. In FACE and Greta, parameters are selected in a postprocessing step. For gesture generation, this would have the advantage that the speaker's natural preferences for one or two hands can be judged from a global perspective, looking at the whole discourse.

Most systems do not consider the problem of generating individual behavior. The authors of VHP acknowledge the importance of individual behavior but see their project as a previous step where they "seek to set a baseline of gesticulatory behavior which can then be parameterized and modified by other means". The FACE authors address individuality and define it by differences in repertoire, frequency and timing: "Individuals differ in the type of facial actions punctuating their speech (one individual may use mainly eyebrow movements, another may use nose wrinkling or eye flashes). They also differ in the number of displayed actions and their place of occurrence" (p. 5). Their approach would theoretically allow to define individualized speaker characteristics by specifying particular sets of type and timing parameters for the facial actions. However, this idea has not been implemented. In BEAT it is argued that another filter could be used to create individuality. This is equivalent to the suggestion of the creators of Greta who propose to encode individual behavior in belief networks. What is still missing, however, is a systematic approach to finding the concrete parameters that would govern such filter and selection procedures. Moreover, individual timing of nonverbal behaviors is not possible by simply filtering behavior.

4.2.3   Gesture Representation

Most systems store their gestures in lexicons. In both MAX and Greta, a mapping from communicative function/intent to a feature-based representation is used. The AC system relies on a dictionary, mapping semantic representations of form to a specific gesture. The VHP system maps gesture commands to gestures. The FACE system, although it uses hard-wired actions, intends to implement a lexicon of emblems for the future.

All systems rely on the literature in determining the lexicon entries. Only REA/P relies on probabilistic rules for posture shift generation that are rooted in empirical data but are generalized across subjects. In all systems, the size of the lexicons is limited to a few specimen. For instance, the VHP knows only five different gestures.

In existing generation systems gestures are stored as motion prototypes with little room for parametrization. However, the same gesture can be performed quite differently: expansive, abrupt, slow or fast, etc. The movement *quality* has found little attention in former approaches because it is difficult both to specify movement quality and to play the same gesture in varying qualities by means of automatic modifications of an existing motion pattern.

To tackle the problem of movement quality specification Chi et al. (2000) introduce two concepts from Laban Movement Analysis (LMA) to animation: *effort* and *shape*. These concepts are believed to reinforce content and contribute to the impression of individuality. The effort dimension has four aspects with two values each (the values are extreme points of a continuum):

- The **space** aspect models how straight a movement is. The value *indirect* refers to flexible, meandering, wandering movements (e.g. waving away bugs), whereas *direct* means single focus, undeviating movement (e.g. pointing to a particular spot).

- The **weight** aspect models how strong a movement is. The value *light* refers to delicate movements that easily overcome gravity and are marked by decreasing pressure (e.g. dabbing paint on a canvas, describing the movement of a feather). The value *strong* means powerful movements with increasing pressure (e.g. punching, pushing a heavy object)

- The **time** aspect models how quick a movement is. The value *sustained* refers to lingering, leisurely movements that indulge in time (e.g. stretching to yawn, stroking a pet), whereas *sudden* means hurried, urgent movements (e.g. grabbing a child from the path of danger)

- The **flow** aspect models how controlled a movement is. The value *free* refers to uncontrolled movement where one is unable to stop in the course of movement (e.g. waving wildly, shaking off water). *Bound* means controlled, restrained movement where one is able to stop (e.g. moving in slow motion, carefully carrying a cup of hot liquid)

The shape component comprises three dimensions: horizontal (spreading vs. enclosing), vertical (rising vs. sinking) and sagittal (advancing vs. retreating).

Chi et al. (2000) implemented the Laban concepts in the EMOTE[12] system that allows to modify existing animations according to user-specified effort/shape parameters. Effort parameters are translated into low-level movement parameters, while shape parameters are used to modify key pose information. Effort parameters only effect the arms, shape parameters mainly effect the torso. EMOTE is used in the Jack system to demonstrate the approach.

4.3   Conclusions

Nine systems were presented, all dealing with the generation of nonverbal behavior. Their underlying principles were identified and discussed. The survey is the basis for the design decisions of this work. Table 4.1 summarizes key properties of the surveyed generation systems.

---

[12]**E**xpressive **MOT**ion **E**ngine

	input	repertoire	model	proc	coord-speech	rendering
PPP	CTG	?	Ru	G	SEQ	○
REA	CTG	?	Gr	G	SSR	○
MAX	CTG	?	Ru	G	SSR	●
AC	CTG	?	Ru	G	SSR	○
VHP	TTG	5	Ru	—	CCS	○
BEAT	TTG	?	Ru	O+F	CCS	○
REA/P	CTG	4	Pr	G	TP	○
FACE	TTG	?	Ru	G	TP	○
Greta	CTG	?	Ru	O+F	CCS	●

input	TTG	text-to-gesture	
	CTG	concept-to-gesture	
repertoire	n	number of gestures/actions	
	?	exact size unknown	
model	Ru	rule-based	
	Gr	grammar-based	
	Pr	probabilistic	
proc	O+F	overgenerate and filter	
	G	generation	
coord-speech	SSR	stroke-stress generation rule	
	CCS	co-concept sync. (less precise than SSR)	
	SEQ	gesture/speech are sequentialized (gesture before/after speech)	
	TP	empirically found timing patterns	
rendering	○	prefabricated motion patterns	
	●	parametrized motion generation	

Table 4.1: *Characteristic features of the surveyed generation systems: input structure, action repertoire, generation model, generation processing (proc), coordination with speech (coord-speech) and rendering.*

The surveyed generation systems are all concerned with finding mechanisms to trigger nonverbal behavior and coordinate it with accompanying speech. They all include visualization devices to show their results. If one considers the process of generating nonverbal actions as a three step pipeline of empiry-modeling-implementation, most systems tend toward the end of the generation pipeline in their focus. As a result, they lack in empirical research and careful, task-oriented modeling. Only for the REA and REA/P systems own empirical studies were conducted. In REA, a qualitative analysis yielded six rules, and the REA/P system was the only one that actually used *quantitative* figures for modeling. Lacking the empirical material, most systems rely on the literature to assemble their gestural lexicons. It is not surprising that therefore all systems incorporate only a few gestures and build on general results instead of considering building individual models of gesturing. Only general results can be found in the literature and moreover, the research community seems to deem the building of general systems at this stage of development more important than investigating individual differences. The systems that used empirical studies, REA/P and Greta, used "normal" subjects. Only the authors of VHP decided for their agent on a more "proficient" speaker profile, that of a professional presenter with "presentation skills". Given that for most computer applications of this research field a communicationally fit synthetic speaker will be required, the interest in the profile of the modeled human speakers is remarkably low. This may be due to the fact that most fundamental research in nonverbal communication has been done in the fields of Psychology, Linguistics and Anthropology/Ethology — all fields interested in the basic mechanisms of human communication. This may also explain why all systems basically use the same timing pattern where gesture and related speech concept simply always co-occur. Anyone trying out different gesture-speech combinations for him-/herself will quickly refute this generalization going back to the influential groundwork by McNeill (1992: 26–29).

All systems include rendering devices to visualize their results. The MAX system renders gestures from feature-based representations that consist of spatial constraints. The FACE and Greta systems build facial expressions by controlling single facial actions. All other systems rely on prefabricated motion prototypes. Gestures are for now still looked upon as non-decomposable entities, thus justifying generation engines that trigger whole gestures as opposed to producing atomic feature specifications like in MAX.

Finally, although all systems render their output, in none of them any kind of evaluation was conducted. This may be due to the fact that the systematic evaluation of nonverbal communication in general and embodied agents in particular is still a quite unexplored research field.

Chapter 5

Video Data Collection

The introductory Chapter 1 laid out the plan for gesture generation: annotation, modeling, generation and implementation. Even before the first step of annotation can be performed, raw data has to be collected. This chapter sets up criteria for the selection of such data and shows that a German TV show, where four speakers discuss recently published books, qualifies as a suitable empirical basis for this work. Two speakers of the show are chosen for gesture annotation.

Empirical data can be obtained in two principle ways. It can be recorded under controlled circumstances, in a laboratory with selected subjects that are instructed in such a way that gestures of the desired type are produced. Alternatively, data can consist of pre-recorded material that was intended for a different purpose like a TV show. The second option was chosen for three reasons: (1) There is plenty of material that is easy to obtain, (2) people starring in the show, *experienced public performers*, would hardly be available for lab experiments, and (3) there are situational factors of a TV show (participants' motivations and situations of conflict) that are hard or impossible to simulate in a lab with the same degree of naturalness and spontaneity, partly due to the *observer effect*, meaning the way subjects are inhibited or otherwise affected by their knowledge of being observed, as is the case under lab conditions. Similar reasons were brought forward by Weinrich (1992: 20) and Linke (1985: 18) who likewise selected TV material for examination of gesture and discourse. The drawbacks are that technical factors cannot be changed (camera angle), a problem that is alleviated by the mass of material that can be chosen from, and that the flow of communication cannot be controlled, which is alleviated by the fact that it is a moderated talk show with a rigid structure (see below).

5.1 Selection Criteria

Since this work aims at generating individual conversational gestures for teams of presentation agents in the human-computer interface, the following criteria had to be fulfilled by the selected material:

(C-App) *Application scenario match*: The constellation of speakers and addressees should match as closely as possible the aimed at application of the generation process. The application in this work consists of a presentation team of embodied agents communicating with each other *and* with the user who sits in front of the screen.

(C-Phen) *Phenomena occurrence*: The phenomena to be analyzed and modeled must occur at all. For this work, the data must contain speech, conversational gestures and interaction between speakers.

(C-Gest) *Conversational gesture properties*: The occurring conversational gestures, being the focus of this work, must have the following properties:

1. Individuality: Each selected speaker should have a way of gesturing that strongly differs from that of the others.

2. Quantity: Gestures should occur frequently, a lower boundary of 20 gestures per minutes was set.

3. Quality: Gesture should be interesting to watch. Raising criteria for the quality of gestures would go beyond the limits of this work. It was assumed that the gestures of those people that are used to acting in public display a sufficient quality of gesture. Such people can be called *experienced public performers*.

(C-Sp) *Speech properties*: The following types of dialog contributions should be represented in the data

1. Monologues: long passages of monologue where gestures are mainly used to illustrate or structure the text

2. Dialog acts: contributions that directly react to other contributions or provoke reactions

3. Turn-taking acts: assigning, holding or yielding a turn (can be considered a subset of dialog acts)

(C-Tech) *Technical requirements*: There are two important technical requirements

1. Visibility: the gestures must be visible, i.e. within the frame or close enough to the frame that the movement is inferable from secondary movement

2. Contiguousness: the material should have a single speaker in the frame for a certain duration without being interrupted for too long by different takes, the maximum interrupt time should be less than 5 seconds

The following sections will apply these criteria the the TV show that was selected as the empirical basis for this work.

5.2 Selected Material

From the TV show *The Literary Quartet* a total number of 23 clips were extracted, each one featuring mainly one single speaker, containing also a few interactions with other speakers. The following sections will justify the choice of show, speakers and clips based on the criteria defined above.

5.2.1 Selected Show

The selected TV show is called *Das Literarische Quartett* or in English: *The Literary Quartet*. In the further discourse, it will be referred to by the English title or by LQ. The Literary Quartet is a highly popular German show, screened in bimonthly intervals. It is a talk show where three permanent hosts and one invited guest discuss five recently published books.

Properties of the Show

The show is situated in a studio with an audience, the *near audience*, and is also broadcast live on TV to the *far audience*. All four speakers are seated, facing each other, in a semi-circle that opens to the near audience. The reviewed books are discussed one at a time. For each book, the discourse runs through three phases. In the *opening phase*, one of the speakers summarizes the book's content. The *discussion phase* consists of free discussion between all four participants and in the *concluding phase*, the debate is closed with some final remarks.

Depending on the discourse phases, the speakers take on different *roles*. One outstanding and permanent role is that of the *talk leader* who has the right to start discussion on a new book, to assign turns and to close the current debate after a certain time limit. The role of the *summarizer* is assumed temporarily for one book and is assigned by the talk leader at the beginning of the opening phase. The summarizer has the right to speak about the book without having to yield the turn. In the discussion phase, every participant fills the role of a *discussionist*, making use of the common turn-taking mechanisms (cf. Sacks et al., 1974, and Duncan and Fiske, 1977).

Suitability of the Show

The LQ show matches the aimed at application in the following manner (C-App): Information is conveyed in the form of a debate, i.e. indirectly – the user (in the show: the audience) is hardly ever directly addressed. The speakers are encouraged, on the one hand, to win over the other debaters in terms of argumentation, and, on the other hand, to produce humor and conflict. The second aspect is driven by the expectations of both audiences, near and far. The near audience gives immediate feedback through clapping and laughter, the far one gives long-term feedback represented by the press. Both audiences are addressed by the speakers by glances toward the auditorium or the camera respectively. Competitive argumentation and the wish to catch an audience's attention by meeting their expectations are central the goal application's scenario.

All sought-after phenomena occur: frequent conversational gestures and speaker interaction (C-Phen). Also, due to the structure and roles of the show's format, all three relevant speech types occur (C-Sp): monologues (in the opening phase, by the summarizer, in the concluding phase, by the talk leader, also in the discussion phase by all discussionists), dialog acts (in the discussion phase, by all discussionists) and turn-taking acts (in the discussion phase, mainly by the talk leader).

Finally, the technical requirements of visibility and contiguousness are met over certain stretches of the show (C-Tech). Long takes show a single speaker with head, torso, arms/hands and often part of the legs. However, such takes can be interrupted by short takes showing another discussionist, the studio audience or the book cover.

5.2.2   Selected Speakers

Two of the three hosts, Hellmuth Karasek (HK) and Marcel Reich-Ranicki (MRR), were selected for gesture annotation. Both are *experienced public performers* since they appear on TV on a regular basis and have been doing so for over 20 years. MRR was selected because he displays strong variation in his gesturing, both in shape and quality, usually energetic and expansive. HK was selected for comparison. His gestures appear to be less varied but not less frequent. Hence, both HK and MRR display the phenomena in question (C-Phen). The gestural properties are also suited (C-Gest): both speakers have a very individual style, gesture frequently and especially speaker MRR's gestures are interesting to watch. An indicator for the latter are audience reactions and comments in the press on his gesture style. Individuality is fostered by the fact that both speakers assume different roles. Since MRR is the permanent talk leader he displays a turn-taking behavior quite different from that by HK. The gesture frequency was pre-tested and found to range between 25–30 gesture per minute for both speakers being beyond the threshold of 20 gestures per minute.

5.2.3 Selected Clips

Video clips of length 0:29 to 4:12 minutes each were taken from three different Literary Quartet shows of the year 1999. The clips show either Marcel Reich-Ranicki (MRR) or Hellmuth Karasek (HK) from an angle that allows observation of face, upper body and both arms. Table 5.1 shows the distribution of material across the three shows. Throughout this work, the single clips will be referred to by

$$LQ<session> - <index>$$

For instance, "LQ2-3" refers to clip #3 of the second session (LQ2 in Table 5.1). For technical reasons, LQ3-1 was taken out so the index numbers for the third session start with 2 to guarantee identification of the clips.

LQ1:

	1	2	3	4	5	6	7
MRR		1:10		3:15		2:14	3:43
HK	2:27		1:23		2:11		

LQ2:

	1	2	3	4	5	6	7
MRR	4:12				2:07		2:20
HK		0:57	2:09	1:09		0:29	

LQ3:

	2	3	4	5	6	7	8	9	10
MRR	1:17	1:35	1:48	4:57	0:49	1:11			2:26
HK							1:27	1:02	

LQ1-3:

	total each	total both
MRR	33:04	
		46:18
HK	13:14	

Table 5.1: *Video clip durations from three Literary Quartet (LQ) shows*

The clips were chosen following the criteria of C-Phen and C-Tech, i.e. the clips should feature the analyzed phenomena and should be technically suited for further analysis, especially the take on the featured speaker should not be interrupted by other takes longer than 5 seconds.

Examples from these clips will be given throughout this work. To specify the location of these examples the following format will be used:

<speaker> LQ<session> - <index> <minutes>:<seconds>

For instance, the reference "MRR, LQ2-1, 2:01" denotes a video featuring speaker MRR in the second session, clip #1, at the time position of 2 minutes and 1 second.

5.3 Technical Preparation

The three shows were first recorded on VHS analog tape in the PAL norm. The clips were then digitized by a process called *capturing* using a PC with *Pinnacle PCTV* TV card.

The settings for capturing were as follows. A screen size of 384x288 pixels and a frame rate of 25 frames per second were selected. The file format for the digital video was set to Microsoft AVI. The codec[1] which is responsible for compressing the size of the final file was set to Intel Indeo 5.1. The resulting files had a size of about 30MB per minute.

After the digitization of all video clips the audio tracks were extracted for the speech labeling with a sampling rate of 22 kHz in 8Bit stereo format using the software *Premiere 5.0* by Adobe. The audio file format was Windows Waveform, i.e. WAV files.

5.4 Summary

For selecting suitable material a set of criteria was devised: how close the material should match the application, which phenomena should occur, and which requirements to gesture, speech and technical frame conditions should be applied. The German TV show *The Literary Quartet* (LQ) matched the application, displayed all phenomena and fulfilled all requirements. Two permanent hosts of the show, named MRR and HK, both experienced public performers, were selected for their highly individual, frequent and interesting display of gestures. Finally, a total of 23 short clips were selected and cut where the technical requirements of visibility and contiguousness were met, resulting in a total of 46 minutes of video material. This material was digitized into Microsoft's AVI format using the Indeo 5.1 codec. In addition, the audio tracks were extracted to WAV files for speech transcription.

---

[1]Short for <u>co</u>mpression/<u>dec</u>ompression

Chapter 6

Research Tool Development:
The ANVIL System

The last chapter showed how suitable primary material in the form of a digital video was selected and obtained. The next step will be, as outlined in Chapter 3, the annotation of gestures and other relevant signals in the video using a suitable coding scheme. For the practical implementation of this step a coding tool is required the design of which will be the topic of this chapter.

The survey of existing tools for manual video annotation in Chapter 3 resulted in the conclusion that no suitable software existed. Therefore, a new tool had to be created. Since this work is concerned with tasks beyond annotation and since these tasks all need software implementations it makes sense to design a single, yet modular software. This software should function as a research *platform* that integrates software solutions to the three tasks of this work: annotation, analysis and generation. The annotation functionality stands out as being of general interest to the research community. This aspect of the tool should therefore be usable by other researchers as well, thus filling a vacuum in the research software market that slows down progress in various disciplines. For this reason the software is conceptualized as an extensible, generic *video annotation tool*. It is called ANVIL, short for **An**notation of **V**ideo and Spoken **L**anguage. The two other core modules for analysis and generation are added via a plug-in interface that allows access to ANVIL's internal structures and graphical components. Integration with external tools for speech transcription and statistics is handled through importing and exporting files.

This chapter describes decisions and solutions for the problem of designing and implementing a generic and extensible annotation tool that can, at the same time, serve as a research platform for gesture generation. A complete description of

ANVIL from the user perspective can be obtained from the ANVIL website[1] in form of a 52-page user manual. In the following, Section 6.1 outlines the necessary and some complementary requirements for such a tool before, in Section 6.2, a concise description of the tool follows, including all functions that meet the requirements. The concluding sections will compare ANVIL with existing tools and point to future directions of development.

6.1 Requirements

This section explores the minimal requirements for the two major roles of ANVIL as a video annotation tool and research platform.

6.1.1 Requirements for a Video Annotation Tool

To define the requirements for ANVIL as a video annotation tool, some terms need to be clarified first. The terms and their relationships are depicted in Figure 6.1. A video annotation tool allows the annotation of primary data in the form of digital video. This annotation follows a certain form with respect to structure and vocabulary that is called a *coding scheme*. The coding scheme reflects the specific objectives of a research project and must be defined before coding by the research team. The unifying structure of multiple possible coding schemes is called a *meta-scheme*. It is an abstract formulation of the facilities an annotation tool offers to define coding schemes, and is often equated with the tool itself. The meta-scheme must provide a *file format* that allows the storage of annotations as *annotation files*.

Coding schemes are specific to individual projects and even within a single project several schemes may be used or explored. Therefore, the foremost requirement for an annotation tool is to be *generic*, i.e. independent of a particular coding scheme. A generic annotation tool lets the user specify the coding scheme and generates the necessary facilities to annotate a video in the coding scheme's vocabulary. Genericness is best achieved by strictly separating the three layers of meta-scheme (the tool), coding scheme (defined by the user) and annotation (the coded data for a single video) as depicted in Figure 6.1. However, genericness comes at a price. The more generic a tool is, the more complicated its concepts become. This can be compensated by investing more time and effort in an intuitive user interface to keep the tool from becoming too difficult for a user to use and to configure. The design must take into account this cost/effect equation to find the right compromise between restriction and genericness so that the tool works for many purposes and many researchers.

---

[1] http://www.dfki.de/~kipp/anvil

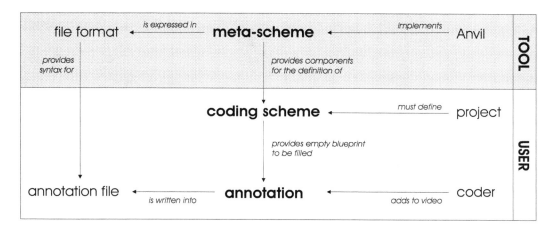

Figure 6.1: *Terms and levels of abstraction in annotation.*

A video annotation tool can be regarded as being a note-pad for temporal information where parallel events are recorded. It has become a common habit to use multiple *layers* for recording these events. Such layers can be used to contain certain event types like words, gestures, posture shifts etc. Since events like gestures can have an internal temporal structure (a gesture consists of one or more phases) some kind of temporal inclusion relationship between layers must be offered: gestures can be coded on one layer, their phases on another, and by establishing the inclusion relationship between a single gesture and its respective phases the internal structure can be correctly encoded. On a more general level, it should also be possible to relate arbitrary annotation elements from different layers with each other, a property called *cross-level coding*. This can be realized by allowing to link up annotation elements across layers. Cross-level coding is especially useful in conjunction with a special layer type for *non-temporal elements*. Non-temporal elements can represent objects that are either permanently absent or permanently present in the video (Martin and Kipp 2002). In both cases, the objects must be represented because they are potential targets for cross-level links while there is no relevant temporal information about them.

During the whole annotation process, the maintenance of consistency is of paramount importance. Consistency means that all annotations conform to the definition specified in the coding manual. The tool can support consistency maintenance by integrating online and offline access to the coding manual. A further auxiliary method is to manage multiple annotations with a single interface that allows browsing and searching. Thus, different instances of the same category can be checked and, if necessary, revised. Consistency can be measured by comparing different annotations of the same material, either by the same coder (intra-coder consistency) or by different coders (inter-coder consistency). For this and other kinds of analysis, the tool must enable the user to compile data from multiple annotations and export this data to a single file.

During annotation, an *intuitive visualization* is key for the tool to be useful to human coders. Associated with the multiple layer paradigm, researchers in Semiotics and Linguistics (Ehlich and Rehbein 1976) suggested the metaphor of a musical score where temporal information (music) of parallel types (instruments) is displayed in human-readable form (cf. Schiel et al., 1998). Therefore, many annotation systems record information along a temporal axis, a *timeline*, that runs from left to right. The multiple layers are listed on top of each other to show the respective events in time-alignment. This allows a quick and intuitive comprehension of the depicted parallel processes and their temporal interrelations (see Figure 6.6 for an impression of ANVIL's implementation of the music score metaphor).

Annotation is used for many purposes. In the field of *Corpus Linguistics* large corpora of annotated data are used to train computers for solving linguistic tasks like part-of-speech tagging, syntax/semantics parsing or language generation (cf. McEnery and Wilson, 1996, or Sampson and McCarthy, 2002). Also in Psychology large bodies of data are needed to satisfy quality standards for statistical analysis. Collecting large corpora requires an efficient coding interface to keep coding cost to a minimum. On the one hand, the most frequently used functions must be quick to access and apply. On the other hand, the evolving annotation must be easy to read during all phases of the coding process.

Annotation is often part of a greater research context. Data from other tools must be integrated, already annotated data must be merged, the completed annotation must be analyzed statistically. The tool must therefore use a standardized data format like XML[2] and offer facilities to import and export data from/to different formats.

To sum up, ANVIL must fulfill the following requirements as a video annotation tool:

- integrated video player
- intuitive visualization
- multiple layers
- genericness
- temporal inclusion relationship between layers
- efficient coding interface
- XML data format
- import/export facilities
- cross-level coding

---

[2]e**X**tensible **M**ark-up **L**anguage

- online and offline access to coding scheme

- management tool for multiple annotations

- search facilities

- non-temporal elements

How these requirements are met by ANVIL will be described in Section 6.2.

6.1.2   Requirements for a Research Platform

In the wider context of a research framework every tool can be looked at on two levels. First, as a separate software tool that needs to build on other software's data and that needs to produce data that can be further processed by other software. Second, as a platform that allows other software to directly connect to this platform, using internal structures and methods.

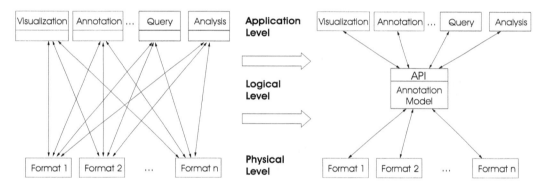

Figure 6.2: *Moving from two levels to three levels.*

These two levels correspond to interactions on the *physical level* (via imported and exported files) and on the *logical level* (via an Application Programmer's Interface or API) of the three-level architecture as proposed by Bird and Liberman (2001). They transferred the concept of a three-level architecture from database software engineering to annotation tools engineering (see Figure 6.2). The three levels of this model are the physical, logical and application level. The *physical level* refers to files on mass storage devices like hard disk, CD-ROM, or DVD. The *logical level* refers to the software's internal representation of an annotation. On this level, a set of standard operations are provided for creating, modifying, and storing annotations. On the *application level*, other software components can directly access the logical level via an API. The range of possible applications includes modules for annotation, visualization, extraction, query and analysis.

The move from a two-level architecture to a three-level architecture is depicted in Figure 6.2. It saves the programmer the work of re-implementing the same core component for each new application. Instead, the core component is factored out, making the system at the same time less error-prone.

To conclude, the requirement for ANVIL as a research platform is to implement a layered architecture that allows external programs direct access to ANVIL's internal structures.

6.2 ANVIL System Description

ANVIL is based on a layered architecture to isolate reusable components for controlled access by other components. As an annotation tool it was crucial to reuse a single annotation representation for all internal and external components in terms of access and manipulation. In ANVIL, the three-level architecture suggested by Bird and Liberman (2001) and outlined in the previous section is extended by a forth level as depicted in Figure 6.3. It has an added *interface level* that shares the benefits of reuse and safety that the logical level exhibits, providing visualization components for annotations. To be useful as a research platform, ANVIL has to provide mechanisms for connecting extensions for the tasks of analysis and generation. A plug-in interface allows access to the annotation framework as well as to the visualization components. Thus, external programs can load, manipulate and save annotations in order to analyze them and even visualize arbitrary portions of the annotation using ANVIL's annotation board. However, to be accessible by ANVIL such components must comply with ANVIL's plug-in interface specification. The user must register new plug-ins in ANVIL so that respective menu items can be automatically created in the GUI.

ANVIL's additional interface level requires that temporal synchronization of all components must be handled in a unified way. This problem is solved by using the currently loaded video clip as a central clock that all other components must synchronize with. As a consequence, loading and viewing multiple videos is not possible without considerable changes in the architecture.

In the next sections, the ANVIL system will be described along the lines of its architectural levels. Section 6.2.1 will deal with the most important level, the logical level, followed by a treatment of the interface level in Section 6.2.2, the application level in Section 6.2.3 and, finally, the physical level in Section 6.2.4.

6.2.1 Logical Level

ANVIL's logical level is solely concerned with the annotation task. It provides a framework for the creation, modification and storage of annotations. To define the task of annotation as general as possible, the terms of *meta-scheme, coding scheme*

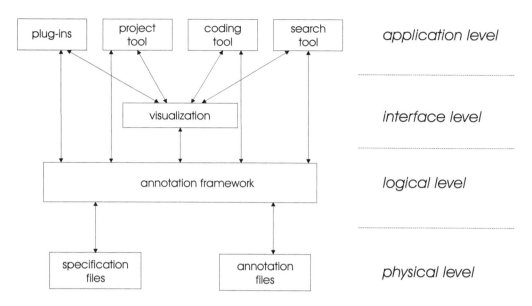

Figure 6.3: *The four architectural levels in ANVIL.*

and *annotation* are borrowed from linguistic annotation and will be used as outlined in Section 6.1.1. The major challenge was to clearly separate the three concepts. How these concepts are realized in ANVIL will be described in the following sections.

Meta-Scheme

A meta-scheme provides a framework that allows the specification of a coding scheme. A coding scheme can be considered a structured, empty blueprint that can be filled with tags from a controlled vocabulary for each new video file. ANVIL's meta-scheme provides two main constructs to define coding schemes: containers and elements. Containers are exactly that: containers. They contain elements. Elements are the basic information carriers that are added in the process of annotation. Both constructs will be described in detail.

ANVIL has two types of containers, tracks and sets. A track is a time-based container. Its elements have a unique temporal position and duration, defined by a start and end time. Example tracks are: words, gestures, head nods, posture shifts. There are three different types of tracks depending on the *anchoring* of their elements. In a *primary track* the elements are directly anchored in time, with a start and end time. In a *span* or *singleton* track elements are not anchored in time but anchored in elements belonging to another track, the *reference* track. In singleton tracks elements point to exactly one partner element in the reference track. For instance, if a primary track contained words, a singleton track could be used to add the words' corresponding part-of-speech label. Each element in a singleton track inherits the start and end time of the associated element in the reference track. In a span track, an element covers a number of contiguous elements in the reference track. It is defined by a start and end element in the reference track and inherits the start time of the associated start element and the end time of the associated end element. Span track can be used to encode dialogue acts or rhetorical relations but also gestures that refer to a primary track with movement phases. Since a singleton track can be considered a special case of a span track both track types are simply referred to as *secondary tracks*.

In complex coding schemes, it can be useful to group tracks together for organizational reasons. For instance, all track referring to speech and all tracks referring to nonverbal behavior could be grouped together, much like in folders in a file directory tree. ANVIL's meta-scheme offers the concept of a *group* to do this. A group can contain a number of tracks and groups so that nested structures are possible.

Apart from tracks there is the second container type, the *set*. The set is a container for *non-temporal* elements. Non-temporal elements can be useful in a number of situations. For instance, consider the scenario of a teacher pointing at various objects on a blackboard (say, a diagram, a sentence and a picture) where his pointing gestures should be linked up with representations of these objects. For these representations temporal information is unnecessary and would even lead to cumbersome workarounds in the annotation process. The set container offers an elegant solution for this case (Martin and Kipp 2002). Note that you could also solve this problem using IDs. However, then you would not be able to store typed information for specifying the properties of these annotations.

All containers, tracks and sets, contain *elements*, the actual content units that are added by the coder during annotation. The content of the elements is not mere text but a typed attribute-value structure. Each element has a set of *attributes* that can each be filled with a value. What kind of value can be used for an attribute depends on the attribute's type. ANVIL offers the following attribute types:

- STRING
- BOOLEAN
- NUMBER
- VALUESET
- LINK

A STRING attribute can store arbitrary alphanumeric sequences. A BOOLEAN attribute accepts one of two values, true or false. A NUMBER attribute expects a number in a pre-defined interval. A VALUESET attribute can be filled with one token from a number of pre-defined ones. Finally, a LINK attribute contains a link to another element. The linked-up element can be located in the same or in a different container. The user must specify the attributes with name and type for each container. These specifications apply to all elements added to this container.

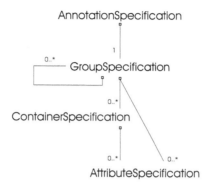

Figure 6.4: *Class diagram of ANVIL's specification structure.*

For instance, for encoding gestures one can define a primary track called "gestures" and specify two attributes: a VALUESET attribute called "category" which will accept one of the following tokens: emblem, deictic, iconic, beat; and a NUMBER attribute called "number of strokes" that expects a number between 1–6.

ANVIL's meta-scheme can be depicted as an object-oriented specification tree (Figure 6.4). The root unit is an AnnotationSpecification. It contains the whole coding scheme. The definition of containers is done with the ContainerSpecification object. It represents the container's name and the attribute specifications. An AttributeSpecification contains name and type of the attribute and additional information depending on the type (e.g., a numeric interval for NUMBER typed attributes). Container specifications can be hierarchically organized in groups using the GroupSpecication object. Group specifications can also have attribute specifications that will be inherited by all containers in the group. Note that the annotation specification contains exactly one group. It is the root group, invisible to the user, that contains all top-level container specifications.

Coding Scheme

By using the concepts of the meta-scheme, reflected in the classes in Figure 6.4, the user can create a coding scheme. A coding scheme is a set of definitions declaring the containers/groups and, for each container, the attribute names and types. In ANVIL, this has to be done in a separate file, called *specification file*, using a special XML language.

Formally, a **coding scheme** $\mathcal{S}$ is a 7-tuple

$$\mathcal{S} = \langle T_p, T_s, S, r, f_n, f_t, V \rangle$$

where T_p is the set of primary tracks, T_s is the set of secondary tracks and S is the set of non-temporal object sets. The union of these sets is the set of containers C, i.e.

$$C := T_p \cup T_s \cup S$$

Furthermore, $r : T_s \to T_p \cup T_s$ is the "referring" relation that defines the hierarchy amongst tracks. $f_n : C \to \mathcal{P}(\{A, \ldots, Z\}^+)$ maps a container to a set of attribute names and $f_t : C \times f_n(C) \to \mathcal{T}$ maps an attribute of a container to an attribute type in $\mathcal{T} = \{\text{STRING, BOOLEAN, LINK, NUMBER, VALUESET}\}$. $V = (V^0, \ldots, V^K)$ is the set of user-defined value sets.

In order for an coding scheme to be valid, all secondary tracks must be *grounded*, i.e. they must eventually refer to a primary track. Only then start and end times can be inherited by a secondary element. One of the following two equivalent conditions must hold:

- **grounding**: Every secondary track must refer to a primary track eventually, either directly or by transition. Formally,

$$\forall\, t \in T_s \quad \exists\, k \in N \quad \exists t' \in T_p : \quad r^k(t) = t'$$

  where r^k is the k-th recursive application of function r on the resulting value.

- **non-circularity**: A secondary track must not refer to itself, neither directly nor by transition. Formally,

$$\forall\, t \in T_s \quad \neg\exists\, k \in N : \quad r^k(t) = t$$

When specifying tracks in an ANVIL specification file, a rule called *ordering condition* ensures that all tracks are grounded. In the specification, all tracks are defined in an order. When defining a secondary track, the user can let the track only refer to previously defined tracks. This restriction can formally be expressed as follows. If the sequence of user-defined tracks is $T = \{t_1, t_2, \ldots, t_n\}$, the ordering condition is:

$$\forall k \in \{1, \ldots, n\} : \quad t_k \in T_s \to (r(t_k) = t_h \wedge h < k)$$

It can be proved by induction that for all tracks t_i the grounding condition holds.

For the base case $i = 0$, the grounding condition is trivially fulfilled because t_0 must be primary (there is no previous track that t_0 could refer to). For $i > 0$, let us look at the case $t_i \in T_s$, since for $t_i \in T_p$ the Grounding condition trivially holds. By the ordering condition it holds that $r(t_i) = t_j$ where $j < i$. Now there are two cases. If t_j is primary, the grounding condition is fulfilled. If t_j is secondary, then by induction precondition the grounding condition holds for t_j as $j < i$ so that $\exists k \in N : \exists t' \in T_p : r^k(t_j) = t'$. Now, $r^{k+1}(t_i) = r^k(t_j) = t' \in T_p$, i.e. the grounding condition holds.

Annotations

The coding scheme acts as an empty blueprint to be filled with *annotations* for a specific video. A single annotation for one video clip has a class structure as depicted in Figure 6.5.

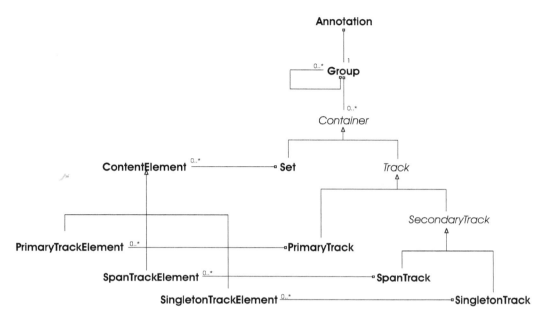

Figure 6.5: *Class diagram of ANVIL's internal representation of an annotation.*

It is modeled with an object that contains a tree of groups and containers. Containers hold content elements, the units that contain the encoded data. Containers come either in the form of tracks where content elements are ordered along the time axis (without overlap), or in the form of sets where content elements are a simple list without temporal anchoring.

Formally, given a coding scheme $\mathcal{S}$, an **annotation in** $\mathcal{S}$ can be defined as a 5-tuple

$$\mathcal{A}^{\mathcal{S}} = \langle E, c, t, r, v \rangle$$

where E is the set of all annotation elements. c is the mapping from elements to their container $c : E \to C$. Let E_p denote all elements of primary tracks and E_s all elements of secondary tracks. Then, t is the mapping from primary track elements to their start and end time $t : E_p \to T \times T$ where T is the ordered set of all possible time-stamps. r is the reference function for secondary elements, pointing to start and end element $r : E_s \rightarrow (E_p \cup E_s) \times (E_p \cup E_s)$, and v is the attribute value function:

$$v : E \times f_n(C) \rightarrow \begin{cases} \text{if } f_t(c) = \text{STRING} : & \mathcal{P}\{A, \ldots, Z\}^+ \\ \text{if } f_t(c) = \text{BOOLEAN} : & \{true, false\} \\ \text{if } f_t(c) = \text{NUMBER} : & \{1, 2, \ldots\} \\ \text{if } f_t(c) = \text{VALUESET} : & V^k \\ \text{if } f_t(c) = \text{LINK} : & \{\langle e_1, \ldots, e_n \rangle : e_i \in E\} \end{cases}$$

For VALUESET attributes the user-defined value set $V^k \in V$ is specified in the coding scheme. Secondary elements have the property of *temporal inheritance* of start and end times. Formally,

$$\forall e \in E : \quad t(e) := t(r^k(e))$$

where $k \in \mathcal{N}$ such that $r^k(e) \in E_{prim}$ which must exist because of the grounding condition.

If an annotation is to be valid, it must fulfill the following **no overlap** condition that two elements in a primary track must not overlap temporally. Formally,

$$\forall \tau \in T_p \quad \forall e \in \tau \quad \neg \exists e' \in \tau :$$

$$\begin{aligned} & t_{start}(e) & < & \quad t_{start}(e') & < & \quad t_{end}(e) \\ or \quad & t_{start}(e) & < & \quad t_{end}(e') & < & \quad t_{end}(e) \end{aligned}$$

If this is true it follows that the same holds for secondary track elements. This condition allows for each track τ to define a strict total order $\prec_\tau$ over all elements in τ:

$$\forall e_1, e_2 \in c : \quad e_1 \prec_\tau e_2 \quad :\Longleftrightarrow \quad t_{start}(e_1) < t_{start}(e_2)$$

This definition of an annotation in ANVIL is responsible for certain limitations in ANVIL's expressive power. Two possible extensions are:

1. **overlapping elements**: Dropping the no overlap condition would allow elements within one track τ to temporally overlap. Note that you would still have a total order $\preceq_\tau$ but not a strict one, i.e. elements can be equal.

2. **nested structures**: Adding a *parent* mapping for all elements E^c of a container $c \in C$

$$p^c : \mathcal{P}(E^c) \rightarrow E^c$$

   would allow a tree-like structure where $p^c(\{e_1, \ldots, e_n\}) = e$ means e **is parent node to elements** $e_1, \ldots, e_n$ $(e, e_1, \ldots, e_n \in E^c)$. Such a structure is prerequisite for syntactic annotation, for instance. An even more general mapping could allow graph structure with or without cycles.

Note that more expressive power comes at a price. First, the user interface must grant the user quick and exhaustive access to all functions as well as intuitive visualizations of the data. Second, in terms of computation, such structures are often harder to search, both in terms of query formulation as well as computation time.

6.2.2 Interface Level

ANVIL's graphical user interface (GUI) is shown in Figure 6.6. To the upper left, the **main window** (1) is located containing the main menu bar (1a) and a text area for trace information (1b). The menu contains all important operations like loading/saving annotations, printing and adjusting view parameters. The controls for video playback can also be found in the main window (1c). The customary VCR functions are offered: play, pause, fast forward/backward and, most importantly, frame-by-frame stepping.

The video is screened onto the **video window** (2), located upper center. A slow motion slider lets the user adjust the playback speed (2a). The video controls were intentionally excluded from the video window because putting them below or above it would have meant less vertical space for the annotation board (3), an important asset in annotation.

The **annotation board** (3) is located below the video window and is the space where the coder views, creates and manipulates his or her video annotation. The track (3b) and group (3c) names are displayed on the left hand side. The tracks' contents, consisting of annotation elements, are displayed in the larger right part of the window, running from left to right in the direction of time. Elements are depicted as colored rectangles, labelled with the value of one of its attributes (user's choice). They are positioned in time-alignment with the timeline (3i), the top bar that gives temporal orientation using ticks to mark seconds and frames. There are special tracks to display the waveform of the video's audio track (3j), and to visualize pitch and intensity from as computed by the PRAAT software (3k). For more or less detail on the annotation board, the user can zoom in or out (3a).

A playback line (3g) slides across the tracks as the video is being played, marking the exact frame position on the board. If the playback line is dragged with the mouse the video adapts continually which allows a quick yet precise video positioning. For coding, a second line, the record line (3f), is used together with the playback line to mark the beginning and end of a new element (see next section). At all times, only one track is active, highlighted blue (3d). In the active track, if the playback line is positioned on an element, this element is the currently selected element (3h) which is also highlighted. Within the active track, the user can jump from element to element using buttons or key commands (3e).

The contents of the selected element is displayed in the upper right **element window** (4). The element's attributes and values are listed in a text area (4a).

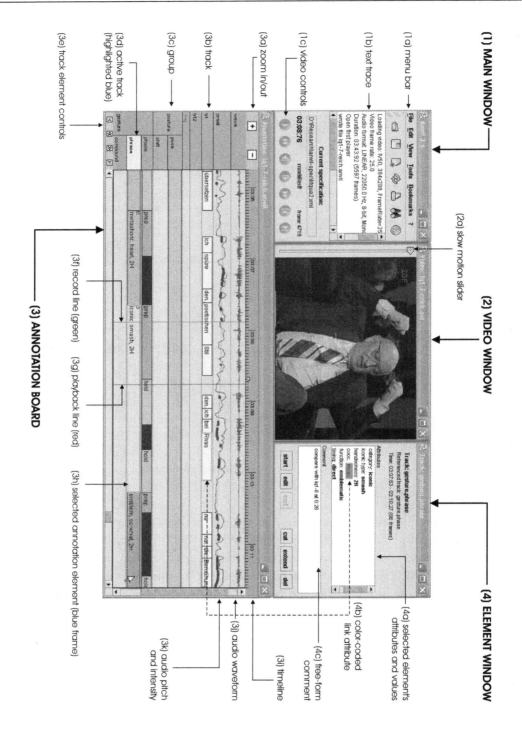

Figure 6.6: *ANVIL's graphical user interface.*

If the selected element has any links to other elements these linked-up elements are highlighted, too, in a color chosen by the user (4b). Apart from user-defined attributes, annotation elements can additionally be described with a free-form comment that appear in the element window (4c). Comments are marked with a small rectangle on the annotation board.

Coding

For annotation, the coder uses the annotation board, marking the start and end of an element with the help of the record and playback lines. When marking the end point, a track-specific edit window appears that is automatically generated from the user-defined coding scheme. The edit window asks for the relevant attributes, offering documentation for each attribute (Figure 6.7). The input method for an attribute depends on the respective value type. A STRING is entered in a string input field, a BOOLEAN with a check box and a VALUESET with an option menu containing the user-defined values. For a LINK attribute, the user clicks on a button to enter the *link mark-up mode*: A new window appears with an editable list of selected elements while on the annotation board the selected elements are highlighted and can be selected and deselected by the user. If the user confirms the selection ANVIL transfers the list of pointers to the currently edited element. Elements of secondary tracks are added similarly. The element's start and end time will be derived from the associated elements. Existing elements can be deleted, edited, cut or extended using the playback line and the context menu. If a secondary element's start or end element is deleted the secondary element would be deleted, too. A warning dialogue informs the coder of this danger and offers to cancel the action.

The main control buttons for coding are located on the element window (upper right) but can also be accessed by context menus on the annotation board that change their options depending on the active track and currently selected element.

Visualization

The visualization of annotation elements is performed in multiple ways. Track elements, which all have a duration, are displayed as rectangles on the annotation board (Figure 6.6). This conforms to the music score metaphor and allows to observe the elements' temporal interrelations. The selected element's attributes and values are listed in the element window (upper right window). A number of attributes can be selected by the user to be displayed on the annotation board as well. Of those attributes only the values are written as labels on the rectangles. Additionally, one attribute can be selected for *color-coding*. It must be of type VALUESET and the user must specify a color for every possible value in the coding scheme. ANVIL will then color the element's rectangle on the annotation board depending on the attribute's value. Attributes of type VALUESET can also assume

attribute of type MultiLink(trl)   clicking on the info button opens
(button for selection)   the associated documentation

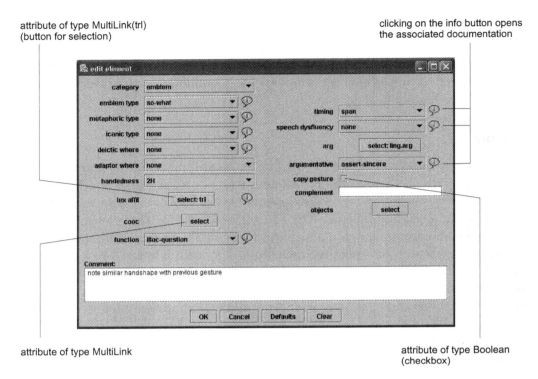

attribute of type MultiLink   attribute of type Boolean
                                                                   (checkbox)

Figure 6.7: *ANVIL sample edit window, automatically generated at runtime from the user-defined coding scheme.*

values that have a *graphical symbol* attached to it. If such an attribute is chosen for labelling, the respective symbol appears on the annotation board. For each element, the coder can attach a free-form comment for arbitrary research notes. Elements containing notes are marked with a small box on the annotation board.

The waveform of the video's audio track can be displayed on a separate track. Pitch and intensity can also be displayed but must have been computed by the external PRAAT[3] tool and imported to ANVIL before. In the annotation shown in Figure 6.6, the waveform is contained in a track called "wave" and pitch and intensity are displayed in the "praat" track.

Navigation

The annotation board can be zoomed in and out. The timeline shows full seconds and, for higher zoom factors, also the single frames with small ticks. For navigation, ANVIL offers jump buttons to move from element to element within one track. For marking important positions in the video *bookmarks* can be inserted, accessed

---

[3]see Section 3.2.1, page 61

and removed through the main menu. They are marked by small triangles in the timeline.

The hierarchical organization of tracks and groups can be exploited by collapsing groups. A collapsed group is reduced to a slim grey bar that needs minimal space and so increases space for the remaining annotation. Groups can be collapsed and expanded with a double-click on the group name (left on the annotation board).

Search

A simple search interface (Figure 6.8) allows to browse a single track for elements that contain specific attribute values. In the interface the user specifies the *goods* list $G = \{g_1, \ldots, g_k\}$ and *nogoods* list $N = \{n_1, \ldots, n_h\}$. A predicate g_i has the structure $A = V$ where A is an attribute and V is a value. For predicates n_j this is a negation $A \neq V$. ANVIL searches for all elements with

$$(g_1 \vee \ldots \vee g_k) \wedge (n_1 \vee \ldots \vee n_h)$$

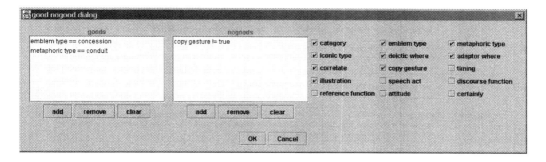

Figure 6.8: *ANVIL search window.*

An upcoming hitlist window shows all the found elements in a table view (bottom right window in Figure 6.12). Which attributes should be included in this table can be specified with the checkboxes on the right of the search window (Figure 6.8). Double clicking elements in the hitlist window makes ANVIL jump to the respective element on the annotation board.

Automatic Coding Manual Generation

Defining a coding scheme necessitates the writing of a coding manual, containing instructions and definitions for the human coder. ANVIL exploits the fact that this coding manual usually has the same structure as the technical coding scheme definition in the specification file. By inserting documentation tags in the specification file, the user can let ANVIL generate a set of HTML pages containing the formatted user documentation in structured form as shown in Figure 6.9.

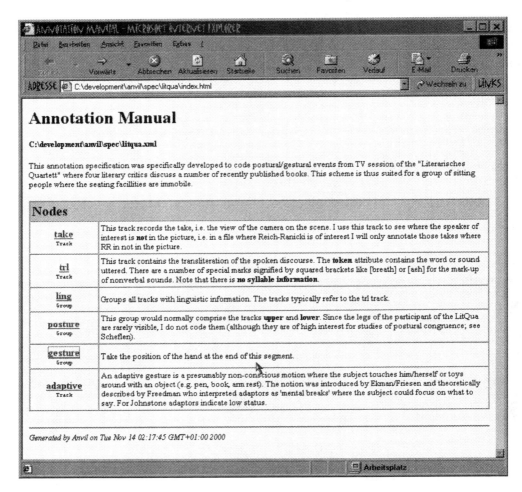

Figure 6.9: *Start page of a coding manual, automatically generated as a set of HTML pages by ANVIL.*

For online access to the documentation, each time an element is created the respective documentation can be accessed by clicking on the "?" buttons (see Figure 6.7 on page 114). The documentation for a single attribute can contain definitions for all possible values as depicted in Figure 6.10.

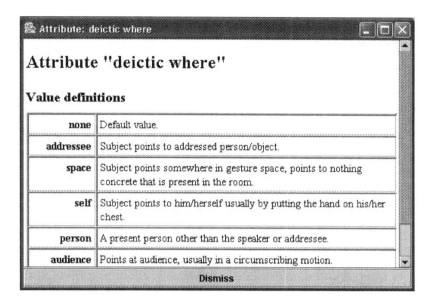

Figure 6.10: *Example attribute documentation window*

6.2.3 Application Level

Project Tool

A research project usually comprises many video files. Consequently, users need to manage more than one annotation. For instance, having annotated a number of videos with a teaching scenario (teacher, students, blackboard) the research team may want to examine the pointing gestures occurring in all videos or in a certain subset of these videos. The respective annotations can be assembled in a list of annotation files that is called a *project*. The project tool (Figure 6.11) allows to assemble such projects and store them for further usage. A necessary condition for a project is that all annotations share the same specification file. This is required for searching a single track in multiple annotations. Equal specifications guarantee that the track exists in all annotations and has the same attributes.

In the project tool, track elements can be searched *across* annotations. Searching is performed as described above for single annotations. The resulting hitlist is also identical to the one used for a single annotation but includes the annotation file name that contains the element. The hitlist window can be used to navigate through annotations by double-clicking hitlist elements. ANVIL loads the respective annotation and jumps to the selected element. This makes comparison of annotated elements across annotations fast and easy (see Figure 6.12).

Finally, with the project tool the contents of a track can be exported to a text table that is readable by statistical analysis software like SPSS or Statistica.

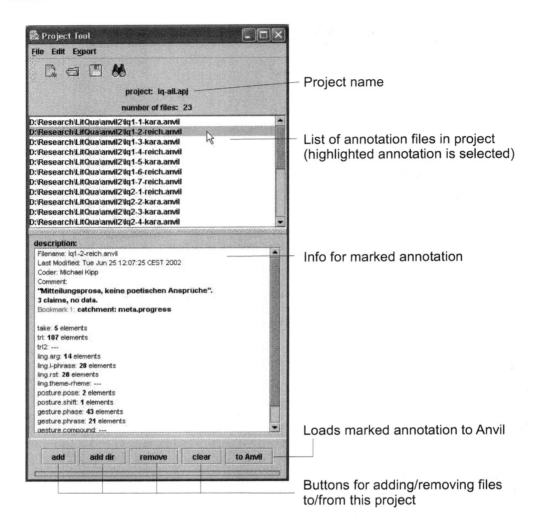

Project name — project: lq-all.apj

List of annotation files in project (highlighted annotation is selected)

Info for marked annotation

Loads marked annotation to Anvil

Buttons for adding/removing files to/from this project

Figure 6.11: *ANVIL project tool GUI.*

Plug-ins

External Java programs can connect to **ANVIL** and directly access its internal struc-
tures via the plug-in interface. Conversely, they can be started and closed from
ANVIL's GUI. To make a program work as a plug-in it must comply with the plug-in
interface specification. Moreover, the user must register the new component so that
ANVIL can offer a menu item in its GUI. Registration can be done directly from
ANVIL's GUI.

Since ANVIL offers an added interface level, another concern emerges: temporal synchronization with ANVIL's main graphical components, i.e. the video player
and the annotation board. This problem is solved by using *listener interfaces* (see

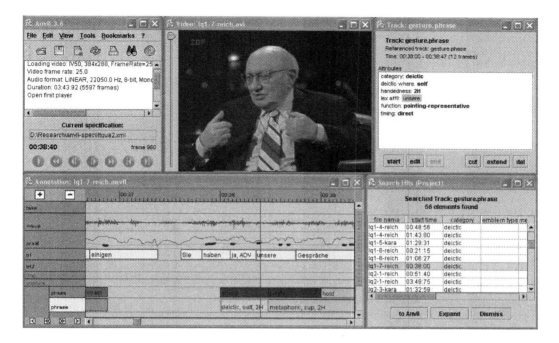

Figure 6.12: *ANVIL with embedded hitlist window (bottom right).*

Figure 6.13). If, for instance, the plug-in P needs a signal each time the video changes to another frame, it registers with **ANVIL** as an `AnvilMediaTimeListener`. Then, each time the video frame changes, **ANVIL** sends out a signal to all registered `AnvilMediaTimeListener` objects, including P. The video can be considered the central "clock". Running multiple videos is not possible without considerable changes in the architecture. The plug-in interface is used for two core components of this work: the analysis and generation modules.

6.2.4 Physical Level

The physical level of **ANVIL** refers to the level of files (see Figure 6.14). It serves the following purposes:

1. storage of primary material in *video files*

2. definition of coding schemes in *specification files*

3. storage of user annotations in *annotation files*

4. storage of multiple annotations in *project files*

5. data exchange with external programs

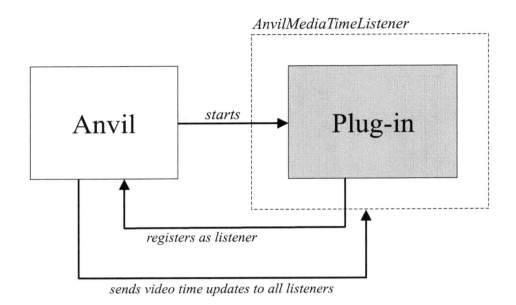

Figure 6.13: *Diagram showing how an* ANVIL *plug-in synchronizes with the video by registering as a media time listener.*

Microsoft AVI	QuickTime (MOV)
Radius Cinepak	Radius Cinepak
Indeo 5.04	Component Video
Indeo R3.2	H-261
	H-263
	Foto JPEG
	RAW Without Compressor

Table 6.1: *List of working codecs in the respective file format, AVI or QuickTime, as tested under Windows platforms.*

ANVIL can read only video files that are based on certain codecs. Table 6.1 lists which codecs in conjunction with which file format works with ANVIL under Windows. ANVIL can work with a video file if two conditions hold. First, it must be supported by the Java Media Framework (JMF). Second, JMF must grant random frame access. For instance, MPEG1 is supported by JMF but does not allow random frame access. Therefore, MPEG1 is not supported by ANVIL.

The file encoding format for all files produced by **ANVIL** is XML because it has become a worldwide standard for data exchange on the physical level. It provides a formalism for syntactic specification called *document type definition* (DTD), also available in an extended type-enabled version called *XML schema definition* (XSD). Both formalisms guarantee generality of syntactic checks. Tools and API components are available for visualization, modification, validation, and transformation of XML files. Programmers can build on existing parsers (e.g. Xerces by IBM Alphaworks) and a standardized internal representation called *document object model* (DOM). **ANVIL** uses DTD, not XSD, for syntax checking. Using XSD would require the automatic generation of a schema file for each new coding scheme. However, the information contained in the schema is subsumed by the data contained in the **ANVIL** specification file. Therefore, it is more elegant to perform the checks like type-checking in the **ANVIL** reader module on the basis of the specification file.

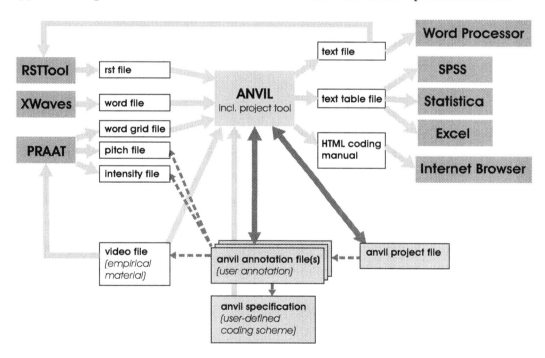

Figure 6.14: *A functional view on ANVIL's relations to the physical level (files) and to external tools. Arrows represent read/write and import/export relations. Dotted arrows are logical links. External tools are shaded in dark gray, whereas ANVIL and its directly associated files are shaded in light gray.*

The coding scheme must be written by the user in XML and serves as a specification and configuration file for **ANVIL**'s annotation facility. It is therefore called the *specification file*. Once a coder has annotated a single video according to his/her coding scheme ANVIL writes the data to an *annotation file*, in XML format. Since the annotation depends on the video file and the specification file (see Section 6.2.1), paths to both files are included in the annotation file (see Figure 6.14).

File exchange with external programs also takes place on the physical level. The import/export file formats depend on the formats of the respective external software, most are text-based. ANVIL can import data from phonetic tools like PRAAT or ESPS/XWaves which produce text files in an individual format. On the other hand, ANVIL can export files for statistical analysis by tools like SPSS or Statistica. To be readable for these tools, ANVIL's data is written to text files as tab-separated tables. Figure 6.14 gives an overview of ANVIL's file organization and how external tools relate to ANVIL.

6.3   Assessment

6.3.1   Requirements Revisited

The requirements assembled in Section 6.1 are all met in the ANVIL system. It offers an integrated video player for digital video and is generic by pursuing a strict separation of meta-scheme, coding scheme and data. It works with multiple layers that can capture the temporal inclusion relationship by the concept of secondary tracks. Tracks can be organized in groups, allowing the elegant annotation of *multi-party* interactions by assigning each speaker an individual group. Coding is possible across levels with the help of links. Non-temporal elements are available, too. The visualization is intuitive with its music score metaphor, the coding interface is efficient through zooming, context menus and navigation support. ANVIL uses the world-wide standard XML for its file exchange and additionally provides import/export facilities for the widely used phonetic software PRAAT and statistical tools SPSS and Statistica. For consistency maintenance, online and offline access to the coding scheme is possible and a project tool ensures that the user can browse the corpus across annotations. A search interface is provided that suffices for simple queries.

For ANVIL as a research platform the requirement of a layered architecture has been met. Connecting to ANVIL from outside is thus possible not only through files (physical level) but also directly through a plug-in interface (logical level).

6.3.2   Comparison with Other Tools

In this section, ANVIL is compared with existing annotation tools that have been presented in Section 3.2. Table 6.2 shows the implemented features in a number of existing annotation tools (for another tool survey cf. Bigbee et al., 2001). In the table a solid circle indicates that the feature is fully implemented and an empty circle means that the feature is only partially present. The features are grouped into four blocks: interface features, annotation model features, output/analysis features and application-relevant features.

	An	CL	MT	MS	Ob	SiS	TX	HI	El	sW
Video player	●	○	●	●	●	●	●		●	●
Timeline view	●			○	○	●	●		●	●
Table view	○			●			●		●	
Color-coding	●			○			●			
Waveform	●						●		●	
Pitch/intensity	●									
Cod. scheme def.	●	●	●	○	●					
Layer dependencies	●	●	●						●	
Complex elements	●			●						
Value dependencies		●		●				●		
Cross-levels links	●									
Non-temporal el.	●									
XML output	●						●		●	
Analysis functions	○	●		●	●					
Platform-indep.	●	mw	m	mw	mw	m	●	w	●	m
Non-Commercial	●	●	●	●		●	●	●	●	

Table 6.2: *Features of the annotation tools ANVIL (An), CLAN (CL), MediaTagger (MT), MacSHAPA (MS), Observer (Ob), SignStream (SiS), TASX (TX), HIAT-DOS (HI), Elan (El) and syncWRITER (sW).*

As concerns the interface, the seamless integration of a digital video player has become standard. Only in older tools like CLAN and HIAT-DOS the integration of digital video is still cumbersome or altogether missing. ANVIL's important contribution is the fine synchronization between the mouse-draggable playback line on the annotation board and the video pane. Another standard is the visualization of temporal data in time-alignment, using the music score metaphor, to show the data's temporal interrelationships, although MacSHAPA and The Observer only offer *passive* views where data cannot be manipulated. These tools rather rely on the table view where annotation elements appear in a sequential list. The table view is preferable when elements are far apart or where the temporal relationship is not relevant. ANVIL uses tables for search results, so when searching for "all elements" the user obtains a complete table view which is, however, passive. Other interface features include color-coding which is surprisingly rare in available tools considering the gain in speed for visual comprehension (MacSHAPA uses graphical patterns like diamonds/stripes to achieve a similar effect). The inclusion of the audio waveform is a more recent development as tools become more general, additionally fostered by the rising interest in the relation between intonation and gesture (cf. McClave, 1994). For the latter the display of pitch and intensity is even more relevant and is only offered by ANVIL to date.

Looking at the tools' underlying annotation model, most tools strive toward genericness, although HIAT-DOS and SignStream still incorporate in parts a fixed coding scheme. A tool to be generic does not imply that a coding scheme can be defined separate from the annotation data. Only ANVIL, CLAN, MediaTagger and The Observer allow a separate coding scheme definition. MacSHAPA offers the definition of vocabularies but not of the layers in a separate file. A separate coding scheme definition means that it can be used for multiple annotations and thus, increase consistency and transparency. Using multiple layers for annotations has also become a standard for annotation tools. But not every tool offers to define dependencies between layers in terms of temporal inclusion, although this feature is already present in the CLAN tool, and was taken over into ANVIL. Less common is the usage of complex elements for annotation. Most tools allow only simple text strings as annotation input. In contrast, complex elements contain attributes and types which makes the coding scheme definition more flexible and the coding more robust because of type-checking. Apart from ANVIL only MacSHAPA offers this feature. In this respect, MacSHAPA is even superior to ANVIL by providing predicate-typed attributes which is a means to change the attribute structure of an annotation element by context (see Section 3.2.2). So, for instance, if an annotation element for gestures contains the attributes "gesture type" and "hand shape" but the second attribute becomes irrelevant for certain gesture types (e.g. beats) this cannot be modeled with ANVIL's coding scheme language and may lead to errors in annotation (when a coder specifies a hand shape for a gesture type "beat"). Modeling such value dependencies is possible with MacSHAPA's predicate attributes but also with the hierarchical values offered by CLAN and HIAT-DOS. ANVIL has one type, however, that is unique for this kind of tools, the LINK type, which allow linkage between arbitrary annotation elements. Cross-level coding is thus possible. Another unique feature of ANVIL's are non-temporal elements which are highly useful in multimodality studies (Martin and Kipp 2002).

As recent developments show, the usage of XML output is becoming the standard. So the most recent tools, ANVIL, TASX and Elan all use XML, and The Observer is being modified to allow XML output. XML allow easy access to the annotation tool's data files *outside* the tool, especially for preparing the files for statistical analysis. Analysis functions inside the tool are offered by a range of tools: CLAN, MacSHAPA and The Observer all offer analysis of data and coding reliability. The latter is very useful and lacking in ANVIL. Other analyses are often too research specific to be worth integrating into an annotation tool. Therefore, most tools, like ANVIL, simply provide export facilities to external statistical analysis programs.

For a widespread use of a software two factors are decisive: which platforms the software runs on and whether it is commercial. Most recent tools, TASX, Elan and ANVIL, rely on Java as the implementation language which makes them run on any platform. Some tools, MediaTagger, SignStream and syncWRITER only run on a Macintosh, a platform quite popular in behavioral research, which severely restricts their use in a PC-dominated world. Concerning the second factor, only two tools are commercial: The Observer and syncWRITER.

To conclude, ANVIL offers a wide range of features and therefore compares well on the tools market. Of course, the features discussed here reflect the specific topic of this work. However, many of them have been reported in other surveys, too, as being essential (cf. Loehr and Harper, 2003, Bigbee et al., 2001, and Soria et al., 2002). ANVIL also has drawbacks not listed in the table. ANVIL only supports a limited range of video codecs, a restriction shared by many other tools. Also, there are limits to the *size* of the video to be analyzed in ANVIL. These limits depend on the computer hardware but a maximum length of about 20 minutes is realistic on modern machines. This restriction is alleviated by the possibility to cut a video into clips while being able to manage the clips in ANVIL's project tool. One last major advantage is ANVIL's robustness. It has been distributed since 2000 and been used by many researchers world-wide. The constant feedback of these users has contributed to eliminating bugs and making extensions/changes which made ANVIL both more usable and robust.

6.3.3   Open Issues

Three extensions are potentially useful and should be mentioned here. First, ANVIL could allow *spatio-temporal annotation*. Currently, ANVIL's annotation model is based on discretized time, usually slices of 1/25th second, and not space. To annotate locations on a picture or video one needs a space-based model. To annotate paths or trajectories one needs a spatio-temporal model. To implement such a model is less a problem of programming but rather of finding an intuitive interface and visualization. A first attempt at this problem has been undertaken by Christoph Lauer (DFKI) who programmed an ANVIL plug-in[4] that allows spatial annotations with boxes on the video pane, called visual mark-up (Soria et al. 2002).

Second, ANVIL could implement image processing methods to detect the location and movement of body parts or to compute motion qualities like speed or intensity (Grammer et al., 1997, and Quek and McNeill, 2000). Such methods can be integrated as the video data is readily available in ANVIL's internal architecture. Such video data manipulations can even be performed through ANVIL's plug-in interface. The challenge would not only be the implementation of known methods but more in the automatic translation of the retrieved data to symbolic informa-

---

[4]Visit http://www.dfki.de/nite and go to *Anvil Tools* to download the plug-in.

tion in one of the annotation tracks. One could imagine that the track for gesture phases could automatically receive an entry for movement intensity from ANVIL's image processor as soon as a new phase element is added.

The third issue is more visionary. ANVIL could support the writing of *coding scheme-specific modules*. At the moment, plug-ins can only be written on the level of the meta-scheme. This is understandable since the coding scheme is the variable factor in a tool, it is highly project-dependent and often changes. However, there are some coding schemes that have developed into quasi-standards. Coding tools could offer to use these coding schemes to automatically compile classes and access methods for writing coding scheme-specific modules that can be used for analysis and other tasks building directly on specific coding schemes. This idea is also brought forward in Bunt et al. (2003).

6.3.4   Impact

ANVIL's distribution started in the year 2000. Since then, it has been requested by more than 350 researchers from over 30 different countries. It is utilized for doctoral studies, institute research and international projects, by researchers from areas as diverse as Computer Science, Psychology, Linguistics, and Dance Choreography, to name a few. This section tries to give an impression of the impact ANVIL has made in the research community since its first release.

The first ANVIL release, version 1.5, was put on a website for distribution in October 2000, the latest release, version 4.0, was uploaded in February 2003. The software is free for research purposes and resides on the ANVIL website. The website offers a general description, a downloadable 51-page user manual in PDF format, a quick-reference card in MS Word format, and a frequently asked questions (FAQ) page. To make ANVIL known in the research community, it has been presented on diverse international conferences (Kipp, 2001b, Kipp, 2001a, Martin and Kipp, 2002) and workshops (Kipp, 2001c, Vintar and Kipp, 2001). The tool was reviewed in published surveys on annotation tools (Bigbee et al., 2001, Dybkjær et al., 2001). By now, it has already become a prototypical representative for annotation tools (Loehr and Harper 2003) and is frequently part of university seminars and conference tutorials[5] dealing with video annotation.

On the ANVIL website, the ANVIL User Web collects contact data of institutes and researchers who have been using ANVIL and are willing to share their expertise. It cannot precisely be measured how many of the 330 downloads resulted in serious use of the tool. However, from e-mail exchanges concerning technical support, requests for new features and general feedback it can be asserted that at least 50

---

[5]For instance, in 2003, ANVIL will be part of a tutorial on *Tools for Annotating Natural Interactivity Corpora* at the 8th European Conference on Speech Communication and Technology (Eurospeech), Geneva, Switzerland.

scientists seriously use ANVIL in their research. This research has already produced a number of publications, including Abrilian et al. (2002), Dellwo (2003), Maeda et al. (2003), Martell (2002), Martin (2002), Martin and Kipp (2002), Magno Caldognetto and Poggi (2002), Pérez-Parent (2002), Vintar and Kipp (2001).

The research institutes where ANVIL is currently in use include LIMSI (France), Chiba University (Japan), MIT Media Lab (US), MITRE (US), OGI (US), University of Shiga Prefecture (Japan), University of Reading (US), University of Chicago (US), Jena University (Germany), Bielefeld University (Germany), University of Ulster (UK), University of Pennsylvania (US), University of Rochester (US), CNR (Italy), University of Bonn (Germany), University at Buffalo (US), University of Paris 8 (France), UC San Diego (US), UC Santa Barbara (US), ICT (US), University of Rome III (Italy), CMU (US), University of Porto (Portugal).

The research areas where ANVIL is utilized are as diverse as Gesture Research, Anthropology, Linguistics, HCI, Ethology, Biology, Psycholinguistics, Semiotics, Robotics, Ergonomics, Psychotherapy, Bioacoustics, Sign Language, Conversation Analysis, Multimedia Summarization, Gesture Recognition, Multimodal Communication, Cross-Cultural Education, Multimedia Information Retrieval, Contrastive Bilingual Communication, Visual Ethnography, Developmental Psychology, Animal/Insect Behavior, Dialogue Systems, Annotation Tools, Talking Heads, Dance Choreography, Ethnomusicology, Augmented Reality, Gestures in Second Language Acquisition, Content-based Image Retrieval, and Multimodal Corpora.

ANVIL continues to draw requests for download and technical support. It has also profited from comments, bug reports and suggestions coming out of its growing user community. The positive response to the tool from a broad variety of fields confirms its declared aims to be intuitive and general enough to be of use in a wide range of areas.

Chapter 7

Speech Transcription:
The NOVACO Scheme I

The last chapter described the design and implementation of the research software
ANVIL which provides a coding tool for video annotation. This chapter introduces
the first part of NOVACO[1], a coding scheme for speech and gesture, specifically
devised for the purpose of gesture generation. This first part of NOVACO deals
with the transcription of speech and related concepts in the LQ data. The second
part, which will be topic of the next chapter, is dedicated to gesture transcription.
In NOVACO, multiple layers contain different kinds of information. These layers,
called *tracks* in ANVIL, are organized in two *groups*, one dealing with speech and
one dealing with gesture. Annotation is performed by coding one track at a time.
The order in which the tracks are presented in this chapter is also the order in
which the annotation process should proceed.

In this chapter, the whole annotation scheme will be described both on an intuitive and a technical level. The technical description includes NOVACO's concrete
application in ANVIL. Since ANVIL is a generic tool suited for many coding schemes,
it must be specifically configured to let coders use the NOVACO scheme. This is
done by writing a specification file for ANVIL in XML syntax. Throughout this
and the next chapter, the complete specification will be provided step by step. The
specification is organized in two groups: speech and gesture. Each group contains a
number of tracks and in each track information is stored in attributes. The speech
group is defined like this:

```
<group name="speech">
  ...
</group>
```

---

[1]**No**nverbal and **V**erbal **A**ction **Co**ding Scheme

This group is centered around the "words" track where the speech transcription of the analyzed speaker is located. The following sections describe all tracks of the speech group in detail.

7.1 Words and Segments

The transcription of the speech stream is usually the first step in any transcription. In the **NOVACO** scheme, words are the basic units for further levels of transcription. It can therefore be called a *word-based* transcription system.

A word is a basic unit of meaning in language. In this work, a word is defined to be an entry in a German dictionary, including all possible word forms. New German Orthography[2] was used for transcription. Punctuation marks were not encoded. Some nonverbal sounds and special phenomena were encoded as shown in Table 7.1.

label	description
[aeh]	German hesitation sound
[aehm]	German hesitation sound
[nid]	not identifiable word
w[-]	word w was not fully articulated

Table 7.1: *Transcription of nonverbal sounds.*

In **NOVACO**, words are represented on a primary track called `trl` for "transliteration". A String-type attribute called `token` contains the word in New German Orthography. Other attributes will be added to this track for further linguistic information on the word level.

```
<track-spec name="trl" type="primary">
  <attribute name="token" display="true" />
</track-spec>
```

Technically, words are transcribed in the PRAAT tool (Section 3.2.1). For this, the sound is first extracted from the video file using Adobe's Premiere 5.0 software. This file is loaded in PRAAT and a *text grid* is created which is a multi-layered annotation construct. Only a single layer of type *interval tier* is needed and named "words". Now the exact word boundaries and tokens can be annotated in PRAAT's graphical environment. The resulting annotation is saved to a *short text file* that can be imported by **ANVIL** to the `trl` track defined above.

---

[2]*New German Orthography* refers to a nation-wide reform of German orthography that was introduced on 1 August 1998.

Words can be grouped to segments which loosely correspond to sentences in written language. In the literature this unit is also called *utterance*. Two alternative theories offer concrete annotation guidelines: the theory of *discourse structure* (Nakatani et al. 1995) and *rhetorical structure theory* or RST (Mann and Thompson 1988). The segmentation guidelines that were used in this work were the ones from RST.

In **NOVACO**, segments are encoded as empty elements on a secondary track, referring to the `trl` track.

```
<track-spec name="segment" type="span" ref="trl" />
```

The elements are empty, their essential information is contained in their pointing to one beginning and one ending word.

7.2 Parts-of-Speech

Parts-of-speech (POS) categorize words according to their syntactic role (McEnery and Wilson 1996). POS also imply certain semantic properties. The POS *noun*, for instance, usually refers to things and living beings. Other well-known POS categories are: verb, adjective, adverb. POS are part of a grammatical theory — the definitions can be derived from Morphology, Syntax, Semantics or Pragmatics, depending on the application. Different categorizations exist, depending on the underlying theory. Since it is a widely established concept, several *automatic* POS taggers[3] have been developed that work statistically or rule-based and achieve an accuracy of over 95% (Brill 1992).

The POS categories of this work were taken from the Stuttgart-Tübingen-Tagset (STTS). Perfect annotation was assumed (100% accuracy). Therefore, annotation was done manually on a list of words found necessary for semantic labelling disambiguation (see Section 11.3). Note that for full automation these tags could be computed with an average accuracy of 96% to 97% using the German TnT (Trigrams'n'Tags) tagger (Brants 2000).

In **NOVACO**, the part-of-speech of a word is encoded in the `trl` track as an additional attribute called `pos`.

```
<track-spec name="trl" type="primary">
  <attribute name="token" display="true" />
  <attribute name="pos" valuetype="posType" display="true" />
</track-spec>
```

The `pos` attribute is a self-defined set of labels called "posType" of type ValueSet, containing the tags listed in Table A.2 in Appendix A.1.

---

[3]For instance, both MORPHIX (Finkler and Lutzky, 1996, Finkler and Neumann, 1986) and TnT (Brants 2000) for German, the Brill tagger (Brill 1992) for English and the Stuttgart Tree-Tagger for German and English (Schmid 1994).

7.3 Theme/Rheme and Focus

Theme, rheme and focus are notions from the theory of *information structure* (Sgall et al., 1973, Hajičová, 1993, Halliday, 1973, Steedman, 2000). Information structure is a theoretical construct that helps to explain how an utterance in a discourse relates to the other utterances, thus explaining how the utterance *coheres* with the larger discourse (Kruijff, 2001: 153). Utterances are divided into several parts which are defined to relate in different ways to the discourse or to each other. In the approach by Steedman (2000) this partition is conducted on two dimensions. The first dimension is that of theme vs. rheme. The second dimension differentiates theme/rheme segments into focus[4] and background.

Theme and rheme

Looking at informal accounts of theme and rheme by Halliday (1967, 1973) and Steedman (2001), the properties of a *theme* can be summarized as follows:

   i) it links the utterance to the previous discourse

   ii) it corresponds to a question or topic that is presupposed by the speaker

   iii) it specifies what the utterance is about

The *rheme* can be characterized as follows:

   i) it relates to the theme

   ii) it specifies something novel or interesting about the theme

To describe theme and rheme more formally, Steedman uses the notion of *alternative sets*. An alternative set contains a number of propositions. Theme and rheme of a single utterance relate to the same rheme alternative set (RAS). The difference is that the theme *presupposes* the RAS, whereas the rheme *restricts* the RAS. Presupposition means that the relevant alternative set is available in the context. Therefore, in a *wh*-question, the question word (e.g. *what* or *which result*) is the theme of the question associated with a set of propositions concerning things, or sorts of result. The rest of the *wh*-question restricts this set to propositions relating to one particular predication. It is this set that in turn typically becomes the set of alternatives associated with the theme in the answer. That does not mean that all answers to questions must necessarily be rhemes. An answer can just as well establish a *new theme*. In the following example, taken from Steedman, 2000, the question projects two alternatives, RAS = {Marcel loves opera, Marcel does not love opera}, neither of which is referred to in the answer. Therefore, the answer constitutes a new theme.

---

[4] Although in more recent work Steedman (2001) has renamed the term focus to *kontrast*, the better known term *focus* will be used here.

Q: Does Marcel love opera?
A: Marcel likes MUSICALS.

Rhemes can be embedded in a theme so that the theme becomes *discontinuous*. See the following example (from Steedman, 2000) where the rheme "a book" (underlined) is embedded in the theme of Marcel giving something to Fred:

Q: I know what Marcel SOLD to Harry. But what did he GIVE to FRED?
A: Marcel GAVE a BOOK to FRED.

Focus

Since only parts of the theme/rheme segments are intonationally marked, Steedman (2000) defines these marked parts to be the *focus*, whereas the rest of the utterance he calls *background*. According to Steedman, the focus consists of words whose meaning contribute to distinguishing the theme or rheme of the utterance from other alternatives that the context makes available. All other words belong to the background. In a theme, the focus is optional, i.e. there need not be a marked segment in the theme.

The focus of the rheme restricts the RAS. In the following example, intonationally marked words are upper case. In the answer, the first square bracket constitutes the theme, the second the rheme — the focus is underlined each and corresponds with the intonationally marked words (taken from Steedman, 2000):

Q: I know that Marcel likes the man who wrote the musical. But who does he ADMIRE?
A: [Marcel ADMIRES]$_{theme}$ [the woman who DIRECTED the musical]$_{rheme}$

The function of the theme focus is to restrict the *theme alternative set* (TAS) which is like the RAS presupposed by the theme. In the example, the TAS contains "Marcel likes X" as an alternative to "Marcel admires X".

Theme/Rheme and Focus in NOVACO

Information Structure is encoded in a secondary track which is called `theme-rheme`. It refers to the `trl` track. Theme and rheme are coded in the `type` attribute. Focus is realized through links to the `trl` track. Background elements are not explicitly marked. The specification is:

```
<track-spec name="theme-rheme" type="span" ref="trl">
  <attribute name="type" display="true">
    <value-el>
      rheme
    </value-el>
    <value-el>
      theme
    </value-el>
  </attribute>
  <attribute name="focus" valuetype="MultiLink(trl)" />
</track-spec>
```

Discontinuous themes are simply marked as two separate spans in the utterance.

7.4 Discourse Relations

Segments in spoken or written discourse relate to each other in various ways: temporally, causally, argumentatively etc. For instance, segment A may deliver the cause for the effect described in the next segment B, or segment A may relate to something that happened *before* what is described in segment B. Such relations are used to describe the structural organization of a text or monologue and are called coherence, rhetorical or discourse relations (Hobbs, 1979, Mann and Thompson, 1988).

Although many such relations can be identified, in **NOVACO** only three relations are used instead of the whole arsenal that can be found in the literature (Hovy 1990). This severe restriction has three reasons. First, to statistically establish the relationship between specific rhetoric relations and specific gestures requires a corpus much larger than the LQ corpus. As exploratory research in the LQ corpus soon made clear, most of the rhetoric relations do not systematically co-occur with specific gestures. Second, encoding rhetorical structure is both time-consuming and difficult in terms of maintaining consistency as existing coding instructions (e.g. by Mann and Thompson, 1988) are very general. Third, since the coding scheme will establish gesture-speech relationships through the word level (see Section 8.4.2), possible correlations between gesture and rhetorical relation can be found via *cue words*. Cue words, like "because", "then", "if" etc., represent rhetorical relations lexically (Knott and Dale 1994). With their help, existing relationships between gesture and rhetorical relations can be established indirectly in the analysis.

The three very simple relations that have been included in the **NOVACO** scheme are: opposition, repetition and list.

Opposition The opposition relation is a binary relation linking two antagonistic segments that contrast each other. This contrast is often intonationally marked and accompanied by gesture (Cassell et al. 2001b). Two examples are:

- "poetisch bezog [ICH]$_1$ auf die Sprache und [SIE]$_2$ beziehen's auf – also gut – geschenkt"[5]

- "...eine [SCHLECHTE]$_1$ Figur oder eine [GUTE]$_2$ Figur?"[6]

Repetition   The repetition relation is an n-ary relation linking two or more repeated instances of the same word or rephrasings that only slightly modify the original word or phrase. Examples are:

- "was tun die beiden Eiswürfel [sie klirren]$_1$ [sie klirren]$_2$"[7]

- "sagt niemals öffentlich [mein Werk]$_1$ [meine Arbeit]$_2$ ist nach dem Muster ...von Bertold Brecht (geschrieben) ..."[8]

List   The list relation is an n-ary relation that links up the items of an enumeration. The relation has been found to be a popular rhetorical device with some relation to nonverbal behavior (Atkinson 1984). This relation includes simple binary conjunctions with connectives "and" or "or". Examples are:

- "das ist ein [hocherfreuliches]$_1$ [wichtiges]$_2$ [lesbares]$_3$ [intelligentes]$_4$ Buch"[9]

- "...sowas wie [Beethoven]$_1$ oder [Brahms]$_2$"[10]

Discourse Relations in **NOVACO**

Discourse relations are modeled in a *set* container (a container for non-temporal objects) called `discourse relations`. The first attribute, called `relation`, holds the relation type. The second attribute, `arity`, contains the number of links to speech segments. Finally, each segment is linked with a reciprocal link to the `trl` track. The container can only model relations with up to six arguments.

---

[5] MRR, LQ1-2, 0:31
[6] MRR, LQ1-6, 0:19
[7] MRR, LQ2-7, 0:05
[8] MRR, LQ3-3, 0:31; verb in brackets was not uttered, sentence was abandoned
[9] MRR, LQ1-2, 0:38
[10] MRR, LQ1-6, 0:57

```
<set-spec name="discourse relations">
  <attribute name="relation" display="true">
    <value-el>opposition</value-el>
    <value-el>list</value-el>
    <value-el>repetition</value-el>
  </attribute>
  <attribute name="arity" valuetype="Number(1,6)" display="true" />
  <attribute name="arg1" valuetype="ReciprocalLink(relation)" />
  <attribute name="arg2" valuetype="ReciprocalLink(relation)" />
  <attribute name="arg3" valuetype="ReciprocalLink(relation)" />
  <attribute name="arg4" valuetype="ReciprocalLink(relation)" />
  <attribute name="arg5" valuetype="ReciprocalLink(relation)" />
  <attribute name="arg6" valuetype="ReciprocalLink(relation)" />
</set-spec>
```

In the LQ data, the number of discourse relation arguments never exceeded six.

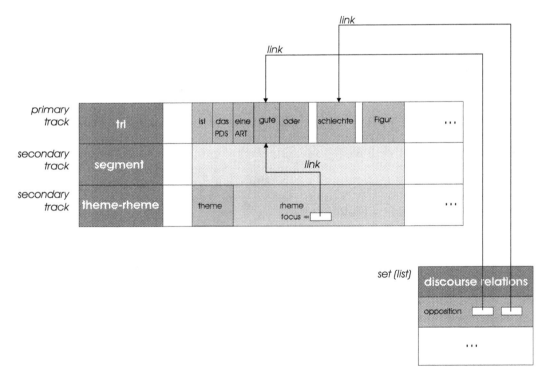

Figure 7.1: *The four ANVIL containers for speech annotation.*

7.5 Summary

This chapter presented the first part of **NOVACO**, a word-based coding scheme specifically designed for the purpose of gesture generation. The first part deals with speech annotation which, in **NOVACO**, is based on the transcription of speech in words. For a number of cases the words were annotated with parts-of-speech to allow disambiguation of singular words without further context at a later stage of processing. Words are grouped to segments that mark the limits of utterances, a construct roughly equivalent to sentences in written language. On another track the concepts of theme and rheme were encoded which relate to the newness of information. A theme's or rheme's focus is the decisive piece of information to make a segment theme or rheme. It is encoded, too. Finally, three discourse relations are coded: opposition, list and repetition. These are relations that pertain to the rhetorical structure of the text.

For **NOVACO**'s definition in **ANVIL**, words are taken as the basic units of speech annotation. Words are encoded in a primary track. All other concepts refer to words and are therefore realized as attributes (parts-of-speech), as a secondary tracks that refers to the words track or as a set where elements point to words via links. Figure 7.1 shows a small sample annotation utilizing all four **ANVIL** containers, demonstrating how the containers relate to each other. The `segment` and `theme-rheme` tracks both refer to the primary `trl` track. The `discourse relations` container consists of a set of non-temporal elements that refer to the `trl` track, too.

Chapter 8

Gesture Transcription: The NOVACO Scheme II

The last chapter presented the first part of **NOVACO**, a word-based coding scheme for conversations. This chapter will extend the **NOVACO** scheme to gestures. The scheme builds on insights from gesture research as presented in Chapter 3. For gestures the scheme will work on both descriptive and interpretative levels. The complete annotation scheme, applied to the LQ data corpus, prepares the way for building gesture profiles and generating gesture in the following chapters.

As in the previous chapter, the order in which tracks are introduced is also the order in which they should be coded. Each track is treated together with its technical realization in **ANVIL**.

8.1 Gesture Structure

In the annotation of gesture one need not only describe features of form but also the temporal structure of the gesture. First of all where they begin and end but also, which part the "meaning-carrying" part is, an essential aspect when synchronizing a gesture with speech. The tool for establishing a gesture's internal structure are *movement phases* that were introduced in Section 3.1.1.

In a hierarchical view on movement structure these phases, small units of movement, form larger units, so-called *phrases*. This approach was introduced by Birdwhistell (1970) who founded the field of *Kinesics* in analogy to the field of *Linguistics*. Although his approach to identify basic units of meaning in motion has not been successful, the movement phases used today are inspired by his endeavor. This section will demonstrate how to segment the gesture stream into phases and how to cluster these phases to phrases.

In **NOVACO**, all tracks encoding gestural information are organized in a single group called **gesture**. The phases, small units of movement, are encoded in the primary track `phase`. These units form larger units, the phrases, that are encoded in the secondary track `phrase`:

```
<group name="gesture">
  <track-spec name="phase" type="primary">
    ...
  </track-spec>
  <track-spec name="phrase" type="span" ref="gesture.phase">
    ...
  </track-spec>
</group>
```

For gestural annotation, both arms are treated in a single track. Consequently, when two arms are moved at the same time this can be encoded in a single gesture only. This makes sense because most of the time these two arms movements belong indeed to the same bi-handed gesture. Although there are cases where two different gestures are performed at the same time with two different hands, it virtually never occurs in the LQ corpus.

8.1.1 Movement Phases

As with words in the speech stream, gestures must first be segmented before they can be classified. From a stream of movement single gestures must be identified. A first delimitation takes a gestural excursion to be the movement between two consecutive *resting positions* of the arms (McNeill, 1992: 376, and Kita et al., 1998: 23). However, these excursions can contain multiple gestures. Exact gesture boundaries together with the gestures internal structure are identified by decomposing an excursion into *movement phases*. The annotation of movement phases is conducted according to the criteria by Kita et al. (1998) that have been described in Section 3.1.1.

Beyond the definitions by Kita and colleagues, a *recoil* phase is defined to be the small recoil motion that can happen after a forceful stroke where the hand lashes back from the stroke-end position. Furthermore, the *beats* phase is what Kita et al. call a *repetitive phase*, i.e. a number of repetitive movements where each movement would qualify as a stroke or preparation. McNeill (1992: 204-205) suggested that beats were *superimposed* on iconic and metaphoric gestures in certain situations. This observation is generalized here insofar as beats are considered part of a gesture's phase structure.

For coding movement phases, the instructions in Section 3.1.1 were used, modified with the recoil and beats phases. Kita et al. (1998) conducted a reliability study where two experienced coders independently annotated about 30 gesture phases, i.e. segmentation and classification were done. They achieved 72% agreement with a tolerance of 2 frames in segmentation (1 frame = 40 msec.) which is a good result showing that this scheme works to a satisfying degree.

In **NOVACO**, the gesture phase is encoded in the `phase` track with the single attribute `type` that holds the phase type as a set of labels:

```
<track-spec name="phase" type="primary">
  <attribute name="type">
    <value-el>prep</value-el>
    <value-el>stroke</value-el>
    <value-el>beats</value-el>
    <value-el>hold</value-el>
    <value-el>indep-hold</value-el>
    <value-el>recoil</value-el>
    <value-el>retract</value-el>
    <value-el>partial-retract</value-el>
  </attribute>
</track-spec>
```

8.1.2 Movement Phrases

A number of movement phases constitute a movement *phrase* (McNeill, 1992: 82–84). A phrase is what would naively be considered a gesture and therefore, the terms phrase and gesture will be used synonymously here. In annotation, phases are coded first. In a second step, the identified phases are grouped together to obtain phrases.

Phases are grouped to phrases according to the following grammar. It is a modified version of the grammar by Kita et al. (1998: 27), including recoil and beats:

phrase	::= (**preparation**) *expressive-phase* (*retraction*)
expressive-phase	::= (**hold**) **stroke** (**recoil**) (**hold**) |
	(**hold**) **beats** (**recoil**) (**hold**) |
	independent-hold
retraction	::= **retraction** | **partial-retraction**

Labels in italics are nonterminals that must be replaced using the given rules. The labels in boldface are terminals, i.e. the actual phases that are not further replaced. All bracketed terminals and nonterminals are optional, i.e. they can be omitted.

The grammar implies that a gesture (a phrase) always contains one expressive phase that can consist of a single stroke, repeated strokes (beats) or a hold. Using the grammar gestures can be reliably segmented, provided that the phases are encoded correctly.

Having defined the temporal limits of a gesture the following sections will deal with adding content to the gestural annotation.

8.2   Gesture Classes

Having identified gestures, the gestures need a classification according to form and function that leads to a lexicon of gestures. Such a lexicon is the basis for a library of gesture clips in the animation phase. Before creating lexicon entries in the next section, a high-level classification of gestures into *gesture classes* serves to divide the lexicon into smaller units. This facilitates creating new lexicon entries by restricting the number of gestures the new gesture has to be distinguished from. It also makes the definition of concepts like *lexical affiliate* clearer (Section 8.4.2).

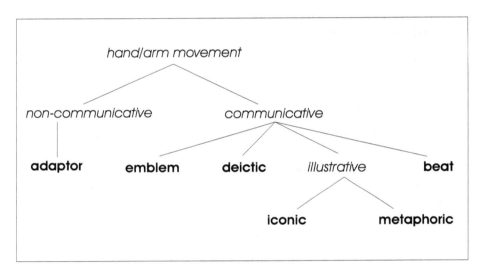

Figure 8.1: *Gesture classes.*

In this work, the following classes, that were introduced in Section 2.1.1, will be used: adaptors, emblems, deictics, iconics, metaphorics and beats. Adaptors are usually not considered gestures at all, while beats are said to bear no communicative content. Iconics and metaphorics are both illustrative gestures. Figure 8.1 graphically shows these relationships, that will be explained below, in a decision tree.

One important property of this categorization is that the classes are *not* orthogonal, i.e. they overlap. This is because different criteria are used for the different classes (see Müller, 1998, for a detailed critique and an alternative model). However, classification is still possible by specifying how to classify gestures in cases of ambiguity. This is achieved by using the decision tree depicted in Figure 8.1. The coder traverses the decision tree from top to bottom and checks which branch to take using the class descriptions below. In cases of doubt the left branch is taken. Ambiguity is thus deleted by prescribing an annotation order. So a gesture is first checked for being an adaptor or a communicative gesture. Kendon (1978) showed in a study that this distinction can reliably be drawn by untrained coders even across cultures. Next, the gesture is checked for being an emblem, a deictic or an illustrative gesture. Illustrative gestures are checked for being either iconic or metaphoric ones. If none of the categories apply the gesture is put into the rest class, the beats.

In **NOVACO**, the class of a gesture is encoded in the `class` attribute of the `phrase` track:

```
<track-spec name="phrase" type="span" ref="gesture.phase">
  <attribute name="class">
    <value-el>beat</value-el>
    <value-el>deictic</value-el>
    <value-el>emblem</value-el>
    <value-el>iconic</value-el>
    <value-el>metaphoric</value-el>
    <value-el>adaptor</value-el>
  </attribute>
</track-spec>
```

The following sections define the class coding criteria. For general descriptions of the gesture classes see Section 2.1.1. The order of the following class descriptions reflects the order in which the coder should traverse the decision tree in Figure 8.1: top to bottom, left to right.

Adaptors

Adaptors are movements that satisfy secondary needs like scratching the cheek or playing around with a pen. They are movements that a recipient would not consider part of the communication (Kendon 1978). In conversations, most self- and object-touches are adaptors. A hand or arm movement must be coded as an adaptor if the following two conditions hold:

(1) The gesture is not considered part of the communication.

(2) The gesture is either a self-touch or an object-touch (e.g. pen, arm-rest, table).

According to Kendon (1978), the first condition can be reliably coded, independent of culture. Pointing gestures (deictics), although they can involve touches when pointing to oneself or others, are excluded from this class due to the first condition.

Emblems

Emblems are gestures that have conventionalized form and meaning and can be used even without speech. Thus, they can be utilized in situations where the speech channel is for some reason restricted, e.g. by noise (construction site) or by convention (library).

However, in this work emblems are seen in a conversational context where they accompany speech. The criterium for a gesture to be an emblem is its conventionalization of form and meaning. A communicative gesture must be coded an emblem if the following three conditions hold:

(1) The form of the gesture is conventionalized.

(2) The meaning of the gesture is conventionalized.

(3) The gesture could be used without speech.

To check the first two criteria, existing emblem dictionaries can be consulted (see Section 2.2.4 for references). In such dictionaries meaning is often defined using either a verbal equivalent or a verbal concomitant utterance.

Pointing gestures (deictics), although they are conventionalized in form and meaning and can be used without speech, are explicitly excluded from this class since they form a large enough category to be separated from other emblems.

Deictics

Deictics are pointing gestures. The arm/hand is used to point at an existing or imaginary object. A *concrete* pointing gesture means to indicate a person, an object, a direction, a location, or a collection of entities. An *abstract* pointing gesture refers to something not present which is either abstract or imaginary (cf. McNeill, 1992: 173).

For coding deictics, a coder must first consider form. In terms of static shape, a single finger, index finger or thumb, or the flat, open hand is extended toward the object. In terms of movement, a movement toward the object is performed, possibly backward over the shoulder.

In a second, interpretative step, it must be checked whether the gesture is actually used to point at something concrete, e.g. hands moving toward addressee. Abstract pointing can be identified by looking at concomitant speech. If there are referents that the pointing refer to the gesture qualifies as a deictic. Excluded from this definition are iconic gestures that illustrate a path or shape of an object.

Iconics

Iconics are movements that serve to illustrate what is being said. Iconic gestures bear some similarity in shape or movement to the speech content. For example, when talking about a picture the hand could form a rectangular frame (shape) or trace an imaginary frame (movement). In both cases the gesture shares the property of rectangularity with the speech referent that is the picture. A gesture must be coded an iconic if both of the following two conditions hold:

(1) There is a referent R that the co-occurring speech utterance refers to.

(2) Some aspect of R, shape or movement, is depicted by the gesture.

The semantic information that the speech utterance transports about R may be identical to the gesture's information or it may complement it, i.e. speech and gesture semantics only partially overlap. This usually occurs when spatial relationships or forms of movement are described which often is more effectively done with gestures (cf. Cassell et al., 1999)

Metaphorics

A metaphoric is a gesture that illustrates a concrete object, the base, which in turn metaphorically refers to something mentioned in speech, the referent. A gesture must be coded a metaphoric if both of the following two conditions hold:

(1) The gesture depicts a concrete object: the base.

(2) The base metaphorically represents a referent that is referred to in the co-occurring speech utterance.

If base and referent are the same or very similar then it is not a metaphoric but an iconic gesture.

Beats

Beats are rhythmic hand movements that accompany speech. The beat gesture is a rest class. A gesture found not to belong to one of the above classes is thus a beat. As opposed to the other classes shape is not a criterium for class membership. Only the phrasal structure that identifies the movement as being a gesture is a minimal criterium for considering the movement a beat.

8.3   Gesture Lexicon and Lemmas

In this work, gesture generation is based on clips, i.e. pre-fabricated movement patterns. Therefore, a principal classification based on form is desirable where each form category has a number of meanings like entries in a dictionary. In Linguistics, dictionary entries are called *lemmas*. Each lemma subsumes variations in form and has a number of different meanings or readings (Levelt 1989). The challenge in gesture annotation is to find gestural equivalents to lemmas, i.e. to identify groups of gesture occurrences that are closely related in surface form. These instances are then labeled with a name that represents a single gesture lemma subsuming all instances. While these instances can have different meanings or functions they cannot belong to different gesture *classes* (Section 8.2). Instead, gesture classes impose a pre-categorization onto the lemmas. Like lemmas in a lexicon are separated by part-of-speech (noun, adjective, verb etc.) gestural lemmas are separated by class, even if the surface form is for some instances identical. This allows, for instance, to keep apart the deictic for pointing up from the emblem called *attention* (raised forefinger) or the adaptor of scratching one's chest from the deictic of pointing to oneself. So gesture lemmas are lexicon entries that subsume variants of form but are themselves part of the superimposed class categorization.

Gesture lexicons have been assembled by various researchers, for instance by Weinrich (1992: 105ff.) for conversational analysis, by Webb (1997: 95ff.) for Psycholinguistic research and by Saitz and Cervenka (1972) as an aid in intercultural understanding. According to the *OED*, the term *lexicon* refers to "the complete set of elementary meaningful units in a language; the words etc. which would be in a complete dictionary (but without definitions)" (Brown 1993). This means that a lexicon does not include the meaning of its entries.

For annotation, first a lexicon of gesture lemmas must be collected from the empirical material. This collection step is done by systematically sifting through the empirical data and cataloguing the gestures by comparing them to the already found ones. Once the lexicon is complete, annotation can begin. During annotation no new gesture lemmas may be added. Otherwise inconsistencies could emerge. Instead, a rest category must serve as a container for gesture lemmas not yet located in the lexicon.

The following sections will explain how to identify a lemma during *collection* as well as during *annotation*.

8.3.1 Identifying a Lemma

A lemma represents a gesture with a tolerance in variation just like entries in a language dictionary allow for variation of intonation and inflection. Gestural lemmas are equivalence classes concerning form and function. A lemma with variations $\{v_1, \ldots, v_n\}$ in form and meanings $\{m_1, \ldots, m_k\}$ is *consistent* if every form v_i can express every meaning m_j.

If a gesture is modified by changing the location or orientation of the hand(s) or by changing the shape of the hand, it may either become a different lemma altogether or it may simply be another formal variation of the same lemma. Hand location, orientation, shape etc. are called *form dimensions*. If changing a gesture along a dimension changes the lemma the dimension is called *formational*[1].

---

[1] The notion of formational parameters was introduced by Stokoe (1960) to describe the meaningful components of sign language. Webb (1997: 18) uses this concept in the context of conversational gestures.

The form dimensions are the following:

- hand shape
- hand location
- hand orientation
- movement
- bi-handedness
- concomitant shoulder movement
- concomitant facial expression

Facial expression must be included as a potentially formational dimension since some emblems cannot be distinguished without it. This necessity has been empirically proved by other researchers in emblem decoding experiments. Bitti (1992) found that two Italian emblems with two differing meanings each could only be identified with the help of facial expression. Calbris (1990) in a decoding experiment of 32 French emblems found facial expression, which she calls a *complementary signifier*, to have a positive effect in recognition in 25% of the cases. However, she also found that in 25% of the cases it had a negative impact. In these negative cases, subjects recognized the purely gestural dimensions very well but were distracted by the facial expression. To avoid this effect, it is therefore important to explicitly state the relevance of facial expression as a formational dimension in the coding manual.

When classifying a gesture g, the collector/annotator checks each lemma L and should act according to the following four cases:

Case 1: Equal Form and Meaning   If the gesture has an instance in the lemma set that equals it in form and meaning, i.e.

$$\text{form}(g) \in \text{form}(L) \quad \wedge \quad \text{meaning}(g) \in \text{meaning}(L)$$

then gesture g is of lemma L, $g \in L$.

Case 2: Equal Form, Different Meaning   If the gesture has an instance in the lemma set that equals it in form but has a different meaning, i.e.

$$\text{form}(g) \in \text{form}(L) \quad \wedge \quad \neg(\text{meaning}(g) \in \text{meaning}(L))$$

then lemma L must be extended by g's meaning but only if all $g' \in \text{form}(L)$ can express this meaning.

Case 3: Different Form, Equal Meaning If the gesture has an instance in the lemma set that is different in form but has equal meaning, i.e.

$$\neg(\text{form}(g) \in \text{form}(L)) \quad \wedge \quad \text{meaning}(g) \in \text{meaning}(L)$$

then lemma L must be extended by g's form but only if all other meanings $f' \in$ meaning(L) can be expressed by this form.

Case 4: Different Form, Different Meaning If there is no lemma where g shares form or meaning with an instance of the lemma, i.e.

$$\neg \exists L : (\text{form}(g) \in \text{form}(L) \quad \vee \quad \text{meaning}(g) \in \text{meaning}(L))$$

then there are two different consequences depending on whether (A) one is collecting the lexicon or (B) doing actual annotation:

(A) A new lemma must be created as described in the following section.

(B) g must be put into the rest category, typically named "unknown".

The following section describes how lemmas must be created depending on the class of the new gesture.

8.3.2 Creating New Lemmas

For each gesture class other criteria were devised how to create new lemmas. The following sections treat the different mechanisms for the five classes, excluding the beat class which is a rest class without further subdivision. A complete list of all lemmas, constituting the shared gesture lexicon of speakers MRR and HK, can be found in Appendix B. Each lemma entry specifies its formational features that serve to distinguish the gesture from other lemmas.

Emblems Emblem lemmas are identified by finding a phrase or word that is equivalent in meaning to the gesture. The following existing gesture inventories were also used to classify emblems: Saitz and Cervenka (1972), Efron (1941), Webb (1997), Calbris (1990), Payrató (1993), Johnson et al. (1975), Weinrich (1992) and Morris (1994).

Adaptors Adaptor lemmas are categorized by the object or body part being touched. Example body parts are: hair, forehead, nose, knee, thigh. Example objects are: pen, table, arm rest.

Deictics A deictic lemma is defined by the person or object being indicated:

- SELF

- ADDRESSEE

- SELF+ADDRESSEE

- AUDIENCE

- SPACE

Locations and inanimate objects are excluded since such cases do not occur in the data. Abstract deictics are considered to be pointing into SPACE. The deictic gesture SELF+ADDRESSEE comprises gestures that flip back and forth between pointing to oneself and to the addressee.

Iconics Iconics are categorized by the illustrated content. This can be an object that is being drawn in the air or represented by a hand shape mimicking the object's shape. Such gestures are also called *pictographs* (Ekman and Friesen 1969). It can also be a part of a movement like drinking (moving an imaginary cup to the mouth) and driving (holding an imaginary steering wheel). Such gestures are called *kinetographs* (Ekman and Friesen 1969).

Some iconic gestures can also be used *metaphorically*, making them metaphorics. For instance, in the gesture ICONIC.EXPLODE the hands start in the lap as fists and fly apart in an abrupt upward/outward movement while the hands open up. The gesture illustrates the pressure wave being set free. It is used both to illustrate the verb "explode" (iconic use) as well as the adjective "huge" (metaphoric use). For such borderline cases the coder has to decide whether to put the gesture into the iconics or metaphorics class. Since iconics and metaphorics are very similar classes, both are subsumed by the notion of *illustrators* by McNeill (1992), the coder does not need to devise two lemmas for the same gesture to distinguish between iconic and metaphoric use.

Metaphorics Metaphorics are categorized by the type of metaphor used. The *conduit* metaphorics, for example, equate the speech content with a solid object that can be held, offered or received (McNeill, 1992: 147ff.). The *progress* metaphorics equate a circular, cyclic movement in the sagittal plane where the upper arc moves away from the body with concepts like progress, future or change (called *metaphors of change* by McNeill, 1992: 159ff.). Moving in the opposite direction makes this metaphoric one of *regress* referring to concepts like regression, past, returning to the origin (Calbris, 1990: 90-93).

8.4 Gesture Properties

Gestures can be annotated with *descriptive* and *interpretative* information. Some argue that only descriptive knowledge may be coded (Jorns 1979), and in the Bern coding system this has been fruitfully done to perfection (Frey 1999). In the Bern system, the coder estimates the position of all joints of all body limbs in discrete units, doing it for each "time slice". Such purely descriptive annotations require large corpora and much time for annotation. Also, data analysis may not result in meaningful interpretations since even simple information like the shape of the hand is hidden in a huge heap of data. Therefore, as in Linguistics, interpretative annotation is usually added that tries to capture the meaning of the gesture based on the coder's own communicative competence (cf. Scherer et al., 1979).

Since gesture generation is the aim of this work, the following requirements emerge. Generation will start from speech input, so the relation to speech must be established by interpretation or temporal co-occurrence. Trying to find relations by analyzing temporal co-occurrence, although intuitively a good idea, is difficult and error-prone. Too many gestures co-occur with speech units without having any relation to them. Therefore, for singling out the meaningful co-occurrences of gesture and speech units, an explicit encoding is needed (Section 8.4.2). Finally, for questions of temporal synchronization of gesture and speech a fine-grained structural view on gestures has to be assumed and the temporal relationship must be explicitly coded (Section 8.4.3). The following sections will first treat the descriptive annotation of handedness ,then proceeded with the interpretative annotation of lexical affiliates and of temporal relationship which requires identification of lexical affiliates.

8.4.1 Handedness

The term handedness refers to whether the gestures relies on the right hand (RH), the left hand (LH) or both (2H). For determining handedness it does not suffice to observe mere movement. One hand being static does not mean it has nothing to do with the gesture. Also, one hand being in motion could stem from small residual movements that bear no relation with the current gesture.

To begin with, one hand can usually be identified that is an integral part of the gesture (LH or RH). Otherwise, the gesture would not have been identified. The question the coder has to answer now is: does the other hand contribute to the gesture? The other hand can contribute by either complementing or duplicating the gesture. Complementing means that omitting the second hand causes the gesture ceasing to function. For instance, in a gesture of prayer the second hand is essential. For such gestures, bi-handedness is said to be a *formational* dimension (Section 8.3). Duplicating means that the second hand does the same as the other. For example, the raised forefinger, a call for attention, can be performed with two hands to make the gesture more visible and emphasized. For both cases, the correct annotation is 2H.

8.4.2   Lexical Affiliation

Words in the speech stream that co-express the same content as an accompanying gesture are often called *lexical affiliates* (Schegloff 1984). McNeill and Duncan (2000) call such related but not identical meanings *co-expressive*, meaning that the gesture and its synchronized co-expressive speech express the same underlying idea unit but do not necessarily express identical aspects of it. This does not imply that gesture and speaking the lexical affiliate are performed at exactly the same time. Co-expression is *not* co-occurrence. Therefore, lexical affiliate annotation cannot be automatized using a temporal synchrony. Instead, the relationship has to be explicitly coded by hand. How are lexical affiliates found for a given gesture? In general, emphasized words are good candidates. And although temporal co-occurrence does not a imply co-expression, it is at least a hint. Lexical affiliates should be looked for in the direct neighbourhood of the gesture. They are usually located within the boundaries of the co-occurring spoken segment.

Lexical affiliates are originally only defined to express the relationship between *iconic* gestures and speech. In this work, an extended definition of lexical affiliation will be used that includes all gesture classes. However, for each class, lexical affiliation is determined differently. Since only communicative gestures can cause lexical affiliation adaptors can be excluded from this examination right away (see Figure 8.1 on page 142). Beat gestures can also be eliminated since, by definition, there is no form-meaning relationship. The remaining classes of emblems, deictics, iconics and metaphorics are treated in separate sections. Since all annotation is done for the specific purpose of generation, only *redundant* lexical affiliates are encoded. Only in cases of redundancy the speech-gesture co-expression relation can be generalized. Other restrictions that arise due to the generation task will be pointed out where applicable. In the example utterances below the underlined portions of text demarcate the duration of the accompanying gesture.

Emblems   Emblems express conventionalized meanings that can be paraphrased in speech. Although one modality would suffice, an emblem is often used in conjunction with its speech paraphrase, increasing the redundancy of the communication. An emblem's lexical affiliate is defined to be this paraphrase. For example, when saying

> "I've always had one single but quite <u>certainly outstanding</u> reader: the censor"[2]

---

[2]MRR, LQ2-1, 2:00

while forming a FINGER-RING gesture the lexical affiliate is constituted by the adjective "outstanding" since it expresses the gesture's conventionalized meaning of "perfection" (Appendix B). The coder must identify phrases that contain the conventionalized meaning of the gesture and annotate these as the lexical affiliate of the gesture. There are borderline cases where lexical affiliation is expressed by a whole sentence like in

"<u>what a book!</u>"

spoken in conjunction with the FINGER-RING gesture. Annotating the whole sentence as a lexical affiliate can easily lead to errors in generation by undue generalization, making the FINGER-RING a likely candidate for accompanying an utterance like "what a mess!" – which is obviously wrong (see Chapter 11).

Deictics   Deictic gesture are pointing gestures that can be divided into concrete and abstract deictics. Concrete deictics in the LQ data exclusively point to a person or the audience as a whole, thereby referring to the person or audience. The lexical affiliate is constituted by the word or phrase in speech that co-refers to the respective person or to the audience. For instance, in the utterance

"and <u>you</u> say, and you are right, that ..."[3]

where the speaker points to an interlocutor, verbal co-reference is achieved with "you". Abstract deictics are harder to annotate. They often co-occur with anaphoric references to the discourse context, like in

"<u>this</u> is shown by Elke Schmitter"[4]

where "this" refers to the previous utterance's content. Here, "this" is co-expressive with the gesture since the deictic abstractly points to the same piece of context that the particle "this" refers to. Other cases involve demonstrative references to objects like in

"<u>these characters</u> we do not have here"[5]

where the whole nominal phrase "these characters" must be annotated as the verbal co-reference to a concomitant abstract deictic. It is the task of the generation algorithm to generalize this information. In the two examples above the part-of-speech helps to disambiguate demonstrative pronouns (PDS) like "this" in the first

---

[3]MRR, LQ1-2, 0:16
[4]MRR, LQ3-2, 1:12
[5]MRR, LQ3-10, 1:01

and attributive demonstrative pronouns (PDAT) like "these" in the second case (Appendix A.1).

Deictics can also be used to illustrate spatial concepts verbalized as "here" and "there", like in

"<u>here</u> there's the following: ..."[6]

where "here" means "in this book/case".

Iconics An iconic gesture visually illustrates an aspect of the spoken content. The gesture can *complement* speech by visualizing aspects that are not expressed verbally which is often done when describing spatial relationships. It can also show *redundant* information by visualizing an aspect that is already encoded in speech, like in the following utterance where the speaker holds both hands in front of him, using them to form a rectangular frame:

"and it is about a <u>picture that plays a role there</u> ..."[7]

The lexical affiliate is "picture" because gesture and speech share the property of rectangularity. Redundant gestures overlap in meaning with the lexical affiliate. The lexical affiliate can be used to generate gestures, it can "trigger" the respective gestures found in the data. Therefore, for the task of generation, lexical affiliates must only be encoded for *redundant* iconics where the gesture captures a prototypical property of the verbal co-expression. In contrast, complementary iconics bear no direct relation to the concomitant speech. Since coding lexical affiliation for complementary iconics can mislead generation such iconics must not be encoded.

Metaphorics Metaphorics refer to the referent metaphorically, i.e. the gesture illustrates the *base* and the base represents the actual content. The lexical affiliation, however, is established directly. In the following utterance the speaker performs a PROGRESS gesture which illustrates a circular motion (base) that metaphorically represents "change":

"but to <u>change the course of art</u>..."[8]

The verb "change" directly expresses the concept of change, thus establishing co-expression.

Many metaphorics illustrate a logical relationship in the rhetoric structure of the discourse like in the following utterance:

---

[6]MRR, LQ3-10, 0:36
[7]HK, LQ1-1, 0:10
[8]MRR, LQ1-4, 0:33

"...and discovering a totally different man for his wife"[9]

where the speaker performs a metaphoric BRIDGE gesture, expressing the rhetoric relationship of *temporal sequence*. The lexical affiliate is the conjunction "and". The gesture is a typical *ideograph* that sketches "a path or direction of thought" (Ekman and Friesen, 1972: 68). In such cases, the *cue word/phrase* for the rhetoric relation is encoded as the verbal co-reference, if such a cue phrase exists (Knott and Dale 1994).

Lexical affiliation in NOVACO

In NOVACO, lexical affiliates have to be grouped to linguistic *phrases*. The following specification provides five attributes that can hold one phrase each:

```
<track-spec name="phrase" type="span" ref="gesture.phase">
    ...
  <attribute name="lexical affiliate phrase 1" valuetype="MultiLink(trl)"/>
  <attribute name="lexical affiliate phrase 2" valuetype="MultiLink(trl)"/>
  <attribute name="lexical affiliate phrase 3" valuetype="MultiLink(trl)"/>
  <attribute name="lexical affiliate phrase 4" valuetype="MultiLink(trl)"/>
  <attribute name="lexical affiliate phrase 5" valuetype="MultiLink(trl)"/>
    ...
</track-spec>
```

In the LQ corpus, the case that more than five phrases of lexical affiliation belong to a single gesture never occurred.

8.4.3 Temporal Gesture-Speech Relation

As mentioned in the previous section, co-expression is not co-occurrence, i.e. the gesture and the speech segment that both refer to the same semantic content are not necessarily synchronized to occur at the same time (see Section 2.2.3). For the purpose of generation, the temporal relationship of co-expressive gestural and speech expressions must be known in order to *position* gestures.

Exploratory analysis of the LQ data revealed four recurring patterns of temporal organization, so-called descriptive *timing patterns*. They will be called *direct*, *indirect*, *span* and *init* timing and must be annotated for every gesture G that has a lexical affiliate L. The following order is also the order of annotation.

Direct timing Direct timing means that gesture G's expressive phase, often a single stroke, co-occurs with the lexical affiliate L. This means that in direct timing co-expression is also co-occurrence. Of course, the onset and offset of the stroke never exactly coincide with the onset and offset of the lexical affiliate. If stroke

---

[9]HK, LQ1-1, 1:31

and lexical affiliate temporally overlap, direct timing can securely be coded. Even if there is no temporal overlap, a tolerance of up to 0.5 seconds distance between stroke offset and lexical affiliate onset, or lexical affiliate offset and stroke onset, can be granted.

The expressive phase may also consist of multiple beats or an independent hold that cover a whole phrase in speech.

Indirect timing   In indirect timing the stroke of gesture G co-occurs with a word or phrase W that is not L but usually bears some relation to L. Often, W is an adjective or negation particle to L. These are cases where G's relation to L is clear so that G's co-occurrence with W may indicate some other communicative function, e.g. to emphasize the negation of L. Consider the following example:

"...hat er <u>nicht</u> selber [angenommen]$_L$ ..."[10]

Here, the gesture ICONIC.GRAB is co-expressive with lexical affiliate "angenommen" while being synchronized with the verb's negation particle. The exact function of this timing pattern is not further analyzed in this work. However, this pattern of timing can be produced in gesture generation.

Span timing   In span timing the gesture covers the length of a whole utterance. Only gestures where the expressive phase consists of multiple beats or an independent hold qualify for this pattern. The expressive phase must start around the first word of the utterance and last almost until the end of the utterance.

Init timing   In cases where a gesture initiates an utterance the timing pattern is called init timing. The gesture's expressive phase occurs around the first word of the utterance and peters off quickly, covering an average number of three words. This average number of words may be dependent on the speaker's speech rate but this will not be further explored here.

If the covered words overlap with the lexical affiliate, it is direct timing. If the utterance is so short that the gesture covers the whole of the utterance it is span timing. The coder should annotate init timing if s/he has the subjective impression that the gesture gives impetus for the initiation of the utterance.

In **NOVACO**, the timing pattern is encoded in the **timing** attribute of the track `gesture.phrase`:

---

[10]MRR, LQ1-4, 1:38

```
<track-spec name="phrase" type="span" ref="gesture.phase">
  ...
  <attribute name="timing">
    <value-el>direct</value-el>
    <value-el>indirect</value-el>
    <value-el>span</value-el>
    <value-el>init</value-el>
  </attribute>
</track-spec>
```

The timing attribute completes **NOVACO**'s gestural part of the coding scheme.

8.5   Summary

In the second part of the **NOVACO** scheme covers the annotation of gestures (see Figure 8.2 for a sample annotation in **ANVIL**). Gesture annotation begins with decomposing movements into *phases* like preparation, stroke, retraction, etc. These basic units of movements are then assembled in a second step to form *phrases*. A phrase is a gesture and is further annotated with class, lemma, handedness, lexical affiliate and timing.

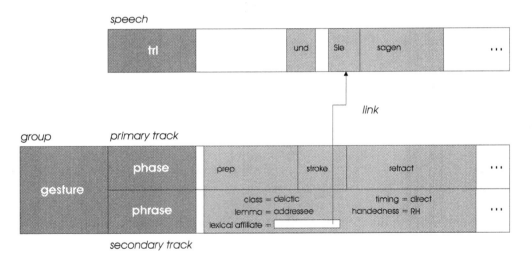

Figure 8.2: *Schematic sample annotation in the gesture annotation group in ANVIL. It consists of one primary track and one secondary track.*

Gestures can be roughly divided into six classes: emblems, deictics, iconics, metaphorics, adaptors and beats. The classes are characterized by degree of conventionalization, illustrative power and communicative intention. They can be further subdivided into lemmas which are equivalence classes of gestures that abstract away from variations in form. Lemmas will later be the entries in the speakers' shared lexicon of gestures. They are defined with the help of formational dimensions and sets of meanings. For each gesture, handedness is annotated (LH, RH or 2H) as well as lexical affiliation. Lexical affiliates are correlates in speech that express the same semantic or pragmatic content as the gestures do. The temporal relation between gesture and verbal correlate is captured by annotating the descriptive timing pattern of which there are four: direct, indirect, span or init timing. Figure 8.2 shows a small sample annotation of a gesture in ANVIL, using the NOVACO scheme. Gesture phases are coded using a primary track. The phrase elements are secondary to this track and contain all the rest of the gestural information, i.e. class, lemma, handedness etc. The lexical affiliate is captured using links to the trl track of the speech annotation.

The NOVACO scheme is now completely defined. The scheme provides the minimal requirements for annotating gesture and speech in such a way that key gestural parameters for gesture generation can be automatically extracted.

Chapter 9

Gesture Analysis

The last two chapters specified the **NOVACO** annotation scheme for speech and gesture. This scheme was applied to the complete LQ corpus using the **ANVIL** tool. This chapter presents an analysis of the annotated LQ corpus. It first shows that the most important and novel part of the scheme, the annotation of gesture lemmas, can be reliably coded. The lemma categorization is key for gesture generation because it is abstract enough to neglect minor formal variations but not so abstract that all relation to form is lost. However, the assembled lexicon of gesture lemmas is quite large and growing with increasing empirical material. In this chapter it will become clear that a subset of highly frequent gestures for each speaker suffices to model the speaker's behavior. This subset can be reduced in size while still covering a large part of the training data. Thus, the feasibility of a generation approach based on motion patterns is granted. Finally, the comparison of the two speakers' individual repertoires as well as key parameters shows that significant individual differences exist that can be exploited for the generation of individual behavior.

This chapter reports on results from analyzing the annotated LQ corpus, starting with studies on the reliability of coding in Section 9.2. Most important, it deals with the selection of a set of gestures best suited for generation in Section 9.3 and investigates parameters that may account for individual differences in Section 9.4. The chapter closes with a summary.

9.1 Annotated Corpus

The annotation scheme specified in Chapters 7 and 8 was applied to the whole LQ corpus, 23 video files featuring one of the speakers MRR and HK each, adding up to 46:18 minutes of data. Table 9.1 shows the amount of movement phases and gesture phrases coded per speaker. The gestures were classified in a lexicon of 68 different gesture lemmas. Of this lexicon, speaker HK used 45 different lemmas while speaker MRR used 64. This difference is due to the larger data corpus for speaker MRR. Measuring the number of lemmas used by MRR with an amount of data comparable to the HK corpus, one arrives at about 50–54 lemmas for MRR.

The annotation of gesture lemmas confirmed findings by Webb (1997) that a shared lexicon of conversational gestures for different speakers can be assembled. However, two questions remain that have not been addressed by her. First, whether the lexical entries can be reliably coded. Second, whether the lexicon is finite or continues to grow with the accumulation of further empirical data. Both issues will be addressed in the following two sections.

	MRR	HK	total
movement phases	1,790	728	2,518
gesture phrases	761	295	1,056

Table 9.1: *Number of encoded movement phases and gesture phrases.*

9.2 Coding Reliability

To check whether the lexicon of 68 gesture lemmas could be reliably coded, two experiments were conducted. In each experiment, both segmentation as well as classification by two independent coders were examined. The result of these experiments yield the degree of *inter-coder* reliability.

In each of the two studies, two coders independently annotated 2:54 minutes (study 1) and 2:26 minutes (study 2) of data. This data contained pre-annotated movement phases of speaker MRR. The task of the coders was twofold. First, to assemble the movement phases to gestures which is called *segmentation*. Then, and to assign a lemma category to each annotated gesture which is called *classification*. In the data, the movement phases were pre-annotated because the reliability for coding these phases was not of interest. Phases were shown to be reliably codable by Kita et al. (1998).

Measures

Both segmentation and classification were examined. Segmentation means grouping movement phases to gestures according to the grammar specified in Section 8.1.2. Errors can occur because, for instance, *hold* phases may belong to either the preceding or the following stroke. If segmentation differed, both gesture were retracted from the count and counted as one "miss". All other remaining gesture pairs were counted as "hits". The segmentation percentage is

$$\frac{\text{hits}}{\text{hits} + \text{misses}} \ 100 \ \%$$

Classification reliability is computed using only the hits in segmentation because only gestures that were segmented equally can be reasonably compared. If the number of these comparable gestures is N, and k is the number of instances where both coders agreed on the lemma, then the reliability percentage is

$$\frac{k}{N} \, 100 \, \%$$

The κ (kappa) value is a measure that gives a more neutral impression of agreement because it evens out the factor of coincidental agreement depending on the data (cf. Boehnke et al., 1990, and Carletta, 1996). If $c_1, \ldots, c_n$ are all possible categories and $f_{i,j}$ is the number of gestures which were classified c_i by coder 1 and c_j by coder 2, then the so-called *confusion matrix* looks like this:

$$
\begin{array}{c|cccc|c}
       & c_1   & c_2   & \cdots & c_n   &   \\
\hline
c_1   & f_{1,1} & f_{1,2} & \cdots & f_{1,n} & f_{1\cdot} \\
c_2   & f_{2,1} & f_{2,2} & \cdots & f_{2,n} & f_{2\cdot} \\
\vdots & \vdots &   & \ddots & \vdots & \vdots   \\
c_n   & f_{n,1} & f_{n,2} & \cdots & f_{n,n} & f_{n\cdot} \\
       & f_{\cdot 1} & f_{\cdot 2} & \cdots & f_{\cdot n} & N
\end{array}
$$

The probability that the two coders pick the same category is

$$p_0 = \frac{\sum_{i=1}^{n} f_{i,i}}{N}$$

whereas the probability that the two coders agree by chance is

$$p_e = \frac{\sum_{i=1}^{n} f_{i\cdot} \, f_{\cdot i}}{N^2}$$

The κ value is now defined as

$$\kappa = \frac{p_0 - p_e}{1 - p_e}$$

and measures the degree of agreement *beyond chance*. The result is a normalized value in $[-1, 1]$ where 1 signifies perfect agreement.

Results

The coders completed the segmentation task, i.e. grouping the pre-coded phases to gestures, to near perfection, as can be seen in the first column of Table 9.2.
In classification agreement, shown in columns two and three of Table 9.2, the first study yielded critical results. A kappa value of 0.6 cannot be considered reliable

	segmentation	classification	
	%	%	κ
study 1	93.0	64.0	0.60
study 2	100.0	79.4	0.78

Table 9.2: *Results of the two reliability studies with respect to segmentation and classification.*

coding. Therefore, insights from the first study were used to revise the lemma lexicon and to extend the coders' training. Subsequently, a second study was conducted using new material. It resulted in a satisfying 79% agreement and a kappa value of 0.78 which is very close to "good agreement" according to Carletta (1996). The changes made after the first study consisted of (1) collapsing several pairs of lemmas to a single one because of too strong similarities in form and function, and (2) adding more verbal explanation about the form (especially the motion) of a gesture.

Looking at the remaining disagreement in lemma classification after the second study, 21% were due to uncertainty when to put a gesture to the "beat" (rest) category, i.e. how degenerated a gesture must look to not try and find a suitable category. 29% were due to fundamental differences in functional interpretation (e.g. taking an emblem for a deictic etc.). Finally, 50% were due to confusions within one category (usually emblems). This last and largest error source can be reduced by more rigid definition and documentation in the coding manual.

To conclude, the experiments show that the devised gesture lemmas can be reliably coded by independent coders. They support the hypothesis that in conversations like the ones in the TV show certain repetitive gesture patterns exist and can be identified by trained coders (cf. Webb, 1997, and Weinrich, 1992).

9.3 Gestures for Generation

Considering the increase of lemmas with increasing empirical material raises the question: Do new lemmas keep emerging as more material is analyzed, ad infinitum, or does the number of lemmas converge to a finite limit at some point? If the first is true, modeling gestures is a futile enterprise since only a small part of all possible gestures can ever be modelled, and probably the ones that are least important. However, if the latter is the case, one ends up with the individual's finite gesture repertoire sooner or later.

In Figure 9.1 the solid line shows the increase of gesture lemmas with increased annotated material for the speakers MRR (top diagram) and HK (bottom diagram). When considering only those lemmas whose instances make up more than 1% of all occurrences we obtain a surprisingly constant amount of 26–28 lemmas

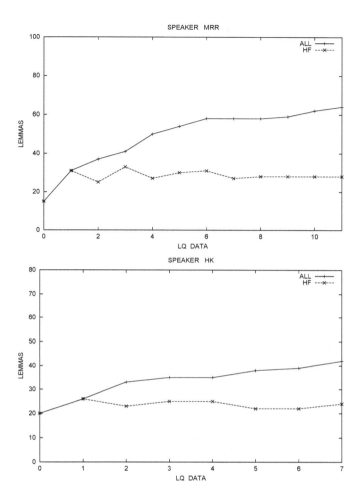

Figure 9.1: *Two diagrams illustrating the number of lemmas in relation to increasing data. The solid line shows the increase of lemmas with increasing material for subjects MRR (top) and HK (bottom). The dashed line shows the number of gesture lemmas whose instances occur with frequency of 1% or more (HF lemmas).*

(dashed lines). These high frequency (HF) lemmas seem natural candidates for being modeled as animations. However, it has to be proven that these HF lemmas are representative enough to be singled out as the only gestures for modeling. A good measure for this aspect is to count how much of the original gesture occurrences this reduced HF lemma set covers. Figure 9.2 shows the coverage of the MRR's and HK's HF lemmas. Although coverage is slightly declining with growing data, the HF lemmas still cover more than 85% of the gesture occurrences in the original data for both speakers. To be precise, speaker MRR has a subset of 28 HF lemmas that cover 86.5% of the original data. Speaker HK has a subset of 26 HF lemmas that cover 90.5% of the data. This shows that a relatively small number of gestural categories covers most part of the gestures that actually occur.

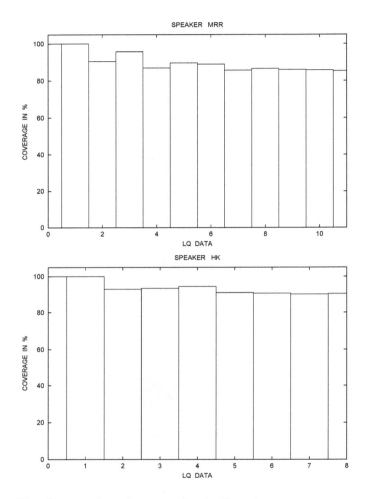

Figure 9.2: *The figures show how much of all gesture occurrences are covered by the HF lemmas (over 1%). Top figure for subject MRR, bottom figure for HK.*

Apart from the danger of insufficient coverage the reduction of a speaker's repertoire could lead to a distortion of his/her overall style. The style is reflected in the distribution of a speaker's gestures over the six gesture classes as shown in Table 9.3. When reducing the gestures to the HF subset the distribution changes as shown in Table 9.4 which shows the absolute number of occurrences, the percentage and the difference to the original distribution. The changes are not dramatic which is not surprising given that the HF subset still covers over 85% of the original data. However, two observations are of interest. First, while most gesture classes increased their share, iconic gestures were reduced for both speakers. This can be explained by their property of having a highly context-specific form that borders on the idiosyncratic. Therefore, many iconic lemmas are not used often enough to cross the 1% threshold. This is good for generation because, due to their context-specificity, iconics are harder to generate than gestures from the other classes. The second observation is that one individual difference between MRR and HK becomes even stronger in the HF subset: the percentage of emblematic gestures. Since emblematic gestures are also the most conspicuous one this may have a positive effect on the perception of individuality between imitations of speakers MRR and HK using the HF subset.

	MRR		HK	
	#	%	#	%
adaptors	15	1.95	5	1.69
emblems	347	45.12	80	27.03
deictics	79	10.37	20	6.76
iconics	32	4.16	18	6.08
metaphorics	239	31.01	130	43.92
beats	49	6.39	42	14.19

Table 9.3: *Distribution of gesture lemma occurrences over the six gesture classes.*

	MRR			HK		
	#	%	Δ%	#	%	Δ%
adaptors	15	2.28	+.33	5	1.87	+.18
emblems	307	46.73	+1.61	65	24.25	-2.78
deictics	72	10.96	+.59	20	7.46	+.7
iconics	0	0	-4.16	12	4.48	-1.6
metaphorics	214	32.57	+1.56	124	46.27	+2.35
beats	49	7.46	+1.09	42	15.67	+1.48

Table 9.4: *Gesture class distribution when taking the high-frequency gestures. The Δ% column shows the difference in percentage to the original distribution.*

9.4 Individuality

One key aspect of this work is to provide synthetic agents with *individual* behavior. Most generation systems for nonverbal behavior utilize the same gestures and the same set of rules for each of their agents which must lead to uniform behavior. Therefore, in this section, the potential sources of individuality are investigated.

First of all, that the two speakers should differ in their behavior was part the selection criteria for the video data in Section 5.1. This subjective judgement can be underpinned by looking at the gesture class distribution showed in Table 9.3. The table shows nicely that speaker MRR uses much more emblems and deictics than HK, whereas HK uses much more metaphorics and beats than MRR. While metaphorics and beats are abstract gestures that often do not trigger an immediate association, emblems are quickly recognized as meaningful gestures. Deictics are in the context of the LQ data also used to assign speaker turns so MRR in his role as the talk leader may have a bias toward using deictics explaining his more frequent deictics. However, deictics, too, are quickly recognized as gestures. In fact, emblems and deictics lie on the high end of the so-called lexicalization continuum which measures how immediate a gesture can be translated to meaning (McNeill, 1992: 37–40). Beats and metaphorics are located on the low end. Beats are hardly perceived as gestures at all since by definition their form bears no relation to the accompanying speech. These arguments aim at supporting MRR's reputation as having a vivid, varied and entertaining gesture behavior, much more so than speaker HK.

Surprisingly, this reputation is not reflected in the measured *gesture rate*. Gesture rate was measured by counting all gestures performed during a speaker's turn while measuring the duration of all turns. MRR performs, on average, 31.1 gestures per minute, whereas HK performs 27.6 gestures per minute. The difference in gesture rate can be statistically examined by applying the Chi-square test (Bortz, 1999: 150–153). The test allows to compare the data with an expected distribution: in this case, uniform distribution. The data had to be brought into a correct format first. Both speakers had differing numbers of turns with differing turn lengths. To obtain comparable frequencies the gesture frequencies were normalized with respect to an equal time span. This was possible since both speakers' gestures were normally distributed over the respective turns. HK performed 296 gestures in 644 seconds, MRR 770 gestures in 1486 seconds. MRR's gesture frequency "normalized" to 644 seconds becomes 334. Comparing the normalized frequencies (296 for HK, 334 for MRR) using the Chi-square test, showed that there is no significant difference in gesture frequency ($\chi^2 = 1.15$, df=1, p=.28). The difference in gesture rate between both speakers can therefore be considered minimal.

This investigation of individuality will be restricted to the HF gestures that were found a workable simplification for generation while not distorting the above

MRR			HK		
lemma	**#**	**%**	**lemma**	**#**	**%**
1 E.Dismiss ↑	61	7.9	1 Beat ↑	42	14.2
2 Beat ↓	49	6.4	2 M.Cup-Flip ↑	34	11.5
3 M.Fling-down	48	6.2	3 M.Frame ↑	20	6.8
4 D.Space ↑	40	5.2	4 E.Finger-Ring ↑	15	5.1
5 M.Frame ↓	35	4.6	5 M.Cup ↑	15	5.1
6 E.Attention ↓	35	4.6	6 E.Attention ↑	14	4.7
7 E.So-What	35	4.6	7 M.Bridge	14	4.7
8 E.Strong ↑	33	4.3	8 E.Dismiss ↓	13	4.4
9 E.Wipe	28	3.6	9 D.Addressee ↑	13	4.4
10 E.Calm	28	3.6	10 M.Walls	10	3.4
11 D.Addressee ↓	23	3.0	11 I.Away	8	2.7
12 M.Dome ↑	21	2.7	12 E.Strong ↓	7	2.4
13 M.Cup ↓	21	2.7	13 D.Space ↓	7	2.4
14 M.Chop ↑	19	2.5	14 M.Dome ↓	6	2.0
15 E.Finger-Ring ↓	18	2.3	15 E.Small	6	2.0
16 M.Heart	18	2.3	16 M.Emerge	6	2.0
17 M.Cup-Flip ↓	17	2.2	17 M.Chop ↓	5	1.7
18 E.One-Hand-Other-Hand	16	2.1	18 Adaptor ↓	5	1.7
19 E.More-Or-Less	15	2.0	19 M.Idea	4	1.4
20 Adaptor ↑	15	2.0	20 I.Merge	4	1.4
21 M.Umbrella	14	1.8	21 M.Aura	4	1.4
22 M.Snatch	12	1.6	22 E.Number	4	1.4
23 E.Hands-Up	11	1.4	23 M.Progress ↓	3	1.0
24 E.Purse ↑	10	1.3	24 E.Purse ↓	3	1.0
25 M.Progress ↑	9	1.2	25 M.Thought-Grip	3	1.0
26 E.Refuse	9	1.2	26 E.Block	3	1.0
27 D.Self	9	1.2			
28 E.Chide	8	1.0			

Table 9.5: *HF gestures for speakers MRR and HK. The 15 gestures shared by both speakers are underlined. For each shared gesture, an arrow signifies how the relative frequency relates to that of the other speaker's gesture: an upward arrow means higher frequency, a downward arrow lower frequency.*

mentioned proportions of gesture class distributions. It also allows a closer comparison of single gesture lemmas without getting lost in detail. The lists of HF gestures for MRR and HK, from now on called their *repertoires*, can be seen in Table 9.5, ordered by frequency. The gestures shared by both speakers are underlined, an arrow indicates whether the gesture is more or less frequent than the other speaker's counterpart. In all, there are 15 gestures shared by MRR and HK. That 54% of MRR's repertoire and 58% of HK's. These shared gestures shall be further analyzed because for all other gestures the simple fact that the other speaker does not use them makes them individual. However, it is the contention of this work that even using the same gestures individuality can be achieved through the aspects of handedness, timing and function.

	MRR			HK		
	RH	LH	2H	RH	LH	2H
E.Dismiss	31	10	59	85	–	15
Beat	13	39	48	98	–	2
D.Space	26	54	21	100	–	–
M.Frame	–	–	100	–	–	100
E.Attention	37	54	9	93	–	7
E.Strong	18	21	61	57	–	43
D.Addressee	65	26	9	100	–	–
M.Dome	5	15	80	–	–	100
M.Cup	10	30	60	100	–	–
M.Chop	–	100	–	100	–	–
E.Finger-Ring	39	39	22	100	–	–
M.Cup-Flip	–	82	18	100	–	–
Adaptor	47	33	20	100	–	–
M.Progress	–	33	67	33	–	67
E.Purse	11	44	44	67	33	–

Table 9.6: *Handedness distribution in % over the HF gestures shared by speakers MRR and HK.*

As concerns handedness, Table 9.6 shows for each gesture of the shared repertoire the distribution of handedness in the corpus. What is evident is that some gestures are exclusively bi-handed, i.e. bi-handedness is a formational feature as defined in Section 8.3.1. Moreover, HK seems to be less inclined to use both hands for gesturing and prefers, most of all, the right hand. MRR is much more flexible but for some gestures also displays clear preferences (for instance, M.Chop preferably LH and D.Addressee preferably RH). Hence, handedness depends not only on the speaker but also on the gesture (and probably other contextual factors). For further analysis, one can look at handedness transitions which will be done in Section 10.4. Apart from handedness, one can examine the timing patterns for each gesture. Table 9.7 is similar to the previous table, only that it shows the distribution over timing patterns used for each gesture. There is hardly one gesture where the two speakers' distributions are similar. Of special interest is the span timing (S) because this timing means that the gesture is performed throughout the duration of the speech segment and is therefore very prominent. Since HK's and MRR's preference for span timing is very different there is a good chance that especially these gestures that are preferably performed with this timing type will be perceived as characteristic for the speaker's imitating agent. Finally, as another

	MRR				HK			
	D	iD	S	I	D	iD	S	I
E.Dismiss	58	12	20	10	62	–	8	31
Beat	62	–	31	8	77	–	19	4
D.Space	79	10	8	3	29	57	–	14
M.Frame	69	25	6	–	55	25	15	5
E.Attention	44	–	50	6	38	–	31	31
E.Strong	71	10	13	6	33	–	50	17
D.Addressee	55	–	35	10	31	–	38	31
M.Dome	43	24	24	10	100	–	–	–
M.Cup	81	10	10	–	53	7	27	13
M.Chop	50	–	43	7	60	–	20	20
E.Finger-Ring	61	–	17	22	53	–	33	13
M.Cup-Flip	93	–	–	7	55	3	–	42
M.Progress	62	38	–	–	33	67	–	–
E.Purse	67	22	11	–	67	–	33	–

Table 9.7: *Distribution of timing patterns in % over the HF gestures shared by speakers MRR and HK. The timing patterns are: direct (D), indirect (iD), span (S) and init (I) .*

source for individual differences is the *function* of gestures. In the annotation, a gesture's function is reflected in the lexical affiliate (Section 8.4.2). For each gesture, all annotated lexical affiliates are collected. Then, they are generalized using a mapping to *semantic tags* as will be described in Section 10.2. Now for each semantic tag the probability that a specific gesture accompanies this tag can be estimated using approximated conditional probabilities (see Section 10.2). These estimated probabilities reflect the individual preferences in terms of function. For instance, speaker HK uses gesture E.Attention to accompany a contrastive conjunction ("but", "however", "nevertheless" etc.) with a probability of 60%, whereas speaker MRR only uses this gesture with 7% probability on this kind of conjunction. In other cases, similarities prevail, like for the gesture D.Addressee which both use on speech segments that address a person ("you") with high probability (75% for HK, 54% for MRR). These examples show that although speaker may use the same gestures, and HK and MRR use half of their HF repertoire conjointly, they use them in different contexts, most likely to serve different functions.

How the individual differences found in the data will be captured in individual profiles will be the topic of Chapter 10. Together with the lexicon the profiles form the basis of gesture generation.

9.5   Summary

This chapter presented an analysis of the LQ corpus annotated with the NOVACO
scheme. The annotation of the two speakers HK and MRR resulted in a total
of 2,518 encoded movement phases and 1,056 annotated gestures. The analysis
consists of three parts. First, the question whether there is a shared and finite
lexicon of gestures can be answered positively. Evidence was provided by showing
that the devised lemma categories could be consistently coded by two independent
coders who achieved a kappa agreement of 0.78. Second, in the generation approach
pursued here, i.e. using pre-fabricated motion patterns, the finiteness of gestural
categories is an important point. Will growing data result in a growing number of
lemmas that have to be graphically modelled with ever increasing expenses? An
analysis of lemma increase with increasing data showed that a relatively small set
of 26–28 lemmas accounted for most of the gesture occurrences (more than 85%).
This strongly suggests that a generation approach with motion patterns is feasible
by relying on a limited amount of highly frequent (HF) lemmas that nonetheless
cover a large amount of all empirical cases. It became clear that the reduction to HF
gestures changes the distribution of gestures over gesture classes in its proportion
only to a negligible degree.

Of the lexicon of HF lemmas 15 entries are shared by both speakers. All other
gestures account for individual differences between the two. Moreover, it was shown
that also handedness, timing and function displayed considerable individual variation that will be exploited for the generation approach. In contrast, the speakers'
gesture rates were found to be quite similar.

Chapter 10

Gesture Profile Modeling: The NOVALIS Module

The last chapter confirmed the possibility of using a subset of the shared gesture lexicon for gesture generation with pre-fabricated motion patterns and suggested parameters for modeling individual differences. This chapter shows how these parameters can be extracted from the annotated LQ data. The main objectives for the selection of parameters are naturalness and individuality. In trying to imitate the original subject a synthetic agent inherits the naturalness and also the individuality of the original.

A model of an individual's gesturing is created by analyzing the annotated gestures. In an offline process, parameters are extracted from the annotated data and stored in data bases, so-called *gesture profiles*. For the modeling of gesture properties, statistical models are used, similar to those used in speech recognition and dialogue act recognition (Reithinger and Klesen 1997). Probabilities are estimated with N-grams and merged in linear combinations. The offline computation of the gesture profiles is done in a software module called NOVALIS (**No**nverbal **A**ction Ana**lysis**). The module is specifically tailored to the NOVACO annotation scheme and connects with ANVIL using the plug-in interface. NOVALIS utilizes ANVIL's internal annotation representation as well as its search engine to compile the figures that are written to the gesture profiles.

After a general introduction of the statistical tools used in Section 10.1, the different components of a gesture profile and the modeling techniques are treated in Sections 10.2 to 10.6. The chapter concludes with a summary of the gesture profile's ingredients in Section 10.7.

10.1 Probability Estimation and Sparse Data

A gesture's probability is scored by summing up individual probabilities with weights, what is called a linear combination (weights sum up to one). The individual probabilities are estimated by counting occurrences in the annotated data. Conditional probabilities are estimated using bigrams, i.e. $P(c_2|c_1)$ is estimated by taking

$$\frac{\#(c_1, c_2)}{\#c_1}$$

If too few occurrences exist, however, the estimation is not reliable. This is called the *sparse data problem*. To sort out such cases, let us define the absolute frequency threshold (AFT). If $\#(c_1, c_2) <$ AFT, the estimation is declared invalid. In order to not produce a serious penalty for all those gestures occurring in below AFT bigrams, a default value is computed for those "missing bigrams". Let N_{AFT} be the amount of (c_1, c_2) bigrams that fulfil the AFT. F_{AFT} is the sum of the absolute frequencies of those bigrams. Let N be the total number of possible bigrams, that is $N = (\#C + 1)\#C$ where C is the set of categories. The $(\#C + 1)$ stems from inclusion of the empty category in the first slot. Let F be the sum of frequencies of all bigrams (below and above AFT). Then the default probability is

$$P(c_2|c_1) = \frac{N - N_{AFT}}{F - F_{AFT}}$$

for all (c_1, c_2) that are below AFT.

10.2 Concept to Gesture

Most gestures have a lexical correspondence in the speech modality. This relation has been annotated in the data as the *lexical affiliate* (Section 8.4.2). The lexical affiliate is identified by finding a shared meaning in the semantic or pragmatic sense. Although it is possible that the meanings of gesture and lexical affiliate do not perfectly match, complementing each other instead, only those cases have been annotated where the same meaning in transported by both gesture and speech. This relation will be used to generate possible gestures when encountering a word or phrase in the speech input. Indirectly, the *function* of a gesture is used as a determinant as the original lexical affiliate manifests a function that underlies it and that is redundantly fulfilled by the generated gesture.

Before exploiting the lexical affiliation relation, however, two generalization steps have to be undertaken. These are: (1) morphological preprocessing (Section 11.2) and (2) a semantic mapping (Section 11.3). Both steps serve to cluster the mostly singular lexical affiliates to greater units in order to exploit the individual relationships for unseen data that differs from the training set.

Morphological Preprocessing

The morphological preprocessing consists of finding the lemma and parts-of-speech of the lexical affiliates. Although both could be done automatically with high reliability (see Section 7.2), tagging was done manually to achieve absolute correctness of 100%. Lemmas were needed to generalize over word inflections, parts-of-speech were needed to disambiguate certain tokens for the semantic mapping. The used parts-of-speech are listed in Appendix A.1.

Semantic Tags

After morphological processing a number of words and phrases are mapped to semantic tags which are meaning clusters that generalize over individual word meaning. The tags are based on the assumption that similar gestural forms can express the meaning of the subsumed words. For instance, the tag INDETERMINATE replaces words like "somewhat" and "some" which are, for speaker MRR, mainly connected to the emblematic gesture MORE-OR-LESS. But the tags not only reflect synonymous relations between words. They also capture beliefs and goals, like the tag CERTAINTY that is similar to a meaning category defined by Poggi et al. (2000), described in Section 4.1.8. The complete mapping is given in Appendix A.2. Future research should strive to find automatic ways of arriving at such mappings, e.g. by collecting words that are realized by similar gestures with clustering algorithms (see Everitt et al., 2001, on clustering methods).

Since the semantic tags are language-independent the generation approach becomes partially language-independent. If the word-to-gesture mapping was restricted to a tag-to-gesture mapping, the algorithm would become totally language-independent.

Model

The mapping is realized using relative frequencies. Let w be a word or phrase. Based on w, the probability that a gesture lemma l of the lexicon L is appropriate to accompany w can be estimated. Let W be the set of words and word stems and let morph: $W \rightarrow W$ be the morphological processing function and sem: $W \rightarrow W \cup S$ be the semantic clustering function where S is the set of semantic tags (listed in Appendix A.2). Let G_t be the set of gesture occurrences in the training data, let lemma: $G_t \rightarrow L$ be the function that maps a gesture onto its lexicon entry, i.e. its lemma, and let lexaffil: $G_t \rightarrow (W \cup S)^*$ be the function associating each gesture occurrence with the respective lexical affiliate. Finally, let W_t be the all words in the training corpus. Then, the probability estimation function is

$$P(l \mid w) = \frac{\#\{g_t \in G_t : \mathrm{lemma}(g_t) = l \wedge \mathrm{lexaffil}(g_t) = \mathrm{sem}(\mathrm{morph}(w))\}}{\#\{w_t \in W_t : \mathrm{sem}(\mathrm{morph}(w_t)) = \mathrm{sem}(\mathrm{morph}(w))\}}$$

In generation, this probability will be used to generate the gestures from scratch depending on words in the speech input.

10.3 Timing

The four gesture timing patterns introduced in Section 8.4.3 are used with different preference depending on the gesture. For instance, speaker MRR uses gesture D.Space almost always with direct timing (79%), whereas he uses gesture E.Attention more often with span timing (50%) than with direct timing (44%). Less obvious is the fact that timing preference for a gesture is speaker-dependent, i.e. speaker MRR uses different timing patterns than speaker HK for the same gesture. This was shown in Section 9.4 (Table 9.7). An individual's gesture profile must contain timing in order to find out *where* to place a gesture once it is selected for generation.

Gesture timing probability

Timing distributions are modeled for each speaker separately. Let us look at the set P containing the four timing patterns and the set G_t of all gesture occurrences. The function timing: $G_t \to P$ yields the timing pattern of a gesture occurrence, whereas function lemma: $G_t \to L$ maps the gesture occurrence to the lexicon, retrieving the respective lemma. Then, for a newly generated gesture whose lemma is l the probability that its timing type is $p \in P$ can be approximated as follows:

$$P(p \mid l) = \frac{\#\{g_t \in G_t : \text{lemma}(g_t) = l \wedge \text{timing}(g_t) = p\}}{\#\{g_t \in G_t : \text{lemma}(g_t) = l\}}$$

This probability will be used to decide where to place gestures in the process of generation.

10.4 Handedness

Throughout this work, *handedness* refers to arms/hands involved in the execution of a gesture: only the left hand (LH), only the right hand (RH), or both hands (2H). The function of handedness is relatively unexplored. One hypothesis is that handedness can create coherence between two gestural events that lie temporally somewhat apart or are separated by a third gesture. McNeill et al. (2001) subsume this under the notion of a *catchment* (Section 2.2.6).

Apart from coherence, other influences on handedness are (1) the location of the addressed interlocutor, whether s/he is left or right of the current speaker and (2) the speaker's original handedness. One would expect left-handers to gesture predominantly with the left hand, right-handers with the right hand. Independent

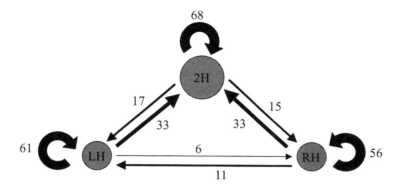

Figure 10.1: *Handedness transition diagram for speaker MRR. Edges are annotated with the traversal probability in percent. The size of the circles reflect the absolute frequency of the respective handedness.*

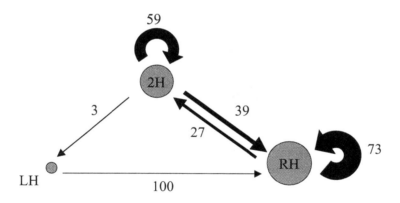

Figure 10.2: *Handedness transition diagram for speaker HK. Edges are annotated with the traversal probability in percent. The size of the circles reflect the absolute frequency of the respective handedness.*

of the speaker's original handedness are bi-handed gestures. They are either inherently bi-handed, i.e. they cannot be performed with a single hand, or they are performed with two hands to accentuate the gesture.

Modeling the above functions is difficult and neither theoretically nor empirically founded. Therefore, the statistical approach in ignoring the underlying functionality of handedness rather approximates the "surface look-and-feel" of a speaker's use of hands. The three aspects of this approximation are:

1. total handedness distribution

2. handedness transitions of each speaker

3. relative handedness distribution (for each gesture lemma)

The first aspect models globally how much a speaker relies on his/her left, right or both hands. For the speaker's general handedness $h \in \{$LH, RH, 2H$\}$, the following simple unigram approximation is used:

$$P(h) = \frac{\#\{g \in G_t : \text{hand}(g) = h\}}{\#G_t}$$

The second important aspect, handedness *transition*, captures the way a speaker shifts from left to right, right to both hands etc. Handedness transition graphs for the two speakers MRR (Figure 10.1) and HK (Figure 10.2) graphically show the different behavioral patterns of the speakers: When a gesture is performed, one of the three handedness *states*, the circles labelled with LH/RH/2H, is assumed. After gesture execution the state is left through one of the arrows with the numerical probability indicated (in percent). Thicker arrows signify higher probability. A transition diagram can be modeled with bigrams. If for an arbitrary sequence of gestures $\langle g_{i-1}, g_i \rangle$ the handedness is given by hand$(g_{i-1})=h_{i-1}$ and hand$(g_i)=h_i$, the transition probability from h_{i-1} to h_i can be approximated by

$$P(h_i \mid h_{i-1}) = \frac{\#(h_{i-1}, h_i)}{\#h_{i-1}}$$

The third aspect, relative handedness distribution, models the probability that for a gesture occurrence g whose corresponding lemma is l the speaker uses handedness h. The following approximation is used:

$$P(h \mid l) = \frac{\#\{g_t \in G_t : \text{hand}(g_t) = h \wedge \text{lemma}(g_t) = l\}}{\#\{g_t \in G_t : \text{lemma}(g_t) = l\}}$$

10.5   Transitions and Frequencies

Looking only at the stream of generated gestures, one can model the "surface structure" of a speaker's gestures without knowledge of the underlying determinants that triggered the gestures. Two aspects of this surface structure are gesture transitions and gesture frequency. The first is a local aspect, the second a global one.

Gesture Transitions

Gesture transitions refer to the probability that gesture occurrence g_i is of lemma category l_i, given that the previous gesture g_{i-1} has been lemma l_{i-1}. When relying only on the direct predecessor g_{i-1} for the estimation of g_i's category probability, one talks of a *bigram* estimation. Theoretically, it is possible to draw on multiple predecessors, using N-grams with $N > 2$, but this inevitably leads into the problem of *sparse data* as explained in Section 10.1. For gesture transitions, the following probability estimation is used:

$$P(l_i \mid l_{i-1}) = \frac{\#(l_{i-1}, l_i)}{\#l_{i-1}}$$

Table 10.1 shows the highest probability estimations for speaker MRR's gesture transitions. Modeling the transitions like this identifies the gestures that are suitable for *repetition*. Additionally, certain idiosyncratic sequences of gestures are captured. For MRR, the gesture sequence dismiss-wipe (both emblems) is especially conspicuous when watching him. Table 10.1 confirms this intuition nicely by giving the sequence the highest score.

l_{i-1}	l_i	$P(l_i \mid l_{i-1})$
E.Dismiss	**E.Wipe**	**0.21**
M.Fling-Down	M.Fling-Down	0.20
E.Dismiss	E.Dismiss	0.20
E.Attention	E.Attention	0.14
E.Dismiss	E.Dismiss	0.14
M.Frame	**I.Strength**	**0.13**
D.Space	D.Space	0.13
M.Frame	M.Frame	0.10

Table 10.1: *Most frequent bigrams of MRR's gestures (lemmas) with estimated conditional probability.*

Gesture Frequency

Gesture frequency gives an impression of the overall quantity of a speaker's gesturing. The amount of gestures a person uses is especially conspicuous if it is very small or very large. It is measured using the *gesture rate*, i.e. the average number of gestures per minute. However, in gesture generation the input consists of words that can only be translated to temporal units if the speech synthesis engine provides special functionality. To make the approach independent of such special circumstances, one can measure gesture rate against speech segments which are annotated as described in Section 7.1. The generation algorithm would also work with the gesture per minute measure.

When measuring gestures against segments, the following definition holds. If G is the set of all gesture occurrences and S the set of all speech segments (utterances), then the gesture rate r is defined as

$$r = \frac{\#G}{\#S}$$

Gesture *lemma* frequency measures the frequency of gestures of a certain category. It models the *variation* of gestures in a speaker's gesture stream. The gesture lemma frequency f_l for category l is defined as

$$f_l = \frac{\#\{g \in G : \text{lemma}(g) = l\}}{\#G}$$

Obviously, all category frequencies add up to one, i.e. $\sum f_l = 1$.

10.6 Long-Distance Relations

So far either neighboring gestures or global parameters have been considered. To capture phenomena like *catchments*, however, where two non-neighboring gestures cohere by a semantic concept, one needs to model long-distance determinants. "Long-distance" refers to relations beyond the direct gesture neighborhood.

One such long-distance determinant are discourse relations, annotated as described in Section 7.4. Discourse relations capture semantic coherence between items of a list, repeated or contrastive items. According to Atkinson (1984) gestures can be used to mark such relations, e.g. by performing a gesture on every item of a list. A first idea is thus to model the probability that a speaker chooses to perform a gesture on an item given that s/he has performed a gesture on a previous item. Now, the theory of *catchments* says that different gestures emerging from the same "idea unit" may share gestural features due to their common origin. Taking a discourse relation as being part of a single idea unit would imply the catchment condition which, in a simplified reformulation (lacking the possibility to control single features of a gesture), would cause the gestures on the different relation items to be of equal lemma category. Aspects of both theories are incorporated by modeling existence and equality probabilities.

In discourse relations only the ordering information can be considered relevant, not the exact temporal position. Thus, a discourse relation R refers to an ordered sequence of words or phrases $\langle s_1, \ldots, s_n \rangle$ where an arbitrary amount of irrelevant words can separate s_i and s_{i+1}. Annotated discourse relations become relevant as soon as $s_1, \ldots, s_n$ contain lexical affiliates of two or more gestures $g_1, \ldots, g_k$ $(k \geq 2)$ which is formally represented by

$$\forall\, i \in \{1, \ldots, k\} \; \exists\, j \in \{1, \ldots, n\} : \; \text{lexaffil}(g_i) \cap s_j \neq \emptyset$$

Let us denote a gesture g_i whose lexical affiliates overlap with s_j by $\text{gest}(s_j)$. Then, two conditional probabilities can be defined, one for gesture existence, one for equality. Given a discourse relation $R(s_1, \ldots, s_n)$, let us define $p = (p_1, \ldots, p_n)$ as a pattern vector where p_i represents whether the speech item s_i has a gesture attached to it ($p_i = 1$) or not ($p_i = 0$). The probability that a gesture is produced on s_i can be estimated in dependence to whether a gesture was produced for s_{i-1}:

$$P_{ex}(p_i = 1 \mid p_{i-1} = 1) = \frac{\#\{(p_1, \ldots, p_{i-1}, p_i, \ldots, p_n) : p_i = 1 \land p_{i-1} = 1\}}{\#\{(p_1, \ldots, p_{i-1}, p_i, \ldots, p_n) : p_{i-1} = 1\}}$$

For those cases where existence of a gesture at s_i has been established because of the existence of a gesture on s_{i-1}, one can additionally check whether the gesture on s_i is equal to the one on s_{i-1}. Let us define the vector $g = (g_1, \ldots, g_n)$ in analogy to p as the gestures on the respective speech segments s_i. If there is no gesture on s_i then $g_i = \emptyset$. Then, the specialization of the above case can be modeled with

$$P_{eq}(g_i = g_{i-1} \mid g_{i-1} \neq \emptyset) = \frac{\#\{(g_1, \ldots, g_{i-1}, g_i, \ldots, g_n) : g_i = g_{i-1}\}}{\#\{(g_1, \ldots, g_{i-1}, g_i, \ldots, g_n) : g_{i-1} \neq \emptyset\}}$$

Computing these scores for the speakers MRR and HK in fact yields some interesting results. For MRR, the discourse relation "list" yields the following probabilities (in a simplified notation):

$$
\begin{aligned}
P_{ex}(g_2 \mid g_1) &= 0.84 \\
P_{ex}(g_3 \mid g_2) &= 0.67 \\
P_{ex}(g_4 \mid g_3) &= 1.0 \\
P_{eq}(g_2 = g_1) &= 0.68 \\
P_{eq}(g_3 = g_2) &= 0.38 \\
P_{eq}(g_4 = g_3) &= 0.67
\end{aligned}
$$

The figures show that on lists there is a high probability of gesture occurrence. Also, there is a 68% chance that the second gesture is the same as the first and even a 100% probability that the forth gesture equals the third which, of course, only applies if the list actually has more than three items.

10.7 Summary

Based on the assumption that empirical material exists with **NOVACO** annotations as described in Chapter 8, this section showed how to extract key parameters for gesture generation. The extraction is performed by a software module called **NO-VALIS** that connects to **ANVIL** via the plug-in interface. Using statistical modeling methods, a number of estimations for local and global parameters and for long-distance relations are defined. Together with a subject's gesture repertoire these parameters make up an individual's *gesture profile*. Individuality is achieved by having different gesture sets and different ways these gestures are used: different

database	formal	description
concept-to-gesture	$P_{sem} := P(l \mid w)$	mapping from phrases of words and/or semantic tags to a gesture lemma l.
gesture timing	$P_{timing} := P(p \mid l)$	distribution of $p \in \{\text{direct, indirect, init, span}\}$ for each gesture lemma l
handedness unigrams	$P(h)$	handedness distribution (AFT 0)
gesture handedness	$P(h \mid l)$	distribution of handedness for each gesture lemma l
handedness bigrams	$P(h_i \mid h_{i-1})$	handedness transitions (AFT 4)
gesture transitions	$P_{bi}(l_i) := P(l_i \mid l_{i-1})$	gesture bigrams (AFT 4)
gesture rate	$\frac{\#G}{\#segments}$	number of gestures per segment
discourse relation (exist)	$P_{rel/ex}(g_i \mid g_{i-1})$	probability that there is a follow-up gesture in a speech relation
discourse relation (equal)	$P_{rel/eq}(g_i \mid g_{i-1})$	probability that follow-gesture equals previous gesture

Table 10.2: *Summary of all parameters in the gesture profile.*

function, different timing and different handedness. Table 10.2 summarizes the relations, their respective mathematical model and purpose.

The parameters fall in two categories. The first kind is *functional* in nature and requires hypotheses on the relation between gesture and speech. Two parameters, the word-to-gesture mapping and the discourse relation modeling belong to this kind. The underlying theories are those of lexical affiliates (cf. Schegloff, 1984) and catchments (cf. McNeill et al., 2001) respectively. All other parameters belong to the second category where the statistical modeling approach is chosen. Here, one tries to approximate a surface behavior without further understanding of the underlying processes. For this statistical modeling, to alleviate the sparse data problem, the absolute frequency threshold (AFT) is introduced as a means to ensure that enough evidence is present to justify the utilization of a bigram.

Chapter 11

Gesture Generation: The NOVA System

The last chapter defined gesture profiles that contain statistical models of individual gesture properties like timing, transitions, handedness etc. This chapter presents an algorithm that uses these profiles to generate gestures from annotated speech input. The final output is an abstract action script that can be used for character animation.

Generation is performed in two steps. In the first step, gestures are overgenerated, i.e. all possible gestures are generated and added to an intermediate graph representation. Scoring functions are used to annotate the graph with probability estimations. Lexical affiliation controls the selection of gestures, whereas the timing profiles determine the gesture's placement within a segment. In the second step, the best gestures are singled out based on the theme/rheme/focus annotations and, more importantly, using the probabilities and that reflect local as well as global properties of the imitated speaker's profile.

The generation algorithm is implemented in a system called **NOVA**, short for **No**n**v**erbal **A**ction Generator, which connects to ANVIL via the plug-in interface. For representing intermediate results during processing a graph structure is used, called *Multimodal Generation Graph* (MuG). **NOVA** accesses ANVIL's internal structures to fill the initial MuG with the annotated input for test runs.

This chapter will first introduce the MuG working representation before describing input structures, algorithm and output of the gesture generation system **NOVA** in separate sections. Screen shots will illustrate the generation procedure. A brief summary closes the chapter.

11.1   Representation

The *Multimodal Generation Graph* (MuG) is a representation structure for both words and nonverbal output. The MuG is an ordered directed acyclic graph (DAG) where the *nodes* represent time points and spoken words are transitions between nodes, called *edges*. The edges have a content and a type. While the exact content depends on the edge type, all edges contain at least the following data:

1. a label (alphanumeric string)

2. a set of probability values, each $\in [0, 1]$

In a MuG with nodes N and edges E, the basic temporal granularity of the graph is defined by words. The nodes N consist of the time points of the words' boundaries, whereas words are represented by edges connecting neighbouring nodes. Time imposes a total order $\preceq$ on all nodes and allows to define a containment relation between edges and nodes as well as between edges and edges. An edge $e = \langle a, b \rangle$ is said to *contain* node n iff

$$a \preceq n \preceq b.$$

Edge e is said to contain edge $\tilde{e} = \langle \tilde{a}, \tilde{b} \rangle$ iff

$$a \preceq \tilde{a} \quad \wedge \quad \tilde{b} \preceq b.$$

Linguistic entities "above" the level of words, such as segments, speech acts, POS or theme/rheme, are represented by edges. Also, nonverbal actions like gestures are represented by edges. A gesture temporally co-occurs with those words that are contained in the gesture's edge.

Because of its graph structure the MuG is similar to *word hypotheses graphs* or *word lattices* known from speech recognition (Schukat-Talamazzini et al. 1994) and to *annotation graphs* known from linguistic annotation (Bird and Liberman 2001). The graph structure is more flexible than a tree because it allows for overlap and parallel edges while preserving the fundamentally temporal nature of the targeted output. Time becomes discrete as word boundaries define the basic granularity. The simplification resulting from this temporal discretization facilitates the detection of gesture collision.

For test runs on annotated data the MuG representation can be extracted online from the **ANVIL** system and fed into the **NOVA** plug-in. A sample MuG, extracted from speaker HK (lq1-1), is shown in Figure 11.1.

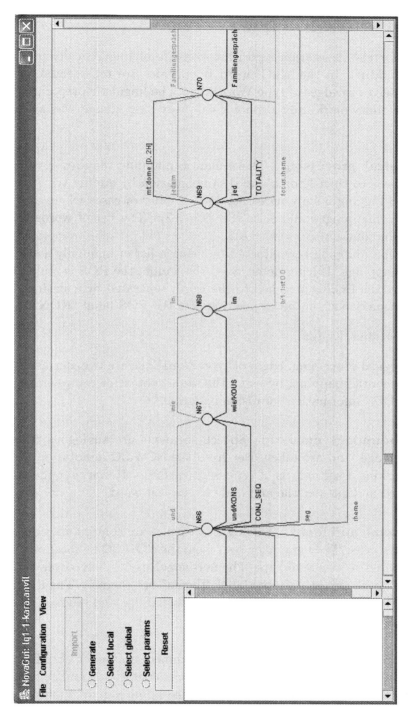

Figure 11.1: *NOVA system with annotated input MuG after semantic tagging.*

11.2   Generation Input

The input for the generation algorithm consists of linguistically prepared words in form of a MuG. In the MuG, word boundaries are represented as nodes, the words themselves as edges of type WordEdge. The linguistic preparation comprises segment boundary mark-up, morphological processing, theme/rheme and discourse relations.

Morphological processing   The semantic mapping requires generalization by mapping words to their lemma and disambiguation by adding the part-of-speech[1] (POS). POS tagging is only necessary in a number of cases where ambiguities for the semantic mapping would arise (Section 7.2). The list of words L where this applies can be found in Appendix A.1.

The lemma mapping is conducted by using a list of manually assembled word-to-lemma mappings. Having determined the lemma the POS is added if the word is in L. If so, the POS is attached to the word, separated by a slash. For example, the conjunction "aber" in initial position gets the POS label "KONS":

aber → aber/KONS

In morphological processing, edges of type WordEdge are transformed in this manner. The semantic mapping, by using the same syntax for representing words, can exploit the POS information for disambiguation.

Segment boundary mark-up   Speech segments are analogous to sentences in written language, and are taken over from the **NOVACO** annotation (Section 7.1). An edge marking a segment is of type SegmentEdge. It starts at the start node of the first word and ends at the end node of the last word.

Theme, rheme and focus   Themes and rhemes are contiguous, non-overlapping sequences of words. They are taken over from the **NOVACO** annotation (Section 7.3) and represented as edges of type ThemeRhemeEdge. They cover the respective sequence of words and contain the label "theme" or "rheme". The theme or rheme focus is imported as a separate edge of type FocusEdge and labelled "focus.theme" and "focus.rheme" respectively.

Discourse relations   Discourse relations connect a number of different word sequences $\langle s_1, \ldots, s_n \rangle$, where each sequence s_i is contiguous and sequences do not overlap (Section 7.4). For each word sequence s_i an edge of type DiscourseRelationEdge e_i is created which contains:

---

[1] See Appendix A.1 for the list of part-of-speech tags and their meaning.

- relation type ∈ {opposition, repetition, list}
- link to previous relation edge e_{i-1} (if $i > 1$)
- exist probability
- equal probability

The two probability values estimate the probability that a gesture occurs on e_i (exist probability) and that this gesture equals the one on e_{i-1} (equal probability) as described in Section 10.6.

11.3 Generation Algorithm

The algorithm proceeds in four steps where each step modifies the MuG to arrive at the final structure. The final MuG can then be translated to a linear action script, called CAML (Section 11.4), that can then be sent to an output renderer.

1. **Semantic tagging**: input is enriched with semantic tags
2. **Gesture generation**: gestures are triggered by lexical affiliation, timing is factored out, theme/rheme prioritizing is done
3. **Gesture selection**: is performed using local and global likelihood
4. **Parameter selection**: handedness is determined

In its actual application the algorithm employs only a subset of the gesture lexicon. As suggested in Section 9.3, this subset consists of the high frequency gestures. In the following, however, *all* gestures will be considered to simplify the situation. The four steps are now explained.

Semantic tagging

In the semantic tagging, the lemmatized and POS-tagged word edges are mapped to edges of type SemanticEdge according to the mapping defined in Appendix A.2, for instance

    Liebe → AFFECT

So that the MuG now contains a mixture of words and semantic tags. For example, the sequence "Sie sagen völlig zurecht..." is mapped in the following manner:

Sie	sagen	völlig	zurecht	
↓	↓	↓	↓	
ADDRESSEE	sagen	TOTALITY	AGREEMENT	...

To simplify the below algorithm, all words not mapped to semantic tags are taken to be semantic tags themselves and are added as edges of type SemanticEdge. Figure 11.1 shows a MuG with all input annotations (POS-tagged and lemmatized words, theme/rheme, focus, discourse relations and segments), including original gestures, and the added semantic edges CONJ_SEQ and TOTALITY.

Gesture generation

The generation algorithm adds gesture edges to the MuG. The algorithm traverses all contiguous sequences of semantic edges $\sigma = \langle s_0, \ldots, s_N \rangle$ that do not cross segment boundaries and have maximum length $N \leq 5$. Let segment(σ) be the corresponding segment edge that contains σ. Let gen(σ) be the set of gestures that are triggered by lexical affiliation to the semantic tags σ (Section 10.2). Let theme_rheme(σ) be the theme or rheme segment that contains σ and let focus(theme_rheme(σ)) be the focus of that theme/rheme segment. Then, for all $g \in \text{gen}(\sigma)$:

> **if** (prob(g) > 0.1) **then begin**
>   **create** gesture edge e_0 with
>   timing(e_0)=DIRECT
>   start(e_0)=start(σ)
>   end(e_0)=end(σ)
> **end**
> **if** (timing_prob(g, SPAN) > 0.1) **then begin**
>   **create** gesture edge e_1 with
>   timing(e_1)=SPAN
>   start(e_1)=start(segment(σ))
>   end(e_1)=end(segment(σ))
> **end**
> **if** (timing_prob(g, INIT) > 0.1) **then begin**
>   **create** gesture edge e_2 with
>   timing(e_2)=INIT
>   start(e_2)=start(segment(σ))
>   end(e_2)=min(start(segment(σ)) + 3, end(segment(σ)))
> **end**
> **if** (timing_prob(g, INDIRECT) > 0.1 **and**
>   exists(focus(theme_rheme(σ))) **and**
>   not(overlap(σ, focus(theme_rheme(σ))))
>   **then begin**
>   **create** gesture edge e_3 with
>   timing(e_3)=INDIRECT
>   start(e_3)=start(focus(theme_rheme(σ)))
>   end(e_3)=end(focus(theme_rheme(σ)))
> **end**

This algorithm generates gestures with timing patterns DIRECT, SPAN, INIT and INDIRECT. The minimum condition for generation is an estimated probability of 10% in dependence of the lexical affiliation strength. For timing patterns SPAN and INIT the conditional timing probability is also tested against the 10% probability threshold. During this step a large number of gestures is created, much more than will "survive" for the final output. Therefore, this step can also be called *overgeneration*.

Gesture selection

Gesture selection consists of two sub-steps, the *local* and the *global* selection step. In local selection, the overgenerated gestures are filtered on the segment level (Figure 11.2). Only the most probable gestures at the most promising locations are selected. Then, in global selection, out of the pool of non-selected gestures the globally most probable ones are added.

During local selection, in an incremental processing approach the selection algorithm traverses all gestures. Only those gestures in a "good" position are considered at all which are those located either in rhemes[2] or in the focus of a theme. For each of these positions exactly one gesture of all candidates is selected. After selection, the next position is processed. The first gesture is selected based only on unigram probability. All following gestures are rated also according to their bigram probability, taking the previously selected gestures into account. The total likelihood is a linear combination of five probability estimations:

$$P(c) := w_{sem}P_{sem} + w_{timing}P_{timing} + w_{bi}P_{bi} + w_{rel/ex}P_{rel/ex} + w_{rel/eq}P_{rel/eq}$$

where the weights are as shown in Table 11.1, and sum up to one.

After local selection all non-selected gestures constitute a set B, the gesture bag. For all members of B, dependent probability scores have to be re-computed according to the selected gestures.

Then, in global selection, the gesture g with the highest probability score is drawn from the bag B. If g does not collide with the already selected gestures, i.e. the edges of the other gestures do not overlap with g's edge, g is added to the selected gestures. Afterwards all probabilities have to be re-computed again. This procedure is repeated, i.e. more gestures are taken from B, until the *average gesture rate* of the imitated speaker is reached within a certain tolerance.

Parameter selection

After generation and selection, some gesture parameters are still left open. In the current version of the NOVA system, only the handedness parameter remains

---

[2]Cassell (1998) hypothesized that "one is most likely to find gestures co-occuring with the rhematic part of speech"

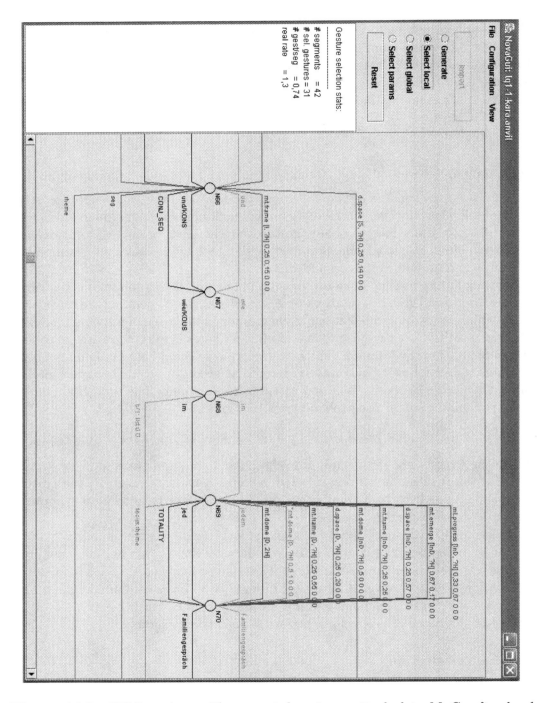

Figure 11.2: *NOVA system with generated gestures attached to MuG, after local selection step.*

weight	value
w_{sem}	0.3
w_{timing}	0.2
w_{bi}	0.2
$w_{rel/ex}$	0.2
$w_{rel/eq}$	0.1

Table 11.1: *Weights used in the central generation equation.*

to be filled. However, in the future, parameters like extension or speed could be determined in this phase as well.

As concerns handedness, in a first run all gestures that are inherently bi-handed (2H) are detected. A gesture is considered inherently bi-handed if it was performed bi-handedly in more than 90% of the occurrences in the training data.

If $\langle g_1, \ldots, g_n \rangle$ is the sequence of generated and selected gestures, handedness is determined by maximum likelihood of the three possible events $h \in \{LH, RH, 2H\}$. Let h_i be the handedness of gesture g_i and c be the category of the current gesture g, then likelihood $P(h|\, g_i)$ for the current gesture g is estimated with

$$P(h|\, g_i) = w_0\, P(h|\, c) + w_1\, P(h) + w_2\, P(h|\, h_{i-1})$$

where all weights w_i are as shown in Table 11.2 and sum up to one, i.e. $\sum w_i = 1$.

weight	value
w_0	0.5
w_1	0.2
w_2	0.3

Table 11.2: *Weights used to score handedness likelihood.*

Once the handedness parameter for all selected gestures is determined, the gesture generation and selection phases are terminated, and the MuG is ready for rendering.

Collision Detection

In the various generation and selection processes described above it can happen that a gesture is generated/selected that overlaps with another gesture. Such gestures are said to *collide*. It is important to get rid of collisions because otherwise the produced gestures may not be visible or recognizable. Therefore, when selecting gestures, a gesture g' selected after gesture g and colliding with it is discarded. The next probable gesture is chosen instead. This is a very simple, incremental processing approach to collision resolution. Other approaches could compare differ-

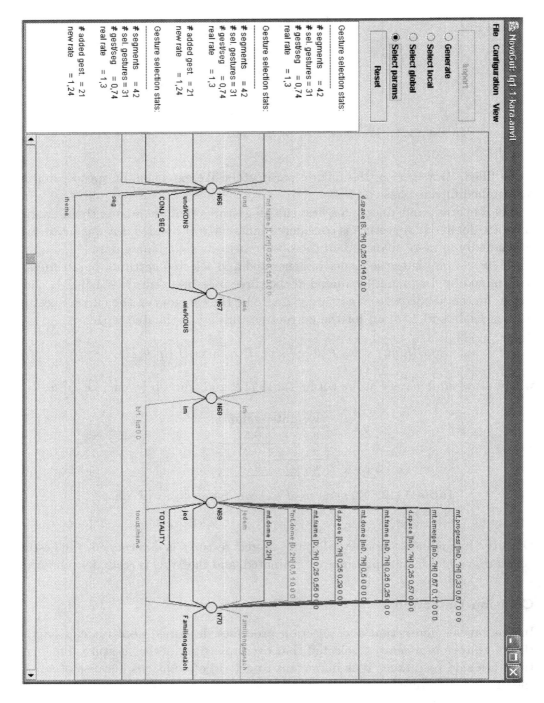

Figure 11.3: *NOVA system with MuG after semantic tagging, gesture generation and gesture selection (both local and global).*

ent solutions in the overall quality, taking a more global but also computationally more expensive approach.

11.4   Generation Output in CAML

In order to be executable by a character animation software the generated gestures must first be transformed from the MuG into an abstract action script. In general, an action script is a linearized specification of speech and actions that can be used to control various rendering devices like speech synthesis and character animation engines. An abstract action script is independent of the concrete rendering software so that it can be considered an *interlingua* for rendering devices. This implies that it must be translated to the specific control language of the output device. However, the structure of the action script should be close enough to most specific control languages that this translation is trivial.

The **C**haracter **A**ction **M**ark-up **L**anguage, short CAML, will be introduced here as such an action script. CAML is an XML language that allows to represent speech and gestures. The overall structure of a CAML script has two blocks for speech and actions each:

```
<caml>
  <speech>
    ...
  </speech>

  <actions>
    ...
  </actions>
</caml>
```

The two blocks are filled with speech and actions respectively. Speech is entered as normal text. To model gestures and their temporal relation to speech, two further tags are used. *Position tags* are entered into the text of the speech block to mark temporal positions for the gestures. They are assigned a unique ID that can be referred to later. In the action block, gestures are specified using *gesture tags*. The gesture tags contain

- lemma: name of the gesture lexicon entry

- handedness: RH, LH or 2H

- timing: direct, init or span

- start: the ID of the position tag at which the gesture should start

- end: the ID of the position tag at which the gesture should end

For example, the generated output shown in Figure 11.3 results in the following CAML script:

```
<caml>
  <speech>
    <pos id="1"/> Und wie <pos id="2"/> in <pos id="3"/>
    jedem <pos id="4"/> Familiengespraech ...
  </speech>

  <actions>
    <gesture lemma="frame" hand="2H" timing="direct" start="1" end="2"/>
    <gesture lemma="dome" hand="2H" timing="direct" start="3" end="4"/>
  </actions>
</caml>
```

Instead of putting the gesture tags directly into the speech block, letting them bracket the covered words, non-bracketing position markers are used. This has the advantage that other speech markers, for instance for intonation, can be used as brackets without running the risk of overlapping with gesture brackets.

The CAML format is kept open in two respects. First, arbitrary speech markers can be added. The input language for the NOVA system when specified in XML using tags for all the necessary linguistic annotations can be fully integrated and retained in the final output script. Second, other action markers, for instance for posture shifts or facial expressions, can be introduced with future extensions or by external tools.

CAML action scripts can be translated to various existing character animation technologies. Two examples are Microsoft's Agent Technology and Charamel's CharActor[3] software (see Figure 11.4). Here, a concrete translation example will be given for the CharActor real-time animation engine.

Given the speech utterance and gestures that were specified above the CharActor command would look like this:

```
SendEvent("Speak", "Und wie $(SingleMotion,emblem/frame) in
                  $(SingleMotion,metaphoric/dome) jedem
                  Familiengespraech.")
Wait("SpeakingEnd")
```

This translation assumes that the motion patterns for the two gestures realize a single stroke. For the timing patterns init and span, however, one needs motion patterns with continual beats. These motion patterns can then be brought to a controlled halt by inserting a command for the default posture at the end point. The CharActor engine will then blend the first motion into the second (which is the resting position) and thus, bring the gesture to a halt:

---

[3]http://www.charamel.de

```
SendEvent("Speak", "$(SingleMotion,emblem/frame) Und wie in
                    $(SingleMotion,special/default) jedem
                    Familiengespraech.")
Wait("SpeakingEnd")
```

The above example is the translation for a single frame gesture used with init timing being brought to a controlled halt after the word "in". Span timing is realized analogously.

Figure 11.4: *Agent Tina animated with two different character animation technologies. Microsoft's Agent Technology animates characters by concatenating pre-fabricated clips (left). Charamel's CharActor player performes rendering at runtime based on a 3D model and pre-fabricated motion patterns (right).*

To conclude, **CAML** offers a simple XML representation of speech and actions where actions are assumed to exist as pre-fabricated motion patterns that are accessed by name. More complexity can be added on demand and a translation to existing scripting languages or concrete rendering software input specifications can be easily developed as was demonstrated for the CharActor software.

11.5 Assessment

The lack of visualization in **NOVA** does not allow an empirical evaluation of the generation system. This chapter therefore concludes with comparing **NOVA** with other generation systems and listing open issues that follow directly from **NOVA**'s approach.

11.5.1   Comparison with Existing Work

Compared to the systems surveyed in Section 4.1 the NOVA system is much more empirically oriented. Hence, the data material of the speaker could be much more specific and a large maximum repertoire of 68 gesture could be assembled. On the other hand, the missing visualization in NOVA makes it difficult to evaluate the system's output.

For generation, NOVA requires annotated input similar to that of AC and REA/P, and can therefore be called a concept-to-gesture system. The model for generating gestures is based on probability estimations like in REA/P but also uses rules for gesture placement similar to BEAT's rules to place gestures on rhematic elements. However, NOVA also uses the notion of theme/rheme *focus* to place gestures. NOVA differs from BEAT in its internal representation which is an ordered acyclic graph as opposed to BEAT's grammar-like tree structure. The advantage of the graph is the possibility of parallel overlapping structures that can be resolved in the filter phase, whereas the tree structure does not allow the representation of such structures in the first place.

	input	repertoire	model	proc	coord-speech	rendering
PPP	CTG	?	Ru	G	SEQ	○
REA	CTG	?	Gr	G	SSR	○
MAX	CTG	?	Ru	G	SSR	●
AC	CTG	?	Ru	G	SSR	○
VHP	TTG	5	Ru	—	CCS	○
BEAT	TTG	?	Ru	O+F	CCS	○
NOVA	CTG	68	Pr+Ru	O+F	TP	—
REA/P	CTG	4	Pr	G	TP	○
FACE	TTG	?	Ru	G	TP	○
Greta	CTG	?	Ru	O+F	CCS	●

Table 11.3: *Comparison of NOVA with existing generation systems. The table is the same as in Section 4.3, p. 90, but extended with NOVA (shaded line).*

The computation of timing models is unique to NOVA. So far, no other system has implemented timing patterns different from what is called *direct* timing in this work. In terms of general architecture, NOVA employs an overgenerate-and-filter approach like the systems Greta and BEAT. In contrast to them, the filter step is used to model *global* parameters like gesture rate. Gesture rate is meant to reflect a speaker's individuality. Individuality is further fostered by individual rules for gesture selection, timing patterns and handedness, and by the fact that separate subsets of the gesture lexicon are used for each speaker. None of the other systems follows this modular approach of exchangeable gesture profiles for individual generation. Table 11.3 summarizes NOVA's properties in direct comparison with the systems surveyed in Section 4.3.

Concerning the CAML action script language, the mechanism of using position tags in the text as reference points for the separate action specification is also used, for instance, in the action specification for the *Max* agent (Kopp and Wachsmuth 2002) called MURML[4] (Krandstedt et al. 2002). This language was developed for a feature-based approach to generation and allows specification of features like hand shape, orientation and movement path. It incorporates much more complexity than needed for NOVA. CAML serves as a simple interlingua to rendering devices and must not be confused with languages that were developed for authoring and thus incorporate all aspects of virtual character modelling plus a range of pre-specified motion patterns. CML[5] is one such example. Other languages like AML[6] are very close to a rendering software and allow fine-grained temporal control of this engine while being useless for other existing rendering software (see Arafa et al., 2002, for an exposition on both CML and AML).

The NOVA approach, in its utilization of individual gesture profiles and with its abstract CAML output, appears to be best fitted to model teams of individual presentation agents that display varied and entertaining nonverbal actions and can be animated with different character players.

11.5.2   Open Issues

The objective for generation was to apply individual gesture profile to speech input to produce gestures. Given the broad scope of this work, many issues on the generation side had to be left open. This section gives a survey of the most important ones.

Text input   Speech input has to be richly annotated. The pre-annotated speech input that is required for NOVA can be justified with the argument that in most speech generation systems the required information is either available or could easily be provided. However, for a real text-to-gesture approach, a pure text input would have to be pre-processed to compute syntactic data, information structure and discourse relations as is done in the BEAT system (Cassell et al. 2001b).

Context   The current approach does not consider context in the sense of world knowledge. For computing handedness it is not considered where the addressee is located. To factor out this context, one would need different settings where the addressee is located to the left/right/in front of the speaker. Alternatively, one can

---

[4]**M**ultimodal **U**tterance **R**epresentation **M**ark-up **L**anguage
[5]**C**haracter **M**ark-up **L**anguage
[6]**A**vatar **M**ark-up **L**anguage

produce context-specific profiles (e.g., a profile for a speaker with addressee to the left). The profiles computed here are actually context-specific. Another alternative is to use rules (see below).

Hidden determinants   In the NOVA system, the relation between gesture and speech drives the whole generation process. However, not always do the functions of gestures have a correlate in speech. Especially functions similar to speech acts (Austin, 1975, and Searle, 1969), including turn-taking acts (Duncan and Fiske 1977), but also semantic information (Cassell et al. 1999) might be encoded in the gesture only. Such determinants would have to be integrated in the NOVACO scheme to be extractable by the NOVALIS module. Moreover, annotated text would not suffice as an input representation for the NOVA generator. Instead, a modality-independent input language like M3L would be necessary (Wahlster 2003).

Rule-based processing   While statistical modeling provides a quick way to model frequently occurring phenomena, rule-based approaches allow to implement more specific but well investigated mechanisms, also integrating world knowledge. Although NOVA already makes use of rules when determining gesture placement or suppressing gesture collision, rules could be integrated in a more modular fashion to override obviously false decisions of the statistical processor or to include specific and context-dependent gesture production rules (for instance, pointing at something) that lack empirical support in the training data.

Rendering   While most other gesture generation systems include rendering, this is lacking here. One important reason is that including rendering often also implies a strong focus on rendering, thus neglecting either the empirical foundation or the generation itself. However, the advantages of including rendering are clear. The produced output can be observed and tested. It can be evaluated by independent subjects to investigate whether the produced gestures are natural, individual and entertaining. Also, generation depends on rendering insofar as the generation engine should at least be as powerful as the rendering engine to exploit all features. For instance, in conjunction with good rendering engines the *segmentation* problem must be solved in detail: how does the gesture's internal structure look like, where does the stroke begin and end, etc.

It must be noted that few systems incorporating rendering make use of the chance of evaluation studies. This may be due to the fact that evaluation of embodied agents is in itself a new and relatively unexplored area of research. For first tentative evaluation approaches see van Mulken et al. (1998), McBreen (2001), McBreen et al. (2001), Nass et al. (2000) and Cassell and Thórisson (1999).

11.6 Summary

This chapter described how the gesture profiles extracted by NOVALIS from the annotated LQ corpus were used to generate gestures in a system called NOVA. Given an annotated speech input, a graph structure called MuG is produced that is processed in two principal steps that can be called generation and selection.

In generation, the MuG is first enriched with semantic tags using a hand-crafted mapping. Then, the actual generation algorithm adds gestures with probabilities triggered by lexical affiliation. These gestures are generated for all four timing types: direct, indirect, init and span. Once all possible gestures are generated, in the selection step only the best ones are chosen for the final output. Selection is first done locally, choosing one gesture per segment according to the maximum likelihood paradigm. Then, a global selection step selects from the set of remaining gestures the ones that are best in global comparison. After selection, some parameters are left to be chosen using a linear combination of unigrams and bigrams.

The generated gestures are written to an action script in the CAML language which is an abstract interlingua for rendering devices. For final rendering in a character animation engine like CharActor or MS Agent Technology, the action script needs to be translated to the software-specific language as was demonstrated for CharActor.

NOVA is a concept-to-gesture system based on probabilistic as well as rule-based processing. Its graph-based working representation allows the processing of parallel structures. NOVA is unique in working with timing patterns and otherwise relies on the well-know overgenerate-and-filter approach. Speaker individuality is especially supported by working with individual gesture profiles. In comparison with existing generation systems, NOVA appears to be best suited for the player-independent generation of individual gestures for a team of presentation agents.

Chapter 12

Conclusion

This chapter starts out with a summary of the complete work. The second section discusses the contributions to current research and the impact that parts of this work already had. The third section reviews open issues and points to future directions.

12.1 Summary

The aim of this work was to generate conversational gestures for a team of embodied agents. The produced gestures should provide a broad base behavior that is both believable and individual. This generation task was approached by imitating specific human speakers who are experienced in performing in public. The generation by imitation approach was pursued in three phases with particular subtasks. These phases were called observation, modeling and generation.

In the observation phase, video clips of two TV speakers to be imitated had to be selected. For the selection process, suitability criteria were developed. These criteria were applied to estimate how close the TV show matches the targeted application, whether the phenomena to be imitated occur in sufficient quantity and quality, whether the right conversational situations are displayed and whether technical requirements like speaker visibility are fulfilled. A digital video corpus, the LQ corpus, was collected by digitizing 23 clips from three recorded sessions of the TV show *The Literary Quartet*. This resulted in a total of 46:18 minutes of material. For the transcription of gesture and speech, annotation schemes and tools were surveyed. The categorial transcription scheme by Webb (1997) was found to be best suited for the generation task, complemented by the structural transcription by Kita et al. (1998) and the concept of lexical affiliation first introduced by Schegloff (1984). The survey of schemes resulted in a number of requirements for a video annotation software tool. Ten existing tools were tested and checked against these requirements: HIAT-DOS, CLAN, Akira, MacSHAPA, MediaTagger,

The Observer, SignStream, syncWRITER, TASX-annotator, and Elan. Each of the tools was found to lack essential features. Therefore, the video annotation tool ANVIL was developed. It is a platform-independent, extensible, general annotation tool that allows user-defined coding schemes and has an intuitive graphical user interface. Using ANVIL and the surveyed coding schemes, the NOVACO scheme was created for the systematic transcription of gesture and speech. The scheme comprises linguistic as well as gestural information like words, information structure, gesture phases, and lexical affiliates. Four timing patterns were devised to capture the temporal relationship between gesture and lexical affiliate. For the transcription in gestural categories, the LQ gesture lexicon had to be created from the LQ data, cross-checking it with published gesture inventories. The lexicon comprises 68 gesture lemmas. Using the ANVIL tool and the NOVACO scheme, the complete LQ corpus was transcribed, resulting in a total of 1,056 transcribed gestures and 2,518 movement phases.

name	description
ANVIL	A generic, extensible video annotation tool with project management and plug-in interface.
NOVACO	A speech and gesture coding scheme, specifically tailored to the purpose of gesture generation.
LQ corpus	A video corpus of a book review TV talk show featuring two speakers, fully annotated with transcribed speech and gesture (23 clips, 46 minutes, 1056 gestures).
LQ gesture lexicon	A lexicon of 68 conversational gestures identified in the LQ corpus.
NOVALIS	A gesture profile extractor, producing statistical models of individual gesture behavior from NOVACO annotations, using a hand-crafted word-to-concept semantic mapping.
NOVA	A generation engine for gestures, producing multimodal output graphs from annotated speech input using gesture profiles extracted by NOVALIS.
CAML	A player-independent action specification language.

Table 12.1: *The tools and data produced in this work.*

In the modeling phase, the annotated LQ corpus was analyzed and gesture profiles for each individual speaker were extracted. To assess the consistency of the **NOVACO** gesture transcription scheme, coding reliability was tested with two independent coders who achieved an agreement of 79.4% (recall) which translates to a kappa value of 0.78. The gesture lexicon was reduced in size, using a frequency criterium, down to 26–28 lemmas that still covered over 85% of the original data. Of these lemmas, 15 are shared by both speakers. It was hypothesized that the remaining gestures account for the individual difference between the speakers. Other factors for individuality were reasoned to be handedness, timing and function. These factors were used to define speaker-individual gesture profiles. The **NOVALIS** module was developed to automatically extract each speaker's profile from the annotated LQ data using statistical models. Each gesture profile contains a probabilistic concept-to-gesture mapping, gesture rate and probability estimations for gesture handedness, timing and discourse relations.

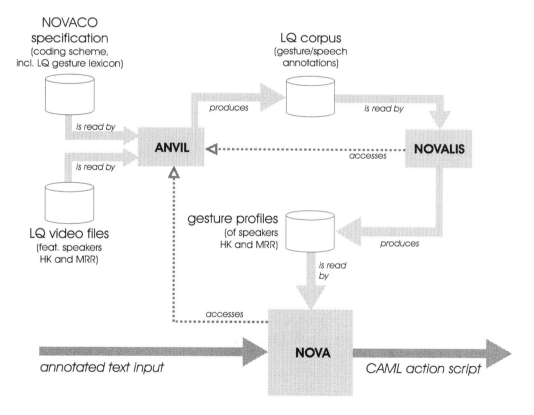

Figure 12.1: *Overall architecture of the tools and data produced in this work. Data is depicted by containers, processing modules by rectangles. Solid arrows indicate data flow, dotted arrows indicate access to software functions.*

For the generation phase, the NOVA gesture generation system was developed. Its generation algorithm works in four stages in an overgenerate-and-filter approach using a graph-based representation. The input is annotated text where the annotation consists of parts-of-speech, segment and theme/rheme/focus mark-up as well as discourse relations. In the first stage, the algorithm enriches the input with semantic tags. In the second stage, gestures are generated using the empirically deduced gesture profile and placement heuristics taken from the literature. In the third stage, gestures are selected according to local and global criteria in a maximum likelihood approach, again based on the gesture profile. In the forth and final stage, gestural parameters like handedness are determined. The resulting gesture graph is translated to the player-independent, XML-based action language CAML. The output scripts can be used to generate instructions for players like MS Agent Technology or CharActor.

The overall design and interplay of the software used in this work is depicted in Figure 12.1. Data is symbolized by containers, processing modules by rectangles. One can see that the processing pipeline starts with ANVIL which is used, together with the NOVACO scheme specification, to annotate the LQ video files, thus creating the annotated LQ corpus. From this corpus, the NOVALIS modules extracts gestural key parameters and stores them in gesture profiles. These profiles are the basis for gesture generation in NOVA. The NOVA system expects annotated text input and produces individual gestures in CAML action scripts that can be forwarded to animation engines like MS Agent Technology or CharActor. The illustration is a slight simplification as all access to LQ data is actually performed through ANVIL. This is indicated by the dotted arrows pointing from NOVA and NOVALIS to ANVIL. ANVIL thus acts as an integrative software platform for all other modules.

The original aim of this work was to collect data, find methods and develop tools for the generation of gestures by imitation. This aim was achieved. The tools and data produced are listed in Table 12.1. The tools work together in a single integrated environment with ANVIL at its core and NOVALIS and NOVA functioning as independent modules communicating with ANVIL via a plug-in interface. All data is stored in XML format.

12.2   Contributions and Impact

On the most general level, the contribution of this work to the research community is that it provides a nearly complete work pipeline, including software tools, for getting from empirical data to generated gestures in an imitation approach. The work is distinct from related work in three major aspects. First, this work focusses on *individual* speakers as opposed to looking at the average behavior of a whole population of subjects. Second, it relies on own empirical analyses instead of resorting to results from the literature. These analyses are used to derive *quantitative* statistical models. Third, the selection of human subjects was guided by the task. The subjects were required to be *experienced public performers*, e.g. TV speakers, as opposed to "normal" people usually examined in similar projects. It was thus ascertained that they display a gestural behavior that is effective, non-monotonous and interesting to watch.

On a more specific level, this work contributes tools, data and insights to the research field of embodied agents. The ANVIL video annotation tool is already being used at various international institutes. The system unites several essential features in a single robust, easy-to-use, non-commercial tool. It keeps a strict separation between coding scheme and tool which makes ANVIL independent of the specific aims of this work. Other important features are the intuitive timeline view, complex coding elements and an efficient coding interface with online access to the user's coding manual. The tool also introduces innovations like cross-level links, non-temporal objects and automatic coding manual generation. ANVIL followed a distribution policy where only stable releases of small download sizes ($< 1MB$) were made publicly available. Distribution started in the year 2000. Since then, more than 350 researchers from over 30 countries downloaded the software, giving numerous feedback, thus making it possible to closely adapt ANVIL's development to the requirements of the various research communities. However, the development philosophy has always been to keep the software as simple as possible but to make it as complex as necessary.

Much more specific to the purpose of this work is the coding scheme NOVACO for the transcription of gesture and speech. It offers mechanisms for coding those aspects that are relevant for gesture generation. A general novelty is the explicit coding of lexical affiliates and their temporal relation to the corresponding gesture by means of timing patterns. While most researchers restrict themselves to the analysis of speech-gesture co-occurrence (McNeill, 1992: 26–29), the NOVACO timing patterns grant a more differentiated picture of gesture-speech synchronization. Although it was created for a very specific purpose, the scheme demonstrates how speech and gesture coding, especially for gesture phase structure and gesture-speech relations, can look like when working with multiple layers and an annotation software like ANVIL. It can thus act as a point of departure for other research projects that conduct gesture annotation with software tools. An integral part of the coding scheme is the LQ gesture lexicon. It is a well-documented inventory of two gesture repertoires of *individuals*. This is unusual as common gesture inventories are collections drawing on whole socio-cultural groups. Also, the fact that all major gesture classes are represented is rare as most published gesture inventories exclusively collect emblems. Both properties are important to applications aiming at a broad, yet individual gestural behavior. Therefore, the LQ gesture lexicon can be the basis for other gesture generation projects that lack the resources to conduct own empirical research. In fact, three projects have already built on this resource.

In these projects, a subset of the LQ gesture lexicon was implemented for an animated agent. First, in the CrossTalk system (Gebhard et al., 2003, and Klesen et al., 2003), an interactive, self-explaining embodied agents installation developed at German Research Center for Artificial Intelligence (DFKI). Second, in the European NECA[1] project which aims at creating embodied agents that can express emotions verbally and nonverbally (Krenn et al. 2002). Finally and most recently, in the VirtualHuman[2] project, a virtual reality tutoring system on topics in Astronomy, developed in a joint effort by several German research institutes working together in a lead project by the German Federal Ministry of Education and Research (BMBF). The LQ gestures were integrated as part of the embodied agents' nonverbal behavior and modeled by a professional graphics designer using video stills from the LQ corpus and textual descriptions like the ones in Appendix B. A subset of the LQ gesture lexicon was incorporated in each of the two embodied agents called Tina and Ritchie. Figure 12.2 shows the metaphoric *Walls* gesture as found in the LQ corpus and transferred to the CrossTalk and VirtualHuman projects, using different character animation technologies.

The annotated LQ corpus of transcribed speech and gesture can become a resource for other projects, as training material or for further exploratory research. The 1,056 annotated gestures are a considerable amount compared to other projects, e.g. 134 annotated gestures in the REA project (Yan 2000). However, the potential as training material is limited by the complexity of the learning task. While the amount of data suffices for statistical modeling as done in the gesture profiles, the data would be too sparse to train, e.g., image-based gesture recognizers. In the field of Gesture Research the LQ corpus can be used to test hypotheses about the relationship between gesture and speech. The precisely annotated temporal boundaries of words and gesture phases have not yet been fully exploited in this approach. They could be useful in an investigation of gestures' relation to intonation. Also, when rendering gestures for implemented embodied agents this fine-grained temporal resolution can be utilized to determine the speech-gesture timing exactly.

The **NOVALIS** component works on the annotated LQ corpus to extract individual gesture profiles, a novel concept in gesture generation. Although quantitative modeling has also been done by Cassell et al. (2001a), their effort aimed at posture, not gesture, and did not model individual but general behavior. Gesture profiles can be compared to individual language models in speech recognition that are created in a personal training period. Both capture individual preferences probabilistically. The captured aspects were chosen to include concept-to-gesture mapping, gesture transitions, handedness preferences and timing preferences. However, which as-

---

[1] **N**et **E**nvironment for Embodied Emotional **C**onversational **A**gents,
see http://www.ai.univie.ac.at/NECA
[2] http://www.virtual-human.org

Figure 12.2: *The metaphoric gesture "Walls" (see Appendix B, page 274) as found in the LQ corpus (top, left) and used for two different implementations of the synthetic agent Tina: in the CrossTalk infotainment installation (top, right) and in the VirtualHuman 3D virtual reality tutoring system (bottom).*

pects of gesture production actually make nonverbal behavior individual must be further explored and confirmed in future research.

The NOVA gesture generation system, using a gesture profile and the word-to-concept mapping, performs shallow generation of gestures. Gestures are triggered by words in the input stream through lexical affiliation. The generated gestures reflect the speakers preferred timing patterns, overall gesture frequency and handedness. In contrast to other, functional oriented systems, the shallow approach models the meaning and function of gestures indirectly with statistical figures in gesture profiles. This has the two drawbacks that the modeled function of the gesture is not precise because context dependencies are usually not captured in this approach and that the function is not explicitly defined. The lack of precision can be tolerated given that the communicative value of the gestures in question are considered very low by some researchers (Krauss et al. 1991). Moreover, Calbris (1990) finds that the "probabilistic nature" of gestures, meaning that it is not possible to exactly decode them, is one of the advantages of the nonverbal channel, enabling speakers to keep meanings ambiguous. Therefore, the focus of shallow generation is to generate a *broad* behavior as opposed to narrow but precise behavior. In the current state of research, generating broad *and* precise behavior is hardly possible since every gesture's various functions would have to be analyzed in-depth and encoded in rules. Thus, shallow generation can provide a base behavior that imitates the behavior of a selected speaker where functional approaches to gesture generation like REA (Cassell et al. 2000a) and MAX (Kopp and Wachsmuth 2000) can be added on top. In this case, functional gestures can be considered to be orthogonal to the base behavior although, of course, the integration of base behavior and functional gestures requires mechanisms for conflict resolution to guarantee a seamless surface behavior.

NOVA provides output in the CAML action language that can be transformed to specific player control languages. CAML is a simple, yet extensible XML language for rendering, not designed to carry functions like M3L or agent behaviors like CML. Neither is it very specific in the control of the output agent; it does not control limbs or joints. However, it is abstract enough to specify the flow of nonverbal body actions and their relation to speech for a number of different animation engines. For instance, both MS Agent Technology as well as CharActor can be used in conjunction with CAML.

12.3 Future Work

In a field as complex as gesture generation, many issues arise that must be left open. It starts with the selection of suitable material where people with effective, entertaining and professional looking gesture behavior must be found. The definition of criteria to measure the effectiveness and entertainment qualities of gestures is a subject of future work. Moreover, to gain a clearer picture on the concept of individuality, systematic analyses must be conducted on how gestures are perceived by the average watcher. One could then pinpoint the factors that reinforce or degrade individuality.

Concerning ANVIL, future work aims at producing a graphical interface for editing the XML specifications, thus facilitating the development of coding schemes. More general and more sophisticated query and analysis functions are other important areas for future improvement. In the long run, one could also consider alternative input media (data gloves) and image processing to obtain exact motion data of the performed gestures. The integration of bootstrapping methods for gesture annotation, using image-based gesture recognition modules connected to ANVIL as plug-ins, is a future vision. A more current issue for the research community is the standardization of coding schemes and metadata. ANVIL is prepared for such standards as it allows the explicit definition of coding schemes in files that can be used to encode standards and easily be distributed to the ANVIL user community. Metadata, as soon as definite standards emerge, can also be integrated in the tool's XML data format without affecting downward compatibility. It can then be comfortably viewed and edited in the Project Tool. A first selection of metadata has already been integrated. Concerning empirical research in general, future research must find workable coding schemes and representations that are applicable for gesture recognition as well as generation systems.

The LQ gesture repertoire has proved to be well-suited for the task of this work. The idea to collect a shared repertoire of gestures while at the same time storing the individual subsets is a valuable approach for the generation of individual gestures. However, more studies must be conducted to arrive at a large database that will slowly converge to a universal repertoire of conversational gestures. The database would include the individual gesture profiles of all studied individuals allowing yet greater variety for teams of embodied agents.

Concerning the modeling of gesture profiles, one could look for a more unified way to integrate the various probability estimations. A future vision for the imitation approach is not only to generate natural and entertaining gestures but to imitate a well-known person to such a degree that she or he is actually recognizable. While the first precondition for recognizability is the realistic rendering of face, body, hair-style, clothes, etc., the truthful rendering of motion (for instance in facial expression) and motion quality (gestures that are imitated using motion capturing techniques) do further enhance the effect. The ultimate step in realistic imitation, however, is the correct coordination of the gestures with the accompanying speech in terms of selection and timing. The results of this work are a first step in modeling this coordination for an individual. Whether the presented techniques suffice to enhance the recognizability of synthetic copies of well-known people like politicians, pop-stars and other celebrities remains to be proven by future systems.

As for generation in NOVA, a more differentiated parametrization of gestures would include motion qualities, i.e. how expansive, fast or smooth a gesture is performed depending on the individual and context. This would require a revision of the NOVACO scheme and the LQ corpus, based on Laban efforts as described in Section 4.2.3. Concerning the generator's input, the currently required annotations can be in part replaced by automatically deduced information as done in the BEAT system (Cassell et al. 2001b). However, a much more important issue is the integration of other approaches like functional generation. Ideally, different approaches, like functional and imitative, could compete in an open generation framework. The open framework of NOVA, based on Java interfaces and XML representations, will facilitate efforts to integrate other approaches.

Most of all, a rendering device is needed to make this work visible. It can then be applied to all kinds of virtual characters, on the web, in movies or as digital guides. For the future, the work may also become relevant to Robotics when humanoid robots are developed to imitate human beings, including their nonverbal behavior.

Several very different disciplines must work together to achieve the single aim of generating gestures. The vision of this work was to choose a human individual and imitate her/his gestures so as to obtain natural nonverbal behavior. This work is a first attempt at running through all stages from observation to generation in a systematic and partially automated way. Although it lacks the detail of existing gesture transcriptions, the depth of existing empirical investigations and the complexity of existing generation systems, the work presented here means to serve as a guideline for future endeavors to get from human behavior to computer character animation.

Bibliography

Abrilian, S., Buisine, S., Rendu, C., and Martin, J.-C. (2002). Specifying cooperation between modalities in lifelike animated agents. In *Proceedings of the International Workshop on Lifelike Animated Agents held in conjunction with the 7th Pacific Rim International Conference on Artificial Intelligence (PRICAI)*, 3–8.

André, E., and Rist, T. (2000). Presenting Through Performing: On the Use of Multiple Lifelike Characters in Knowledge-Based Presentation Systems. In *Proceedings of the Second International Conference on Intelligent User Interfaces (IUI 2000)*, 1–8.

André, E., Müller, J., and Rist, T. (1996). WIP/PPP: Automatic Generation of Personalized Multimedia Presentations. In *Proceedings of Multimedia 96, 4th ACM International Multimedia Conference*. Boston, MA: ACM Press. 407–408.

André, E., Rist, T., and Müller, J. (1999). Employing AI methods to control the behavior of animated interface agents. *Applied Artificial Intelligence* 13:415–448.

André, E., Rist, T., van Mulken, S., Klesen, M., and Baldes, S. (2000). The Automated Design of Believable Dialogues for Animated Presentation Teams. In Cassell, J., Sullivan, J., Prevost, S., and Churchill, E., eds., *Embodied Conversational Agents*. Cambridge, MA: MIT Press. 220–255.

Arafa, Y., Kamyab, K., Mamdani, E., Kshirsagar, S., Magnenat-Thalman, N., Guye-Vuillème, A., and Thalman, D. (2002). Two approaches to scripting character animation. In *Proceedings of the Workshop on "Embodied Conversational Agents" held in conjunction with The First International Joint Conference on Autonomous Agents and Multi-Agent Systems (AAMAS)*, 11–19.

Atkinson, M. (1984). *Our Masters' Voices. The language and body language of politics*. London and New York: Methuen.

Austin, J. L. (1975). *How To Do Things With Words*. Oxford: Oxford University Press.

Axtell, R. E. (1998). *Gestures - The Do's and Taboo's of Body Language Around the World*. New York: John Wiley & Sons, Inc. First published in 1991.

Badler, N. I., Philips, C. B., and Webber, B. L. (1993). *Simulating Humans: Computer Graphics, Animation and Control*. New York, Oxford: Oxford University Press.

Badler, N., Webber, B., Becket, W., Geib, C., Moore, M., Pelachaud, C., Reich, B., and Stone, M. (1995). Planning and parallel transition networks: Animation's new frontiers. In Shin, S. Y., and Kunii, T. L., eds., *Computer Graphics and Applications:*

Proceedings of Pacific Graphics '95, 101–117. River Edge, NJ: World Scientific Publishing.

Bakeman, R., and Gottman, J. M. (1986). *Observing Interaction: An Introduction to Sequential Analysis*. Cambridge: Cambridge University Press.

Barakat, R. A. (1973). Arabic Gestures. *Journal of Popular Culture* 6(4):749–892.

Bergmann, J. R. (1994). Ethnomethodologische Konversationsanalyse. In Fritz, G., and Hundsnurscher, F., eds., *Handbuch der Dialoganalyse*. Tübingen: Niemeyer. 3–16.

Bigbee, T., Loehr, D., and Harper, L. (2001). Emerging requirements for multi-modal annotation and analysis tools. In *Proceedings of the 7th European Conference on Speech Communication and Technology (Eurospeech)*, 1533–1536.

Bird, S., and Liberman, M. (2001). A Formal Framework for Linguistic Annotation. *Speech Communication* 33(1–2):23–60.

Birdwhistell, R. L. (1970). *Kinesics and Context: Essays on Body Motion Communication*. Philadelphia: University of Pennsylvania Press.

Bitti, P. E. R., and Poggi, I. (1991). Symbolic nonverbal behavior: Talking through gestures. In Feldman, R. S., and Rimé, B., eds., *Fundamentals of Nonverbal Behavior*. New York: Cambridge University Press. 433–457.

Bitti, P. E. R. (1992). Facial and Manual Components of Italian Symbolic Gestures. In Poyatos, F., ed., *Advances in Nonverbal Communication*. Amsterdam/Philadelphia: John Benjamins. 187–196.

Boehnke, K., Bortz, J., and Lienert, G. A. (1990). *Verteilungsfreie Methoden in der Biostatistik*. Berlin: Springer.

Boersma, P. (2002). Praat, a system for doing phonetics by computer. *Glot International* 5(9/10):341–345.

Bolt, R. A. (1980). Put-that-there: Voice and gesture at the graphics interface. *Computer Graphics* 14(3):262–270.

Bortz, J. (1999). *Statistik für Sozialwissenschaftler*. Berlin, Heidelberg: Springer.

Brants, T. (2000). TnT - a Statistical Part-of-Speech Tagger. In *Proceedings of the Sixth Applied Natural Language Processing Conference (ANLP-2000)*, 224–231.

Breazeal, C., and Scassellati, B. (1999). A context-dependent attention system for a social robot. In *Proceedints of the Sixteenth International Joint Conference on Artificial Intelligence (IJCAI 99)*, 1146–1151.

Brill, E. (1992). A simple rule-based part-of-speech tagger. In *Proceedings of the Third Conference on Applied Computational Linguistics (ACL)*, 152–155.

Broide, N. (1977). *Israel Emblems — Israeli Communication Units: Emblems Repertoire of "Sabras" of East European Descents*. Ph.D. Dissertation, Tel-Aviv University, Tel-Aviv.

Brown, L., ed. (1993). *The New Shorter Oxford English Dictionary*. Oxford: Clarendon Press.

Brugman, H., Russel, A., Broeder, D., and Wittenburg, P. (2000). EUDICO. Annotation and Exploitation of Multi Media Corpora. In *Proceedings of LREC 2000 Workshop*.

Bunt, H., Kipp, M., Maybury, M. T., and Wahlster, W. (2003). Fusion and Coordination For Multimodal Interactive Information Presentation. In Stock, O., and Zancanaro, M., eds., *Intelligent Information Presentation*. Kluwer Academic Publishers. submitted.

Calbris, G. (1990). *Semiotics of French Gesture*. Bloomington, Indiana: Indiana University Press.

Campbell, W. N. (1996). CHATR: A high-definition speech re-sequencing system. In *Acoustical Society of America and Acoustical Society of Japan, Third Joint Meeting*, 1223–1228.

Carletta, J. (1996). Assessing Agreement on Classification Task: The Kappa Statistics. *Computational Linguistics* 22(2):249–254.

Cassell, J., and Thórisson, K. R. (1999). The power of a nod and a glance: envelope vs. emotional feedback in animated conversational agents. *Applied Artificial Intelligence* 13:519–538.

Cassell, J., Pelachaud, C., Badler, N., Steedman, M., Achorn, B., Becket, T., Douville, B., Prevost, S., and Stone, M. (1994). Animated Converstaion: Rule-Based Generation of Facial Expression, Gesture & Spoken Intonation for Multiple Conversational Agents. In *Proceedings of SIGGRAPH '94*, 413–420.

Cassell, J., McNeill, D., and McCullough, K.-E. (1999). Speech-gesture mismatches: Evidence for one underlying representation of linguistic & nonlinguistic information. *Pragmatics & Cognition* 7(1):1–33.

Cassell, J., Stone, M., and Yan, H. (2000a). Coordination and context-dependence in the generation of embodied conversation. In *Proceedings of International Natural Language Generation (INLG)*.

Cassell, J., Sullivan, J., Prevost, S., and Churchill, E. (2000b). *Embodied Conversational Agents*. Cambridge, MA: MIT Press.

Cassell, J., Nakano, Y. I., Bickmore, T. W., Sidner, C. L., and Rich, C. (2001a). Non-verbal cues for discourse structure. In *Proceedings of 39th Annual Meeting of the Association for Computational Linguistics (ACL)*, 106–115.

Cassell, J., Vilhjálmsson, H., and Bickmore, T. (2001b). BEAT: the Behavior Expression Animation Toolkit. In *Proceedings of SIGGRAPH 2001*, 477–486.

Cassell, J. (1998). A framework for gesture generation and interpretation. In Cipolla, R., and Pentland, A., eds., *Computer Vision in Human-Machine Interaction*. New York: Cambridge University Press. 191–215.

Cassell, J. (2000). Embodied conversational interface agents. *Communications of the ACM* 43(4):70–78.

Chi, D., Costa, M., Zhao, L., and Badler, N. (2000). The EMOTE Model for Effort and Shape. In *Proceedings of SIGGRAPH 2000*, 173–182.

Collier, G. (1985). *Emotional Expression*. Hillsdale, NJ: Lawrence Erlbaum.

de Ruiter, J.-P. (1998). *Gesture and Speech Production*. Ph.D. Dissertation, Katholieke Universiteit Nijmegen, Wageningen.

Dellwo, V. (2003). Tools for a combined analysis of speech and gestures. In *Proceedings of the 15th International Congress of Phonetic Sciences*, 351–354.

DePaulo, B. M., and Kirkendol, S. (1989). The motivational impairment effect in the communication of deception. In Yuille, J., ed., *Credibility assessment*. Norwell, MA: Kluwer Academic. 51–70.

DePaulo, B. M. (1992). Nonverbal behavior and self-presentation. *Psychological Bulletin* 111(2):203–243.

Duncan, S., and Fiske, D. W. (1977). *Face-to-Face Interaction: Research, Methods and Theory*. Hillsdale, New Jersey: Lawrence Erlbaum.

Duncan, S. (1983). Studies of structure and individual differences. In Wiemann, J. M., and Harrison, R. P., eds., *Nonverbal Interaction*. London: Sage. 149–177.

Dybkjær, L., Berman, S., Kipp, M., Olsen, M. W., Pirrelli, V., Reithinger, N., and Soria, C. (2001). ISLE Deliverable D11.1: Survey of Existing Tools, Standards and User Needs for Annotation of Natural Interaction and Multimodal Data. Technical report, NISLab, Denmark.

Efron, D. (1941). *Gesture and Environment*. New York: King's Crown Press.

Efron, D. (1972). *Gesture, Race and Environment*. Den Haag: Mouton, second edition. New edition of "Gesture and Environment".

Ehlich, K., and Rehbein, J. (1976). Halbinterpretative Arbeitstranskiptionen (HIAT). *Linguistische Berichte* 45:21–41.

Ehlich, K. (1992). HIAT – a transcription system for discourse data. In Edwards, J. A., and Lampert, M. D., eds., *Talking Data: Transcription and Coding in Discourse Research*. Hillsdale, NJ: Erlbaum. 123–148.

Ekman, P., and Friesen, W. V. (1969). The Repertoire of Nonverbal Behavior: Categories, Origins, and Coding. *Semiotica* 1:49–98.

Ekman, P., and Friesen, W. V. (1972). Hand movements. *Journal of Communication* 22:353–374.

Ekman, P., and Friesen, W. V. (1975). *Unmasking the Face: A guide to recognizing emotions from facial clues*. New York: Prentice-Hall.

Ekman, P., and Friesen, W. V. (1978). *Facial Action Coding System*. Palo Alto, CA: Consulting Psychologists Press, Inc.

Ekman, P., Friesen, W. V., and O'Sullivan, M. (1988). Smiles When Lying. *Journal of Personality and Social Psychology* 54(3):414–420.

Everitt, B. S., Landau, S., and Leese, M. (2001). *Cluster Analysis*. Edward Arnold, forth edition.

Fast, J. (1970). *Body Language*. New York: M. Evans and Company.

Finkler, W., and Lutzky, O. (1996). MORPHIX. In Hausser, R., ed., *Linguistische Verifikation. Dokumentation zur ersten Morpholympics 1994*, 67–88. Tübingen: Niemeyer.

Finkler, W., and Neumann, G. (1986). MORPHIX. ein hochportabler Lemmatisierungsmodul fr das Deutsche. Technical Report Forschungsbericht (8), Universität des Saarlandes, FB Informatik, Saarbrücken.

Freedman, N., and Hoffman, S. (1967). Kinetic behavior in altered clinical states: Approach to objective analysis of motor behavior during clinical interviews. *Perceptual and Motor Skills* 27:527–539.

Freedman, N. (1977). Hands, words and mind: On the structuralization of body movements during discourse and the capacity for verbal representation. In Freedman, N., and Grand, S., eds., *Communicative Structures. A Psychoanalytic Interpretation of Communication*. New York: Plenum Press. 219–235.

Frey, S., and Pool, J. (1976). A new approach to the analysis of visible behavior. Technical Report 1976-2, University of Berlin.

Frey, S., Hirsbrunner, H. P., Florin, A., Daw, W., and Crawford, R. (1983). A unified approach to the investigation of nonverbal and verbal behavior in communication research. In Doise, W., and Moscovici, S., eds., *Current Issues in European Social Psychology*. Cambridge: Cambridge University Press. 143–199.

Frey, S. (1999). *Die Macht des Bildes: der Einfluß der nonverbalen Kommunikation auf Kultur und Politik*. Bern: Verlag Hans Huber.

Gebhard, P., Kipp, M., Klesen, M., and Rist, T. (2003). Authoring scenes for adaptive, interactive performances. In *Proceedings of the Second International Joint Conference on Autonomous Agents and Multiagent Systems*, 725–732.

Gebhard, P. (2001). Enhancing embodied intelligent agents with affective user modelling. In Vassileva, J., and Gmytrasiewicz, P., eds., *Proceedings of the 8th International Conference on User Modeling (UM2001), Doctoral Consortium Summary*, 271–273. Berlin, Heidelberg: Springer.

Gottlieb, H. (2002). The jack principles of the interactive conversation interface.

Gottman, J. M., and Roy, A. K. (1990). *Sequential Analysis: A Guide for Behavioral Researchers*. Cambridge: Cambridge University Press.

Grammer, K., Filova, V., and Fieder, M. (1997). The communication paradox and possible solutions. towards a radical empiricism. In Schmitt, A., Atzwanger, K., Grammer, K., and Schaefer, K., eds., *New Aspects of Human Ethology*. London, New York: Plenum Press.

Gratch, J., Rickel, J., André, E., Badler, N., Cassell, J., and Petajan, E. (2002). Creating interactive virtual humans: Some assembly required. *IEEE Intelligent Systems* 54–63.

Grosz, B. (1981). Focusing and description in natural language dialogues. In Joshi, A., Webber, B., and Sag, I., eds., *Elements of Discourse Understanding*. New York: Cambridge University Press. 84–105.

Hajičová, E. (1993). *Issues of sentence structure and discourse patterns, volume 2 of Theoretical and Computational Linguistics*. Prague, Czech Republic: Charles University Press.

Halliday, M. (1967). *Intonation and Grammar in British English*. The Hague: Mouton.

Halliday, M. A. K. (1973). *Explorations in the Functions of Language*. London: Edward Arnold.

Hanke, T., and Prillwitz, S. (1995). SyncWRITER: Integrating video into the transcription and analysisof sign language. In Bos, H., and Schermer, G., eds., *Sign Language Research 1994: Proceedings of the Fourth European Congress on Sign Language Research*, 303–312. Hamburg: Signum.

Hienz, H., Bauer, B., and Kraiss, K.-F. (1999). HMM-based continuous sign language recoginition using stochastic grammars. In Braffort, A., Forest, F., Gherbi, R., Gibet, S., Richardson, J., and Teil, D., eds., *Proceedings of the 3rd Gesture Workshop: Towards a Gesture-Based Communication in Human-Computer Interaction (GW99)*, 185–196.

Hobbs, J. R. (1979). Coherence and coreference. *Cognitive Science* 3:67–90.

Hofmann, F. G., Heyer, P., and Hommel, G. (1998). Velocity profile based recognition of dynamic gestures with discrete hidden markov models. In Wachsmuth, I., and Fröhlich, M., eds., *Gesture and Sign Language in Human Computer-Interaction: International Gesture Workshop Bielefeld 1997, Proceedings*. Berlin: Springer. 81–95.

Hovy, E. H. (1990). Parsimonious and profligate approaches to the question of discourse structure relations. In *Proceedings of the 5th International Workshop on Language Generation*, 128–136.

Izard, C. (1990). Facial expressions and the regulation of emotions. *Journal of Personality and Social Psychology* 58(3):487–498.

Janin, A., Baron, D., Edwards, J., Ellis, E., Gelbart, D., Morgan, N., Peskin, B., Pfau, T., Shriberg, E., Stolcke, A., and Wooters, C. (2003). The ICSI Meeting Corpus. In *Proceedings of the International Conference on Acoustics, Speech and Signal Processing*.

Jelinek, F. (1990). Self-organized language modeling for speech recognition. In Waibel, A., and Lee, K.-F., eds., *Readings in Speech Recognition*. San Mateo, California: Morgan Kaufmann. 450–506.

Johnson, H. G., Ekman, P., and Friesen, W. V. (1975). Communicative Body Movements: American Emblems. *Semiotica* 15:335–353.

Jorns, U. S. (1979). Kodierung und Sinnzuschreibung bei der Notation nichtverbaler Phänomene dargestellt an Beispielen von Kopfhaltungen und Gesichtsbewegungen. *Zeitschrift für Semiotik* 1:225–249.

Joshi, A. K., Levy, L., and Takahashi, M. (1975). Tree adjoining grammars. *Journal of the Computer and System Sciences* 10:136–163.

Kendon, A. (1978). Differential perception and attentional frame: Two problems for investigation. *Semiotica* 24(3/4):305–315.

Kendon, A. (1980). Gesticulation and speech: Two aspects of the process of utterance. In Key, M. R., ed., *Nonverbal Communication and Language*. The Hague: Mouton. 207–227.

Kendon, A. (1981). Geography of gesture. *Semiotica* 37(1/2):129–163.

Kendon, A. (1983). Gesture and Speech. How They Interact. In Wiemann, J. M., and Harrison, R. P., eds., *Nonverbal Interaction*. London: Sage. 13–45.

Kendon, A. (1995). Gestures as illocutionary and discourse structure markers in Southern Italian conversation. *Journal of Pragmatics* 23:247–279.

Kendon, A. (1996). An Agenda for Gesture Studies. *The Semiotic Review of Books* 7(3):8–12.

Kipp, M. (2001a). Analyzing Individual Nonverbal Behavior for Synthetic Character Animation. In Cavé, C., Guaïtella, I., and Santi, S., eds., *Oralité et Gestualité. Actes du colloque ORAGE 2001*, 240–244. Paris: L'Harmattan.

Kipp, M. (2001b). Anvil – a Generic Annotation Tool for Multimodal Dialogue. In *Proceedings of the 7th European Conference on Speech Communication and Technology (Eurospeech)*, 1367–1370.

Kipp, M. (2001c). From Human Gesture to Synthetic Action. In *Proceedings of the Workshop on "Multimodal Communication and Context in Embodied Agents" held in conjunction with the Fifth International Conference on Autonomous Agents (AGENTS)*, 9–14.

Kita, S., van Gijn, I., and van der Hulst, H. (1998). Movement phases in signs and co-speech gestures, and their transcription by human coders. In Wachsmuth, I., and Fröhlich, M., eds., *Gesture and Sign Language in Human-Computer Interaction*, 23–35. Berlin: Springer.

Klesen, M., Kipp, M., Gebhard, P., and Rist, T. (2003). Staging exhibitions: Methods and tools for modeling narrative structure to produce interactive performances with virtual actors. *Virtual Reality. Special Issue on Storytelling in Virtual Environments* 7(1). To appear.

Knott, A., and Dale, R. (1994). Using linguistic phenomena to motivate a set of coherence relations. *Discourse Processes* 18(1):35–62.

Koons, D. B., Sparrell, C. J., and Thórisson, K. R. (1993). Integrating simultaneous input from speech, gaze and hand gestures. In Maybury, M., ed., *Intelligent Multimedia Interfaces*. Cambridge, Mass.: MIT Press. 257–276.

Kopp, S., and Wachsmuth, I. (2000). A knowledge-based approach for lifelike gesture animation. In *Proceedings of the 14th European Conference on Artificial Intelligence (ECAI)*, 661–667.

Kopp, S., and Wachsmuth, I. (2002). Model-based animation of coverbal gesture. In *Proceedings of Computer Animation*, 252–257. Geneva, Switzerland: IEEE Computer Society.

Krandstedt, A., Kopp, S., and Wachsmuth, I. (2002). MURML: A multimodal utterance representation markup language for conversational agents. In *Proceedings of the Workshop on "Embodied Conversational Agents" held in conjunction with The First International Joint Conference on Autonomous Agents and Multi-Agent Systems (AAMAS)*, 29–34.

Krauss, R. M., Morrel-Samuels, P., and Colasante, C. (1991). Do Conversational Hand Gestures Communicate? *Journal of Personality and Social Psychology* 61:743–754.

Krauss, R. M., Dushay, R. A., Chen, Y., and Rauscher, F. (1995). The Communicative Value of Conversational Hand Gestures. *Journal of Experimental Social Psychology* 31:533–552.

Krauss, R. M., Chen, Y., and Chawla, P. (1996). Nonverbal behavior and nonverbal communication: What do conversational hand gestures tell us? In Zanna, M., ed., *Advances in experimental social psychology*. San Diego, CA: Academic Press. 389–450.

Krauss, R. M., Chen, Y., and Gottesman, R. F. (2000). Lexical Gestures and Lexical Access: A Process Model. In McNeill, D., ed., *Language and Gesture*. New York: Cambridge University Press. 261–283.

Krenn, B., Pirker, H., Grice, M., Baumann, S., Piwek, P., van Deemter, K., Schröder, M., Klesen, M., and Gstrein, E. (2002). Generation of multimodal dialogue for net environments. In Busemann, S., ed., *Proceedings der 6. Konferenz zur Verarbeitung natrlicher Sprache (KONVENS'02)*, 91–98.

Kruijff, G.-J. M. (2001). *A Categorial-Modal Architecture of Informativity: Dependency Grammar Logic and Information Structure*. Ph.D. Dissertation, Charles University, Prague, Czech Republic.

Kruppa, M., Krüger, A., Rocchi, C., Stock, O., and Zancanaro, M. (2003). Seamless personalized TV-like presentations on mobile and stationary devices in a museum. In *Proceedings of The Seventh International Cultural Heritage Informatics Meeting (ICHIM)*.

Laird, J. E., Newell, A., and Rosenbloom, P. S. (1987). SOAR: An architecture for general intelligence. *Artificial Intelligence* 33:1–64.

Latoschik, M. E., Fröhlich, M., Jung, B., and Wachsmuth, I. (1998). Utilize speech and gestures to realize natural interaction in a virtual environment. In *Proceedings of the 24th Annual Conference of the IEEE Industrial Electronics Society IECON98*, 2028–2033.

Lee, S., Badler, J., and Badler, N. (2002). Eyes alive. In *ACM Transactions on Graphics - Special Issue, Proceedings of SIGGRAPH 2002*, 637–644. San Antonio, TX: ACM Press.

Lester, J. C., Converse, S. A., Kahler, S. E., Barlow, S. T., Stone, B. A., and Bhogal, R. (1997a). The persona effect: Affective impact of animated pedagogical agents. In *Proceedings of CHI'97 Human Factors in Computing Systems*, 359–366. New York: ACM Press.

Lester, J. C., Converse, S. A., Stone, B. A., Kahler, S. E., and Barlow, S. T. (1997b). Animated pedagogical agents and problem-solving effectiveness: A large-scale empirical evaluation. In *Proceedings of the Eighth World Conference on Artificial Intelligence in Education*, 23–30. Amsterdam: IOS Press.

Lester, J. C., Voerman, J. L., Towns, S. G., and Callaway, C. B. (1997c). Cosmo: A life-like animated pedagogical agent with deictic believability. In *Proceedings of the Workshop on Animated Interface Agents: Making them intelligent (IJCAI 1997)*, 61–69.

Lester, J. C., Stone, B. A., and Stelling, G. D. (1999). Lifelike pedagogical agents for mixed-initiaitive problem solving in constructivist learning environments. *User Modeling and User-Adapted Interaction* 9:1–44.

Levelt, W. J. M. (1989). *Speaking: From Intention to Articulation*. ACL-MIT Press Series in Natural-Language Processing. Cambridge, MA: MIT Press.

Lindner, C. (2003). *Avatare – Digitale Sprecher für Business und Marketing*. Berline: Springer.

Linke, A. (1985). *Gespräche im Fernsehen. Eine diskursanalytische Untersuchung. (Züricher Germanistische Studien; Bd. 1.)*. Bern, Frankfurt, New York: Peter Lang.

Loehr, D., and Harper, L. (2003). Commonplace tools for studying commonplace interactions: practitioners' notes on entry-level video analysis. *Visual Communication* 2(2):225–233.

MacWhinney, B. (1995). *The CHILDES Project*. Hillsdale, NJ: Lawrence Erlbaum.

Maeda, M., Horiuchi, Y., and Ichikawa, A. (2003). Analysis of correlation between interlocutors' gestures in spontaneous speech. In *Information Processing Society of Japan (IPSJ) SIGNotes Contents, Human Interface*, volume 102.

Magnenat-Thalmann, N., and Moccozet, L. (1998). Virtual Humans on Stage. In Heudin, J., ed., *Virtual Worlds: Synthetic Universes, Digital Life and Complexity*. New England Complex Systems Institute Series on Complexity. 95–126. Chapter 4.

Magno Caldognetto, E., and Poggi, I. (1999). The score of multimodal communication and the goals of political discourse. *Quaderni dell'Istituto di Fonetica e Dialettologia* 1. CD-ROM.

Magno Caldognetto, E., and Poggi, I. (2002). Una proposta per la segmentazione e l'etichettatura di segnali multimodali. In *Proceedings of the VIIIth Congress AI*IA (Associazione Italiana Intelligenza Artificiale)*.

Mann, W. C., and Thompson, S. A. (1988). Rhetorical Structure Theory: Toward a functional theory of text organization. *Text* 8(3):243–281.

Martell, C. (2002). FORM: An extensible, kinematically-based gesture annotation scheme. In *Proceedings of the Seventh International Conference on Spoken Language Processing (ICSLP 02)*, 353–356.

Martin, J.-C., and Kipp, M. (2002). Annotating and Measuring Multimodal Behaviour – Tycoon Metrics in the Anvil Tool. In *Proceedings of the Third International Conference on Language Resources and Evaluation (LREC)*, 31–35.

Martin, J.-C. (2002). Measuring cooperations between modalities in human multimodal behavior. In *Proceedings of the 4th International Conference on Methods and Techniques in Behavioral Research (MB 2002)*, 164–165.

McBreen, H., Anderson, J., and Jack, M. (2001). Evaluating 3D embodied conversational agents in contrasting VRML retail applications. In *Proceedings of the Workshop on "Multimodal Communication and Context in Embodied Agents" held in conjunction with the Fifth International Conference on Autonomous Agents (AGENTS)*, 83–87.

McBreen, H. (2001). Embodied Conversational Agents in E-Commerce Applications. In Dautenhahn, K., ed., *Socially Intelligent Agents: building relationships with computers and robots*. Dordrecht: Kluwer. 267–274.

McClave, E. (1994). Gestural beats: The rhythm hypothesis. *Journal of Psycholinguistic Research* 23(1):45–65.

McEnery, T., and Wilson, A. (1996). *Corpus Linguistics*. Edinburgh: Edinburgh University Press.

McGinley, H., LeFevre, R., and McGinley, P. (1975). The Influence of a Communicator's Body Position on Opinion Change in Others. *Journal of Personality and Social Psychology* 31(4):686–690.

McNeill, D., and Duncan, S. D. (2000). Growth points in thinking-for-speaking. In McNeill, D., ed., *Language and Gesture*. Cambridge: Cambridge University Press. 141–161.

McNeill, D., Quek, F., McCullough, K.-E., Duncan, S., Furuyama, N., Bryll, R., Ma, X.-F., and Ansari, R. (2001). Catchments, prosody and discourse. *Gesture* 1(1):9–33.

McNeill, D. (1985). So you think gestures are nonverbal? *Psychological Review* 92:350–371.

McNeill, D. (1992). *Hand and Mind: What Gestures Reveal about Thought*. Chicago: University of Chicago Press.

Mehrabian, A. (1972). *Nonverbal Communication*. Chicago: Aldine Atherton Inc.

Milde, J.-T. (2002). Creating multimodal, multilevel annotated corpora with TASX. In *Proceedings of the International CLASS Workshop on Natural, Intelligent and Effective Interaction in Multimodal Dialogue Systems*, 120–126.

Miller, G. A., Beckwith, R., Felbaum, C., Gross, D., and Miller, K. (1990). Introduction to WordNet: an on-line lexical database. *International Journal of Lexicography* 3(4):235–244.

Molcho, S. (1983). *Körpersprache*. München: Mosaik Verlag.

Molet, T., Aubel, A., Capin, T., Carion, S., Lee, E., Magnenat-Thalmann, N., Noser, H., Pandzic, I. S., Sannier, G., and Thalmann, D. (1999). Anyone for tennis? *Presence* 8(2):140–156.

Morris, D. (1994). *Bodytalk. The Meaning of Human Gestures*. New York: Crown Trade Paperbacks.

Müller, C. (1998). *Redebegleitende Gesten: Kulturgeschichte, Theorie, Sprachvergleich.* Berlin: Berlin Verlag.

Müller, J. (2000). *Persona: Ein anthropomorpher Präsentationsagent für Internet-Anwendungen.* Ph.D. Dissertation, Universität des Saarlandes, Saarbrücken.

Nakatani, C., Grosz, B., Ahn, D., and Hirschberg, J. (1995). Instructions for annotating discourses. Technical Report TR-21-95, Center for Research in Comp. Tech., Harvard University, MA.

Nass, C., Isbister, K., and Lee, E.-J. (2000). Truth is beauty: Researching embodied conversational agents. In Cassell, J., Sullivan, J., Prevost, S., and Churchill, E., eds., *Embodied Conversational Agents.* Cambridge, MA: MIT Press. 374–402.

Noma, T., and Badler, N. (1997). A Virtual Human Presenter. In *Proceedings of the Workshop on "Animated Interface Agents" held in conjunction with the Fifteenth International Joint Conference on Artificial Intelligence (IJCAI)*, 45–51.

Noma, T., Zhao, L., and Badler, N. (2000). Design of a Virtual Human Presenter. *IEEE Journal of Computer Graphics and Applications* 20(4):79–85.

Paiva, A., Machado, I., and Martinho, C. (1999). Enriching Pedagogical Agents with Emotional Behavior: The Case of Vincent. In *AI-ED 99 Workshop Proceedings "Animated and Personified Pedagogical Agents"*, 47–55.

Payrató, L. (1993). A pragmatic view on autonomous gestures: A first repertoire of Catalan emblems. *Journal of Pragmatics* 20:193–216.

Pedelty, L. L. (1987). *Gesture in Aphasia.* Ph.D. Dissertation, Department of Behavioral Sciences, University of Chicago.

Pelachaud, C., and Poggi, I. (2002). Subtleties of facial expressions in embodied agents. *Journal of Visualization and Computer Animation* 13(5):301–312.

Pelachaud, C., Badler, N. I., and Steedman, M. (1996). Generating Facial Expressions for Speech. *Cognitive Science* 20:1–46.

Pelachaud, C., Carofiglio, V., Carolis, B. D., de Rosis, F., and Poggi, I. (2002). Embodied contextual agent in information delivering application. In *Proceedings of the First International Joint Conference on Autonomous Agents and Multi-Agent Systems (AAMAS 02)*, 758–765.

Pelachaud, C. (2003). Communicative functions. Slides for the Tutorial on "Virtual Characters" at the 16th International Conference on Computer Animation and Social Agents (CASA 03).

Pérez-Parent, M. (2002). Collection, handling, and analysis of classroom recordings data: using the original acoustic signal as the primary source of evidence. *Reading Working Papers in Linguistics* 6:245–254.

Perlin, K., and Goldberg, A. (1996). Improv: A System for Scripting Interactive Actors in Virtual Worlds. *Computer Graphics* 29(3).

Pierrehumbert, J., and Hirschberg, J. (1990). The meaning of intonational contours in the interpretation of discourse. In Cohen, P. R., Morgan, J., and Pollack, M. E., eds., *Intentions in Communication*. Cambridge, MA: MIT Press. 271–311.

Poggi, I., and Magno Caldognetto, E. (1999). A procedure for the generation of gesture in bimodal communication. In Santi, S., Guaitella, I., Cavé, C., and Konopczynski, G., eds., *Proceedings of "Oralité et Gestualité"*.

Poggi, I., Pelachaud, C., and de Rosis, F. (2000). Eye Communication in a Conversational 3D Synthetic Agent. *AI Communications* 13(3):169–181.

Poggi, I. (1983). La mano a borsa: Analisi semantica di un gesto emblematico olofrastico. In Attili, G., and Bitti, P. E. R., eds., *Comunicare senza parole*. Rome: Bulzoni. 219–238.

Posner, R. (1993). Believing, causing, intending: The basis for a hierarchy of sign concepts in the reconstruction of communication. In Jorna, R. J., van Heusden, B., and Posner, R., eds., *Signs, Search, and Communication: Semiotic Aspects of Artificial Intelligence*. Berlin, New York: deGruyter. 215–270.

Poyatos, F. (1975). Gesture inventories: Fieldwork, methodology and problems. *Semiotica* 13:199–227.

Prendinger, H., and Ishizuka, M., eds. (2003). *Life-Like Characters – Tools, Affective Functions, and Applications*. Heidelberg: Springer.

Quek, F., and McNeill, D. (2000). A multimedia system for temporally situated perceptual psycholinguistic analysis. In *Proceedings of the 3rd International Conference on Methods and Techniques in Behavioral Research, Measuring Behavior 2000*, 215.

Reeves, B., and Nass, C. (1996). *The Media Equation: How People Treat Computers, Television, and New Media Like Real People and Places*. Stanford, CA: CSLI Publications.

Reithinger, N., and Klesen, M. (1997). Dialogue act classification using language models. In Kokkinakis, G., Fakotakis, N., and Dermatas, E., eds., *Proceedings of the 5th European Conference on Speech Communication and Technology (Eurospeech 97)*, 2235–2238.

Rickel, J., and Johnson, W. L. (1999). Animated agents for procedural training in virtual reality: Perception, cognition, and motor control. *Applied Artificial Intelligence* 13:343–382.

Rickel, J., Marsella, S., Gratch, J., Hill, R., Traum, D., and Swartout, W. (2002). Toward a new generation of virtual humans for interactive experiences. *IEEE Intelligent Systems* 17(4):32–38.

Rimé, B., and Schiaratura, L. (1991). Gesture and speech. In Feldman, R. S., and Rimé, B., eds., *Fundamentals of Nonverbal Behavior*. New York: Cambridge University Press. 239–281.

Rist, T., André, E., Baldes, S., Gebhard, P., Klesen, M., Kipp, M., Rist, P., and Schmitt, M. (2003). A review of the development of embodied presentation agents and their application fields. In Prendinger, H., and Ishizuka, M., eds., *Life-Like Characters – Tools, Affective Functions, and Applications*. Heidelberg: Springer. 377–404.

Sacks, H., Schegloff, E. A., and Jefferson, G. (1974). A Simplest Systematics for the Organization of Turn Taking for Conversation. *Language* 50:696–735.

Saitz, R. L., and Cervenka, E. J. (1972). *Handbook of Gestures: Colombia and the United States*. The Hague: Mouton, second edition.

Sampson, G., and McCarthy, D. (2002). *Readings in Corpus Linguistics*. London and NY: Continuum International.

Sanderson, P. M., Scott, J. J. P., Johnston, T., Mainzer, J., Watanabe, L. M., and James, J. M. (1994). MacSHAPA and the enterprise of Exploratory Sequential Data Analysis (ESDA). *International Journal of Human-Computer Studies* 41:633–668.

Schaumburg, H. (2001). Computers as tools or as social actors? – the users' perspective on anthropomorphic agents. *International Journal of Cooperative Information Systems. Double Special Issue on "Intelligent Information Agents: Theory and Applications"* 10(1,2):217–234.

Scheflen, A. E. (1964). The Significance of Posture in Communication Systems. *Psychiatry* 26:316–331.

Schegloff, E. A. (1984). On some gestures' relation to talk. In Atkinson, J. M., and Heritage, J., eds., *Structures of Social Action*. Cambridge: Cambridge University Press. 266–296.

Scherer, K. R., Wallbott, H. G., and Scherer, U. (1979). Methoden zur Klassifikation von Bewegungsverhalten: Ein funktionaler Ansatz. *Zeitschrift für Semiotik* 1:177–192.

Scherer, K. R. (1979). Personality markers in speech. In Scherer, K., and Giles, H., eds., *Social Markers in Speech*. Cambridge: Cambridge University Press. 147–209.

Schiel, F., Burger, S., Geumann, A., and Weilhammer, K. (1998). The Partitur Format at BAS. In *Proceedings of the First International Conference on Language Resources and Evaluation (LREC 98)*, 1295–1301.

Schiel, F., Steininger, S., and Türk, U. (2002). The SmartKom Multimodal Corpus at BAS. In *Proceedings of the Third International Conference on Language Resources and Evaluation (LREC 02)*.

Schiller, A., Teufel, S., Stckert, C., and Thielen, C. (1995). Vorläufige Guidelines für das Tagging deutscher Textcorpora mit STTS. Technical report, Universität Stuttgart, Institut fr maschinelle Sprachverarbeitung, and Seminar fr Sprachwissenschaft, Universität Tübingen.

Schmauks, D. (1991). *Deixis in der Mensch-Maschine Interaktion*. Tübingen: Niemeyer.

Schmid, H. (1994). Probabilistic part-of-speech tagging using decision trees. In *Proceedings of the International Conference on New Methods in Language Processing*.

Schröder, M., Cowie, R., Douglas-Cowie, E., Westerdijk, M., and Gielen, S. (2001). Acoustic correlates of emotion dimensions in view of speech synthesis. In *Proceedings of the 7th European Conference on Speech Communication and Technology (Eurospeech)*, 87–90.

Schukat-Talamazzini, E. G., Kuhn, T., and Niemann, H. (1994). Speech recognition for spoken dialogue systems. In Niemann, H., de Mori, R., and Hanrieder, G., eds., *Progress and Prospects of Speech Research and Technology: Proceedings of the CRIM/FORWISS Workshop*, 110–120. St. Augustin: Infix.

Searle, J. R. (1969). *Speech Acts*. London: Cambridge University Press.

Sgall, P., Hajičová, E., and Benešová, E. (1973). *Topic, Focus, and Generative Semantics*. Kronberg/Taunus.

Soria, C., Bernsen, N. O., Cadée, N., Carletta, J., Dybkjær, L., Evert, S., Heid, U., Isard, A., Kolodnytsky, M., Lauer, C., Lezius, W., Noldus, L. P. J. J., Pirelli, V., Reithinger, N., and Vögele, A. (2002). Advanced tools for the study of natural interactivity. In *Proceedings of the Third International Conference on Language Resources and Evaluation (LREC 02)*, 357–363.

Steedman, M. (2000). Information structure and the syntax-phonology interface. *Linguistic Inquiry* 34:649–689.

Steedman, M. (2001). Information-structural semantics for english intonation. Paper to LSA Summer Institute Workshop on Topic and Focus.

Steininger, S., Schiel, F., and Louka, K. (2001). Gestures during overlapping speech in multimodal human-machine dialogues. In *Proceedings of the International Workshop on Information Presentation and Natural Multimodal Dialogue*.

Steininger, S. (2001). Labeling of gestures in SmartKom - concept of the coding system. Technical Report Nr. 2, SmartKom.

Stokoe, W. C. (1960). Sign language structure: An outline of the visual communication system of the American deaf. *Studies in linguistics, Occasional papers* 8.

Swartout, W., Hill, R., Gratch, J., Johnson, W. L., Kyriakis, C., LaBore, C., Lindheim, R., Marsella, S., Miraglia, D., Moore, B., Morie, J., Rickel, J., Thiébaux, M., Tuch, L., Whitney, R., and Douglas, J. (2001). Toward the holodeck: Integrating graphics, sound, character and story. In *Proceedings of the Fifth International Conference on Autonomous Agents*, 409–416.

Thomas, F., and Johnston, O. (1981). *The Illusion of Life: Disney Animation*. New York: Hyperion Press.

Tomkins, S. (1962). *Affect, Imagery, Consciousness. Vol. 1 + 2*. New York: Springer.

Tuite, K. (1993). The production of gesture. *Semiotica* 1/2:83–105.

van Hooff, J. A. R. A. M. (1982). Categories and sequences of behavior: methods of description and analysis. In Scherer, K. R., and Ekman, P., eds., *Handbook of Methods in Nonverbal Behavior Research*. Cambridge: Cambridge University Press. 362–439.

van Meel, J. M. (1984). Kinesic strategies in representation and attention-deployment. In *Paper presented at the Symposium on the Relation of Language, Thought and Gestures*.

van Mulken, S., André, E., and Müller, J. (1998). The Persona Effect: How Substantial is it? In *Proceedings of the British Computer Society Conference on Human Computer Interaction (HCI 98)*, 53–66.

Vintar, Š., and Kipp, M. (2001). Multi-track annotation of terminology using anvil. In *Eurolan Workshop on Multi-layer Corpus-based Analysis*, 1–13.

Wachsmuth, I., and Fröhlich, M., eds. (1998). *Gesture and Sign Language in Human Computer-Interaction: International Gesture Workshop Bielefeld 1997, Proceedings.* Berlin: Springer.

Wahlster, W. (1991). User and discourse models for multimodal conversation. In Sullivan, J., and Tyler, S., eds., *Intelligent User Interfaces.* Reading, Mass.: Addison-Wesley. 45–67.

Wahlster, W., ed. (2000). *Verbmobil: Foundations of Speech-to-Speech Translation.* Berlin: Springer.

Wahlster, W. (2002). SmartKom: Fusion and fission of speech, gestures, and facial expressions. In *Proceedings of the First International Workshop on Man-Machine Symbiotic Systems*, 213–225.

Wahlster, W. (2003). SmartKom: Symmetric multimodality in an adaptive and reusable dialogue shell. In *Proceedings of the Human Computer Interaction Status Conference*, 47–62. Berlin: DLR.

Walker, P. M. B., ed. (1991). *Chambers Science and Technology Dictionary.* Edinburgh, New York: Chambers.

Webb, R. (1997). *Linguistic Properties of Metaphoric Gestures.* New York: UMI.

Weinrich, L. (1992). *Verbale und nonverbale Strategien in Fernsehgesprächen.* Tübingen: Max Niemeyer Verlag.

Witkin, A., and Kass, M. (1988). Spacetime Constraints. *Computer Graphics* 22:159–168.

Yan, H. (2000). Paired speech and gesture generation in embodied conversational agents. Master's Thesis, MIT Media Lab.

Appendix A

Linguistic Preprocessing

A.1 Part-of-speech Tagging

For a number of words it is necessary annotate the part-of-speech (POS). The POS describes a word's grammatical function and can be found by looking at the word's direct surroundings. Therefore, the POS encodes a certain amount of a word's context which in some cases allows to disambiguate words that have different meanings when considered in isolation. The *Stuttgart-Tübingen Tagset* (STTS) is a widely used set of POS categories. A subset of STTS, plus one new tag, was taken to encode POS. Table A.1 shows the words coded, their possible POS categories and an example for each category to demonstrate the ambiguity of the words. Table A.2 summarizes and explains the POS categories. The descriptions were taken from Schiller et al. (1995). The tag marked with an asterisk is new.

word(s)	tag	example
aber	ADV	das ist **aber**/ADV nett
	KONS∗	**Aber**/KONS als ich nach Hause kam
als	KOKOM	er arbeitet **als**/KOKOM Bauer
	KOUS	**als**/KOUS er heimkam
	KON	sowohl Kinder **als**/KON auch Frauen
doch	ADV	das geht **doch**/ADV nicht
	PTKANT	**Doch**/PTKANT
da	KOUS	**da**/KOUS du kommst, bleibe ich
	ADV	ich bin **da**/ADV
der, die, das	ART	**die**/ART Frau
	PRELS	der Mann, **der**/PRELS **das**/PDS gesagt hat
	PDS	**das**/PDS weiß ich nicht
		der/PDS, der **das**/PDS sagt, lügt
dies	PDAT	**dieses**/PDAT Buch
	PDS	**dies**/PDS ist ein Buch
ein	ART	ich habe **eine**/ART Frage
	CARD	**ein**/CARD oder **zwei**/CARD Dinge
	ADJA	der **eine**/ADJA und der **andere**/ADJA Arm
	PDS	das ist **einer**/PDS, der ihr gefällt
	PIS	die **einen**/PIS und die **anderen**/PIS sind weg
		ich habe **eins**/PIS gesehen
ja	ADV	das ist **ja**/ADV komisch
	ITJ	**ja**/ITJ, was ich sagen wollte…
	PTKANT	**Ja**/PTKANT
nein	ITJ	**nein**/ITJ, was ich sagen wollte…
	PTKANT	**Nein**/PTKANT
nur	KONS∗	**Nur**/KONS was kann ich dafür?
	ADV	es ist **nur**/ADV sehr wenig
und	KON	du **und**/KON ich
	KONS∗	**Und**/KONS was soll man machen
		Er hat gesagt **und**/KONS es ist geschehen
was	PRELS	das/PDS, **was**/PRELS er gesagt hat
	PWS	er fragt, **was**/PWS es gibt
		was/PWS ist los?
		er weiß, **was**/PWS er will
	PIS	er hat schon **was**/PIS gemacht (etwas, sowas)
welche	PRELS	die Frage, **welche**/PRELS gestellt wurde
	PWAT	**welchen**/PWAT Hut hast du ausgesucht
	PWS	**welchen**/PWS von beiden hast du gesehn?
wie	KOKOM	er ist nicht so schnell **wie**/KOKOM du
	PWAV	**Wie**/PWAV geht es dir?
	KOUS	**wie**/KOUS vorhin gesagt…
zu	PTKA	er ist **zu**/PTKA groß
	PTKZU	er bittet ihn **zu**/PTKZU **kommen**/VVINF
	PTKVZ	das trifft **zu**/PTKVZ
	APPR	ich gehe **zu**/APPR meiner Mutter

Table A.1: *Words that were additionally coded with POS.*

POS tag	description
ADJA	attributing adjectives
ADV	adverb
APPR	preposition
ART	article
CARD	cardinal number
ITJ	interjection
KOKOM	comparison particle
KON	coordinating conjunction
KONS*	leading conjunction (or between two full SV clauses)
KOUS	subordinating conjunction
PDS	demonstrative pronoun
PDAT	attributing demonstrative pronoun
PIS	substituting indefinite pronoun
PRELS	substituting relative pronoun
PTKA	particle next to adverb/adjective
PTKANT	response particle
PTKVZ	separated verb prefix
PTKZU	particle for infinitive verbs
PWAT	attributing interrogative pronoun
PWAV	adverbial interrogative pronoun
PWS	substituting interrogative pronoun

Table A.2: *Description of all used part-of-speech (POS) tags.*

A.2 Semantic Tags

Tables A.3 to A.11 show the semantic tags used in offline processing (see Section 10.2) and online generation (see Section 11.3). It is essentially a clustering of words that serves the generalization of concepts. Note that this mapping makes the generation algorithm in principle language-independent. The first column shows the semantic tag or cluster name. The second column lists the member of this tag/cluster. Sometimes, whole phrases were mapped to a single tag. In this case, words were concatenated with underscores to protect the phrase from being dissembled during the mapping. When the POS was needed to disambiguate words the POS is included in the form "word/POS". There are still ambiguities in the sense that a word belonging to a semantic tag has readings not subsumed by the tag. These cases were not disambiguated here (with POS or otherwise) because in the LQ data the respective words occurred only in the reading reflected by the tag. In this sense, the semantic tags need some reworking to make them applicable to other data.

tag	members
ADDRESSEE	Ihnen
	Sie
AFFECT	liebend
	möchten
	Gefühl
	Liebe
	Wehmut
	sehnen
	spüren
AFTER_BEHIND	nach
AGGRESSION	Aggressivität
	Held
	provozierend
	Barrikade
	Temperament
	aggressiv
	kämpfend
	widersetzen
	zwingen
AGREEMENT	Recht geben
	einverstanden
	ja/PKANT
	jawohl
	können man erlauben
	nicht zu unrecht
	richtig
	zu Recht
	zu recht
	zurecht
	zutreffen
APOLOGY	Entschuldigung
	entschuldigen
	mit Verlaub
	zugeben
ART	künstlerisch
	literarisch
	musikalisch
ATTENTION	aufmerksam
	aufpassen
	hinweisen
	interessant
	vor_allem
	vorsichtig
	wichtig

Table A.3: *All semantic categories and members.*

tag	members
BOOK	Buch
	Roman
	Werk
BOOKTITLE	Napoleanspiele
	Tristanakkord
CERTAINTY	eins/PIS v(sein) sicher
	wirklich
COGNITIVE	Phantasie
	begreifen
	denken
	hören
	kapieren
	lernen
	schreiben
	stumpf
	verblüfft
	verrückt
	verstört
	überlegen
CONJ_CAUSAL	also/KONS
	damit/KONS
	denn/KONS
	deshalb
	deswegen
	weil
CONJ_CONTRAST	aber/KONS
	allerdings/KONS
	dennoch/KONS
	jedoch
	nur/KONS
CONJ_SEQ	dann/KONS
	und/KONS
CONTAINER	Band
	Kapitel
DEFINITE	das/ART
	der/ART
	die/ART

Table A.4: *All semantic categories and members (ctd).*

tag	members
DEIC_HERE	daran
	darauf
	darüber
	heute
	hier
	jetzt
	da/ADV
	jenseits
	später
DEMONSTRATIVE	das/PDS
	dies/PDAT
	dies/PDS
	solch
DESTRUCT	Luft
	auflösen
	beenden
	gleichgültig
	streichen
	untergehen
	verbrennen
	zerfetzen
DISTANCE	Zwischenraum
	Zwischenzeit
	lang
	so weit
	soweit
	zwischen
DRINK	besaufen
EXTRAORDINARY	Ausbruch
	Explosion
	Höhepunkt
	ausgeprägt
	dramatisch
	eigen
	groß
	stark
	ungeheuer
	unglaublich

Table A.5: *All semantic categories and members (ctd).*

tag	members
GEO_LOCATION	Amerika
	DDR
	England
	Heidelberg
	Holland
	Land
	München
	New York
INDEFINITE	ein/ART
INDETERMINATE	Unterschied
	etwa
	etwas
	ich_glaube
	leise
	mag_sein
	manch
	mehr oder weniger
	oszillieren
	schwanken
	so_ungefähr
	unterschiedlich
	verschieden
INIT	zunächst einmal
INSULT	du Schwein
LOCATION	im Mittelpunkt
	in der Mitte
	ins Quartett
MANY	lauter
	recht_viel
	viel
MOREOVER	außerdem
	noch etwas
MOVEMENT	fahren
	fallen
	gehen
	geraten
	heranrücken
	kommen
	rausfliegen
	rauslenken
	rausschleudern
	verlaufen
	weglaufen
	zusammentun

Table A.6: *All semantic categories and members (ctd).*

tag	members
NEGATION	kein
	nein/PKANT
	nicht
	ohne
NEG_AFFECT	Eintönigkeit
	Hass
	Leiden
	Traurige
	Unglück
	abstoßend
	anwidern
	ekeln
	leiden
	unangenehm
	widerlich
	widert mich an
	Überdruss
	übel
NEG_ATTRIBUTE	Schuld
	eitel
	gering
	leichtsinnig
	schuld
	zu_schnell
NEG_EVAL	Kritik
	Unwillen
	abscheulich
	furchtbar
	hässlich
	leider
	maniriert
	nicht_gut
	schlecht
	schrecklich
	schwach
	unerträglich
NEG_TOTALITY	gar_nicht
	gar_nichts
	garnicht
	kein_Mensch
	nichts
	nie
	niemand
	überhaupt nicht
	überhaupt nichts

Table A.7: *All semantic categories and members (ctd).*

tag	members
NUMBER	dreihundert
	ein/CARD
	erst
	fünf
	hundert
	vier
	vierzehn
	zwei
	zweihundert
	zweit
OBJECT	Bild
	Figur
OTHER	ander
OTHER_HAND	andererseits
PAGE	Titelseite
	Umschlagseite
PERMANENCY	immer
	immer_wieder
	unentwegt
PERSON	Autor
	Erzähler
	Frau
	Frau_Löffler
	Hauptfigur
	Herr Busche
	Herr Karasek
	Ich-Erzähler
	Japaner
	Karasek
	Mann
	Romancier
	Tochter
	Vater
PERSUASION_PART	eigentlich

Table A.8: *All semantic categories and members (ctd).*

tag	members
PERS_NAME	Bertold Brecht
	Byron
	Carver
	Conrad
	Flaubert
	Ford Meadow Ford
	Gounaud
	Heine
	Hemingway
	Hölderlin
	Leon de Winter
	Margeriet de Moor
	Maupassant
	Mulich
	Noteboom
	Rilke
	Rivas
	Thomas Bernhard
	Wagner
PERS_PRONOUN_OTHER	er
	sie
PERS_PRONOUN_SELF	ich
	wir
POSSESSIVE_OTHER	deren
	dessen
	ihr
	sein
POSSESSIVE_SELF	mein
	unser
POS_AFFECT	Spaß
	erleichtert
	herrliche Atmosphäre
POS_ATTRIBUTE	Freundlichkeit
	fleißig

Table A.9: *All semantic categories and members (ctd).*

tag	members
POS_EVAL	Beste
	Vorliebe
	Vorzug
	beachtlich
	best
	fabelhaft
	gefallen
	gern
	glänzend
	großartig
	gut
	gut_sein
	hervorragend
	hocherfreulich
	hochinteressant
	intelligent
	lesbar
	nicht_schlecht
	ordentlich
	poetisch
	schön
	unvergesslich
	wunderbar
PRAYER	um Gotteswillen
PRECISION	bestimmt
	kurz
	rein
	wohl
PROCESS	anregen
	aufbrechen
	hervorbringen
	konzipieren
	machen
	produzieren
	schaffen
	spielen
	verändern
	übersetzen
QUEST_PART	warum
	was/PWS
RECEIVE	annehmen
SIMPLE	nur/ADV
	offenbar

Table A.10: *All semantic categories and members (ctd).*

tag	members
SPATIAL_FLAT	Ebene
	Niveau
	flach
	plan
SUBTLE	unaufdringlich
	zart
THERE_IS	es geben
	geben es
TOTALITY	all
	ganz
	gar
	jed
	voll
	völlig
	überall
TRANSCENDENCE	Dämonie
	Meisterwerk
TRASH	Mumpitz
	Quatsch
	dummes Zeug
UNIT	Jahr
	Seite
VERY	besonders
	deutlich
	sehr
	weitaus
	äußerst

Table A.11: *All semantic categories and members (ctd).*

Appendix B

LQ Gesture Lexicon

This section presents the shared gesture lexicon, i.e. all gesture lemmas, of the speakers MRR and HK, as assembled from the LQ data. This section displays 64 entries. Note, however, that the entry "Adaptors" represents five different subtypes that were used in annotation. The original annotation lexicon contains 68 entries.

The lexicon is structured according to the gesture classes: adaptors, emblems, deictics, iconics, metaphorics and beats. The order of classes follows the order of class annotation (Section 8.2). Within each class the lemmas are ordered alphabetically by name. Each gesture has the following information:

- **Video stills**: One or two frames from the LQ data that show MRR or HK perform the gesture. Not all gestures are documented with pictures.

- **Description**: A verbal description of the gesture.

- **Speech Sample**: A speech sample that co-occurred with this gesture in the LQ data. The underlined part is the part where the gesture's expressive phase (stroke, beats or independent hold) was performed. Only the current gesture is marked by underlining, other gestures are ignored for the sake of clarity. Nonverbal sounds are transcribed with square brackets. Commas and colons were added for readability. Question and exclamation marks indicate the respective intonational contours. Note that the picture must not necessarily be taken from the same stretch as the speech sample. Both were selected separately to obtain the most representative picture and speech sample each.

- **Features**: Description of the gesture's formational features. This point does not apply to adaptors (since there are no sub-categories) and to beat (since it is a rest class). The formational dimensions are

    - Hand shape (HS)
    - Hand location (Loc)

- Hand orientation (Orient): PTB = palm towards body, PAB = palm away from body, PU = palm up, PD = palm down, PI = palm sideways inward
- Hand/arm movement (Move): TB = towards body, AB = away from body, TS = to the side
- Bi-handedness (2H)
- Shoulder movement (Sh)
- Facial Expression (FE)

If the hand moves during the gesture, sometimes start and end position/shape are specified using an arrow symbol in-between. If only the end position/shape is a formational feature the end position/shape is signified with an arrow up front.

- **References**: References to this gesture in the research literature with names and possibly information on its meaning (decoding).

- **Similar**: List of gestures in the inventory that are similar to this one and could be possibly confused with it. However, similar gestures must be distinguishable in at least one formational feature.

- **LitQua**: Absolute and relative frequencies for speakers MRR and HK.

Note that this lexicon does not describe the meaning of its entries. In the approach of this work, gesture meaning is implicitly coded in the probabilistic rules contained in the gesture profiles. However, the speech sample given for each gesture usually gives a good impression of how the gesture might function in a conversation.

B.1   Adaptors

Description	Touching one's own body parts, for instance scratching the nose, rubbing the neck, touching one's ear lobe, hair, forehead. Also, touching objects like pen, cup, rubbing the chair's arm or the table surface.
References	Morris (1994: 42) lists the *ear scratch* as an "involuntary action" indicating confusion, and the *head scratch* (p. 143) as a "natural reaction to conflict" indicating puzzlement.
LitQua	MRR: 20 (2.6%), HK: 5 (1.7%)

B.2   Emblems

Emblem.Anticipation

Description	Open hand rotates back and forth at wrist. Palm directed away from body on the level of the head or slightly lower. Face may look sceptical.
Speech Sample	"man muss sehr aufpassen" (MRR, LQ2-1, 2:25)
Features	HS: open, Orient: PI, Loc: head, Move: wrist rotation.
References	—
Similar	Emblem.Chide, Emblem.More-or-less, Emblem.Wave
LitQua	MRR: 3 (0.4%)

Emblem.Attention

Description	Forefinger is shaken at someone or simply displayed, pointing up.
Speech Sample	"mir gefällt ganz besonders die letzte Geschichte" (MRR, LQ3-10, 0:09)
Features	HS: Forefinger.
References	Calbris (1990) finds two version: shaking for warning (see Emblem.Chide) and static for advise (Emblem.Attention). Saitz and Cervenka (1972) call it *attention* (Colombian gesture). Efron (1941) calls it *hey!* (Italian gesture). Webb (1997: 98) calls it *important point*. Morris (1994: 87) calls it *forefinger raise*, decoded as "pay attention!".
Similar	Emblem.Chide, Deictic.Addressee, Deictic.Space
LitQua	MRR: 35 (4.5%), HK: 14 (4.7%)

Emblem.Big

Description	Both hands are held at head level one shoulder width (or more) apart, palms facing each other.
Speech Sample	"und das ist wirklich ein so großer Roman in dem Zwischenraum" (HK, LQ3-8, 0:52)
Features	HS: open, Orient: PI, Loc: head-level/side, 2H
References	Efron (1941) calls it *so big!* (Italian gesture)
Similar	Meta.Frame, Meta.Walls
LitQua	HK: 1 (0.3%)

Emblem.Block

Description	Hand is positioned in front of the speaker, palm toward addressee, possibly in a straight movement to the side.
Speech Sample	"bitte schimpfen Sie mich nicht gleich aus" (HK, LQ1-5, 0:13)
Features	HS: open, Orient: PAB.
References	Saitz and Cervenka (1972) call it *stop* (US gesture). Weinrich (1992: 117) calls it *halt hand*. Webb (1997: 99) subsumes it under *none*.
Similar	Emblem.Refuse, Emblem.Wave
LitQua	MRR: 2 (0.3%), HK: 3 (1.0%)

Emblem.Chide

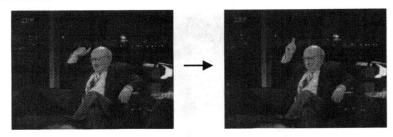

Description	Open hand (or forefinger) is shaken at somebody in an almost threatening manner.
Speech Sample	"<u>schreibt nicht über New York!</u>, es ist <u>sehr gefährlich</u> über New York zu schreiben" (MRR, LQ1-6, 2:05)
Features	HS: open or forefinger, Orient: PTB or PI.
References	Calbris (1990) ascribed the meaning *warning* to this gesture. Saitz and Cervenka (1972) call it *warning*. Payrató (1993) calls it *threat*.
Similar	Emblem.Anticipate, Emblem.Attention.
LitQua	MRR: 8 (1.0%)

Emblem.Calm

Description	Open hands, palms pointing down, are outstretched to addressee as if to calm him/her down. Also performed by pressing down hands repetitively.
Speech Sample	"<u>richtig, ja ja</u>" (MRR, LQ3-10, 0:32)
Features	HS: open, Orient: PD, Move: down.
References	Efron (1941) listed it under *go slowly, take it easy, be calm, wait, listen!* (Italian gesture). Payrató (1993) calls it *calm*. Johnson et al. (1975) list a gesture called *be calm* that may be equivalent to this. Morris (1994: 188) calls it *palm lower*, decoded as "less, please", or *palms down*, decoded as "calm down".
LitQua	MRR: 28 (3.6%), HK: 2 (0.7%)

Emblem.Despair

Description	Both hands are raised, palm facing each other, and the face makes a lamentable expression.
Speech Sample	"er ist unglaublich eitel" (MRR, LQ1-6, 1:43)
Features	HS: open, Orient: PI, Loc: head-level, FE: despair.
References	—
LitQua	MRR: 1 (0.1%), HK: 1 (0.3%)

Emblem.Dismiss

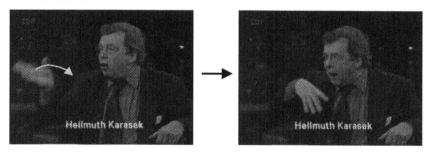

Description	Hand is wipes through the air in a downward arc as if chasing away a fly. Motion from the wrist or elbow if more expansive.
Speech Sample	"aber das ist eigentlich unser Problem nicht" (MRR, LQ2-1, 4:05)
Features	HS: open, Orient: PD, Move: downward arc.
References	Saitz and Cervenka (1972) call it *disbelief* (US gesture) and *emphasis* (Colombian gesture). Efron (1941) calls it *rejection*. Subsumes *effeminate neg* found by Webb (1997: 97) and is identical to her *sweep away* (p. 103).
Similar	Meta.Fling-Down
LitQua	MRR: 61 (7.9%), HK: 13 (4.4%)

Emblem.Doubt-Shrug

Description	Hands are opened in an outward arc, ending in a palm-up position, usually accompanied by a slight shrug and a face saying "I don't know".
Speech Sample	"daran ist der Autor schuld oder nicht schuld, ich weiß es nicht" (MRR, LQ3-6, 0:04)
Features	2H, HS: open, Orient: PU, Move: TS/arc.
References	Saitz and Cervenka (1972) call it *no information* (Colombian gesture). Payrató (1993) calls it *doubt, ignorance, impotence*. Johnson et al. (1975) have two gestures called *I don't know* and *I doubt it* which could both apply. Webb (1997: 98) calls it *no idea*. Morris (1994: 137) calls it *hands shrug*, decoded as "disclaimer", or *shoulders shrug*, decoded as "I do not know".
Similar	Emblem.So-What
LitQua	MRR: 4 (0.5%), HK: 2 (0.7%)

Emblem.Finger-Ring

Description	Forefinger and thumb touch to form a ring.
Speech Sample	"...hat das Auto <u>gut</u> verkauft" (HK, LQ3-8, 0:44)
Features	HS: finger ring, Orient: PI or PAB.
References	Saitz and Cervenka (1972) call it *perfection*. Efron (1941) calls it *just, friendship, love, marriage, precision* (Italian gesture). Kendon (1981: 154) calls it *good, perfect, OK*. Payrató (1993) calls it *all right, perfect, OK*. Weinrich (1992: 119) calls it *finger ring*. Webb (1997: 100) calls it *ring*. Morris (1994: 118) calls it *hand ring*, decoded as "OK, good" or "perfection".
Similar	Emblem.Purse
LitQua	MRR: 18 (2.3%), HK: 15 (5.1%)

Emblem.Hand-Clap

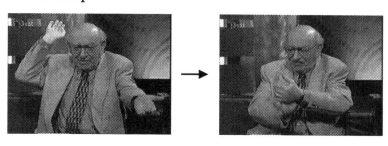

Description	Clapping both hands together or slapping the arm rest or table with one hand.
Speech Sample	"ich <u>wette</u>, Frau Löffler wird diesen Roman zerfetzen" (MRR, LQ2-5, 0:20)
Features	HS: open, Move: straight together, Loc: hands touch.
References	Saitz and Cervenka (1972) call it *emphasis* or *agreement* (the latter only Colombian).
LitQua	MRR: 2 (0.3%)

Emblem.Hand-Rub

Description	Rubbing both hands together.
Speech Sample	"sie hat <u>immer</u> feuchte Hände" (MRR, LQ2-7, 2:06)
Features	2H, Move: rubbing, Loc: hands touch.
References	Saitz and Cervenka (1972) call it *anticipation* or *thought* (the latter only US). Johnson et al. (1975) call it *anticipation*, too.
LitQua	MRR: 4 (0.5%)

Emblem.Hands-Up

Description	Hands are thrown up into the air, palms to the front.
Speech Sample	"ein manirierter <u>Stil, der nicht erträglich ist</u>" (MRR, LQ2-7, 0:52)
Features	2H, HS: open, Orient: PAB, Loc: above head.
References	Johnson et al. (1975) call it *happy hands*, decoding it as "I give up". Magno Caldognetto and Poggi (1999) call it *hands up*, decoding it as "I resign, I do not oppose you". Morris (1994: 5) calls it *arms raise* (I surrender).
Similar	Emblem.Wave
LitQua	MRR: 11 (1.4%)

Emblem.Indignation

Description	Hands are abruptly thrown up and to the side.
Speech Sample	"<u>ach</u> Kinder!" (MRR, LQ3-5, 4:48)
Features	2H, HS: open, Orient: PI, Loc: head, Move: up.
References	—
Similar	Emblem.Hands-Up
LitQua	MRR: 3 (0.4%)

Emblem.Invitation

Description	Arms are opened as if to embrace somebody. Often accompanied by a smile.
Speech Sample	"<u>kein Land</u> auf Erden hat eine so herrliche Atmosphäre" (MRR, LQ3-5, 4:44)
Features	2H, HS: open, Orient: PAB, Move: TS/arc, Loc: center → side.
References	Payrató (1993) calls it *invitation, to pass, "come in!"*.
Similar	Emblem.So-What
LitQua	MRR: 2 (0.3%)

Emblem.Knee-Slap

Description	Hand hits own knee with emphasis.
Speech Sample	"so, <u>jetzt</u> gehen wir zum nächsten Buch über" (MRR, LQ3-4, 0:09)
Features	HS: open, Move: down, Loc: center → knee.
References	—
Similar	—
LitQua	MRR: 6 (0.8%)

Emblem.More-Or-Less

Description	The open hand, palm down, swivels around the wrist.
Speech Sample	"<u>es ist da eine leise</u> oder <u>mehr</u> oder weniger starke Enttäuschung" (MRR, LQ2-1, 0:14)
Features	HS: open, Orient: PD, Move: wrist rotation.
References	Saitz and Cervenka (1972) call it *more or less*. Johnson et al. (1975) call it *so-so, about average*, decoding it with "don't know", "uncertainty". Payrató (1993) calls it *Approximately*.
Similar	—
LitQua	MRR: 15 (1.9%), HK: 1 (0.3%)

Emblem.Number

Description	Fingers stick out from the otherwise closed hand to indicate a number.
Speech Sample	"es heißt aber nicht, dass zweimal bei einem eingebrochen wird" (HK, LQ2-4, 0:58)
Features	HS: closed apart from fingers, Orient: PAB, Loc: chest/head.
References	Johnson et al. (1975) call it *counting.*
Similar	Emblem.Attention
LitQua	MRR: 6 (0.8%), HK: 4 (1.4%)

Emblem.One-Hand-Other-Hand

 →

Description	Hand shifts location from one side to the other.
Speech Sample	"was ist der Unterschied zwischen einer journalistischen und einer epischen Begabung?" (MRR, LQ3-5, 0:55)
Features	2H, Loc: center → side, Move: straight.
References	Subsumed by *location* of Webb (1997: 99).
Similar	Deictic.Space
LitQua	MRR: 16 (2.1%)

Emblem.Pray

Description	The palms of the two hands touch, finger tips pointing up, like in prayer.
Speech Sample	"diese Klischees sind ziemlich peinlich" (HK, LQ2-2, 0:33)
Features	2H, HS: open/flat, Orient: PI, Loc: palms touch
References	Kendon (1995) calls it *praying hands*. Saitz and Cervenka (1972) call it *saintliness*. Johnson et al. (1975) have a gesture called *pleading* that may be this one. Efron (1941) calls it *prayer, plea* or *pleading*. Morris (1994: 140) calls it *hands wring*, decoded as "please help me", or *palms contact*, decoded as "prayer".
Similar	—
LitQua	MRR: 1 (0.1%), HK: 2 (0.7%)

Emblem.Purse

Description	All fingertips of the hand touch and point up.
Speech Sample	"die Zensur zwingt einen, vorsichtig zu schreiben" (MRR, LQ2-1, 2:15)
Features	HS: finger-bunch, Orient: PU, Move: up/down.
References	Called *mano a borsa* by Poggi (1983), *tulip hand* by Bitti and Poggi (1991), *purse hand* by Kendon (1995). Efron (1941) calls it *what do you want?*. Kendon (1981: 154) calls it *good, query, criticism*. Weinrich (1992: 115) calls it *pointed hand*. Morris (1994: 110) calls it *hand purse*, decoded as "query" or "good".
Similar	Emblem.Finger-Ring
LitQua	MRR: 10 (1.3%), HK: 3 (1.0%)

Emblem.Refuse

Description	Flat hand with palm toward addressee or hand with extended forefinger is moved outward in a wiping motion.
Speech Sample	"das soll der Journa<u>list</u> nicht tun" (MRR, LQ3-5, 1:27)
Features	HS: open or forefinger, Orient: PAB, Loc: center → side, Move: straight.
References	Saitz and Cervenka (1972) call it *no* (Colombian gesture): index finger is moved from side to side. Efron (1941) calls it *no, no!* (Italian gesture): index finger moved slowly from side to side. Payrató (1993) calls it *negation*. Webb (1997: 99) subsumes it under *none*. Subsumes *forefinger wag* by Morris (1994: 89), decoded as "no!".
Similar	Emblem.Wipe, Emblem.Block
LitQua	MRR: 9 (1.2%), HK: 2 (0.7%)

Emblem.Small

Description	Forefinger and thumb almost touch, leaving only a small space in-between, while the rest of the hand is closed.
Speech Sample	"beim Romancier kommt es auf jeden Zwischenraum, zwischen den Zeilen, darauf kommt es an" (MRR, LQ3-5, 1:10)
Features	HS: thumb and forefinger almost touch, Orient: PI, Loc: chest/head.
References	Johnson et al. (1975) have a gesture called *something small*. Payrató (1993) calls it *little*.
Similar	Emblem.Finger-Ring
LitQua	MRR: 2 (0.3%), HK: 6 (2.0%)

Emblem.So-What

Description	Hands are opened and moved outward in an arc as if to show the empty palms.
Speech Sample	"warum versagt er im Westen?" (MRR, LQ2-1, 0:48)
Features	HS: open, Orient: PU and PAB, Loc: center → side, Move: TS/arc.
References	Payrató (1993) calls it *indifference, ignorance* or *innocence*. Morris (1994: 197) calls it *palms up*, decoded as "I swear!".
Similar	Emblem.Doubt-Shrug
LitQua	MRR: 35 (4.5%), HK: 2 (0.7%)

Emblem.Strong

Description	Hand is formed to a fist.
Speech Sample	"…dass Sie eine Vorliebe haben für kämpfende <u>Frauen</u>" (MRR, LQ1-7, 0:52)
Features	HS: fist.
References	Saitz and Cervenka (1972) call it *anger*. Efron (1941) calls it *absolutely no/yes* (Italian gesture). Morris (1994: 70) calls it *fist clench*, decoded as "power", or *fist shake*, decoded as "threat" or "we won!".
Similar	—
LitQua	MRR: 33 (4.3%), HK: 7 (2.4%)

Emblem.Wave

Description	The flat hand is outstretched, upward, palm toward the addressee with small sideways movements, like waving somebody hello.
Speech Sample	"wie ein Autor einen Roman beginnt ist sehr wichtig" (MRR, LQ2-7, 0:32)
Features	HS: open, Orient: PAB, Move: waving, Loc: above head.
References	Webb (1997: 96) calls it *attention*. Morris (1994: 1) calls it *arm raise* (request for attention).
Similar	Emblem.Block
LitQua	MRR: 4 (0.5%), HK: 1 (0.3%)

Emblem.Wipe

Description	Flat hands, palms down, start near (above) each other and move apart in a straight, wiping motion.
Speech Sample	"er hat keine Zeit für sowas" (MRR, LQ1-4, 1:42)
Features	HS: open, Orient: PD, Loc: center → side, Move: TS/straight.
References	Saitz and Cervenka (1972) call it *termination*. Johnson et al. (1975) have a gesture called *finished* that could be this one. Efron (1941) calls it *finished, through* (Italian gesture). Payrató (1993) calls it *enough, end*. Webb (1997: 99) subsumes it under *none*.
Similar	—
LitQua	MRR: 28 (3.6%), HK: 1 (0.3%)

B.3   Deictics

Deictic.Addressee

Description	Hand is pointing toward the addressee, possibly with forefinger outstretched.
Speech Sample	"ich <u>will Ihnen</u> gerne recht geben" (HK, LQ1-5, 0:36)
Features	HS: open or forefinger, Orient: pointed at addressee
References	Efron (1941) calls it *you, this, that* (Italian gesture). Magno Caldognetto and Poggi (1999) call it *accusative index finger* on a second-layer interpretation. Weinrich (1992: 113) calls it *stretch hand* or *forefinger*. Subsumes *to you* by Webb (1997: 103). Morris (1994: 85) calls it *forefinger point*, decoded as indicating direction or "threat".
Similar	Meta.Cup
LitQua	MRR: 23 (3.0%), HK: 13 (4.4%)

Deictic.Person

Description	Hand points toward a person that is neither the speaker him-/herself nor the addressee, possibly with forefinger outstretched.
Speech Sample	"... und <u>eigentlich, wie Karasek gesagt hat</u>, drei-, dreihundert Seiten lang total unlesbar" (MRR, LQ3-5, 0:40)
Features	HS: open or forefinger, Orient: pointed at a person (neither speaker nor addressee)
References	—
Similar	—
LitQua	MRR: 3 (0.4%)

Deictic.Self

Description	Speaker points with one hand or both hands to him-/herself, using the flat hand, forefinger or thumb, usually on the height of the chest.
Speech Sample	"<u>mir</u> persönlich gefällt ganz besonders die letzte Geschichte" (MRR, LQ3-10, 0:08)
Features	HS: open or forefinger, Orient: PTB and pointing at oneself
References	Saitz and Cervenka (1972) call it *self*. Johnson et al. (1975) call it *me*. Efron (1941) also calls it *me* (Italian gesture). Payrató (1993) calls it *sincerity, oath*. Webb (1997: 102) calls it *self/to self*. Morris (1994: 23, 24) calls it *chest hold, chest point*, or *chest tap* (me?).
Similar	—
LitQua	MRR: 9 (1.2%)

Deictic.Self+Addressee

Description	Hand alternates between pointing at the addressee and the speaker.
Speech Sample	"unsere Gespräche, die waren ja dramatisch, <u>als wir allein</u> uns darüber unterhielten" (MRR, LQ1-7, 0:38)
Features	HS: open or forefinger, Orient: pointing at oneself → pointing at addressee, Move: back and forth.
References	Webb (1997: 102) calls it *self-other*.
Similar	—
LitQua	MRR: 2 (0.3%)

Deictic.Space

Description	Hand or forefinger points into the space in front of the speaker, usually down.
Speech Sample	"<u>diese</u> Figuren haben wir hier bei ihm nicht mehr" (MRR, LQ3-10, 1:01)
Features	HS: open or forefinger, Orient: PD or PI (pointing into center space).
References	Efron (1941) calls it *here, now, down* or *you, this, that* (Italian gestures). McNeill (1992: 173, 154) calls it *abstract pointing*.
Similar	—
LitQua	MRR: 40 (5.2%), HK: 7 (2.4%)

B.4   Iconics

Iconic.Away

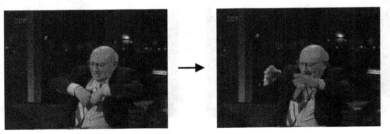

Description	Hand makes a movement away from the speaker.
Speech Sample	"und mitten aus diesem zweiten Liebesfrühling einfach wegläuft" (HK, LQ1-1, 2:09)
Features	Orient: PI, Loc: stomach level, Move: AB/straight.
References	Efron (1941) calls it *go away, get out, he got out, he got away* (Italian gesture). Payrató (1993) calls it *to pass, move along!*.
Similar	—
LitQua	MRR: 3 (0.4%), HK: 8 (2.7%)

Iconic.Drink

Description	Hand performs action as if speaker would drink from a glass.
Speech Sample	"...ich kann die Männer um die Finger <u>wickeln</u>, und der Mann besäuft sich" (HK, LQ3-8, 0:38)
Features	HS: holding a glass, Loc: center → mouth, Move: short tilt at mouth
References	A *kinetograph* according to Ekman and Friesen (1969). Called *drink* by Saitz and Cervenka (1972) (Colombian gesture), Efron (1941) (Italian gesture) and Poyatos (1975). Morris (1994: 106) calls it *hand 'drink'*, decoded as "drink".
Similar	—
LitQua	HK: 1 (0.3%)

Iconic.Explode

Description	Hands start at stomach level and move abruptly upward and outward as if propelled by an explosion.
Speech Sample	"zwischen den Zeilen sind Explosionen" (MRR, LQ3-10, 1:20)
Features	2H, Orient: PI, Loc: center → side, Move: TS/arc.
References	Efron (1941: 101) calls it *a tremendous explosion* (Jewish gesture).
Similar	Meta.Emerge
LitQua	MRR: 5 (0.6%)

Iconic.Fall

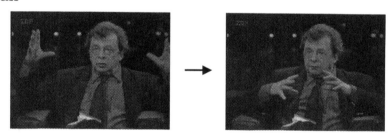

Description	Hands with palms down fall from chest level down to stomach level.
Speech Sample	"und fällt den Frauen dann umso heftiger in die Hände" (HK, LQ1-1, 1:52)
Features	2H, HS: open, Orient: PD, Loc: chest → stomach, Move: straight.
References	—
Similar	Meta.Umbrella
LitQua	HK: 2 (0.7%)

Iconic.Front-Back-Distance

Description	One hand is positioned in front of the other, both parallel to the speaker's body, with a small distance in-between.
Speech Sample	"soweit man das in dieser Übersetzung merkt" (HK, LQ2-4, 0:11)
Features	2H, HS: open, Orient: PTB, Loc: stomach.
References	—
Similar	—
LitQua	MRR: 1 (0.1%), HK: 1 (0.3%)

Iconic.Grab

Description	The open hand contracts all fingers in a grabbing motion.
Speech Sample	"den Booker-Preis, den er bekommen hat, hat er nicht selber angenommen" (MRR, LQ1-4, 1:37)
Features	HS: open → fist.
References	A *kinetograph* according to Ekman and Friesen (1969). Webb (1997: 101) calls it *grasp-1 hand* or *graph-2 hand*.
Similar	—
LitQua	MRR: 5 (0.6%)

Iconic.Merge

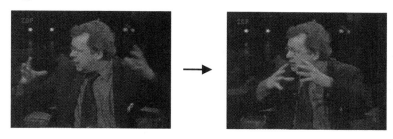

Description	The two claw-like hands, palms facing each other, are moved toward each other and back multiple times.
Speech Sample	"...dieser Situation, die er da schildert, <u>das hat sich mir</u> nicht zusammengetan" (HK, LQ1-3, 1:03)
Features	2H, HS: claw, Orient: PI, Loc: side → center, Move: back and forth.
References	Could be *each other* or *together* found by Webb (1997: 97).
Similar	—
LitQua	MRR: 5 (0.6%), HK: 4 (1.4%)

Iconic.Page

Description	The open, flat hand is shown as if to represent a page while the other hand points toward it.
Speech Sample	"...indem er auf <u>die</u> Titelseite drucken lässt: Roman" (MRR, LQ3-6, 0:41)
Features	2H, HS1: open, HS2: open or forefinger, Orient1: PI or PAB, Orient2: pointing at other hand.
References	—
Similar	—
LitQua	MRR: 4 (0.5%)

Iconic.Sway

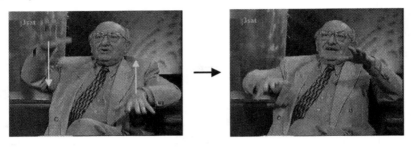

Description	Both open hands, palms down, alternate in an up-down movement.
Speech Sample	"das <u>Buch</u> [äh] oszilliert" (MRR, LQ2-7, 0:40)
Features	2H, HS: open, Orient: PD, Move: hands alternate in up-down motion.
References	—
Similar	—
LitQua	MRR: 3 (0.4%), HK: 1 (0.3%)

Iconic.To-Fro

Description	Both hands move from one side to the other.
Speech Sample	"das Buch [äh] oszilliert, <u>es es</u> schwankt zwischen verschiedenen sprachlichen Ebenen" (MRR, LQ2-7, 0:40)
Features	2H, HS: open, Orient: PI, Loc: center → side → other side
References	Webb (1997: 96) calls it *alternate*.
Similar	Emblem.One-Hand-Other-Hand
LitQua	MRR: 2 (0.3%)

Iconic.Write

Description	Hand imitates the act of writing.
Speech Sample	"es heißt <u>immer: J. M.</u>" (MRR, LQ1-4, 1:22)
Features	HS: holding a pen, Move: writing.
References	A kinetograph according to Ekman and Friesen (1969). Payrató (1993) calls it *bill, to write*. Morris (1994: 132) calls it *hand 'write'*, decoded as "please bring me the bill".
Similar	—
LitQua	MRR: 2 (0.3%)

B.5   Metaphorics

Meta.Aura

Description	Both hands are held at head level as if touching a sphere around the head.
Speech Sample	"weil man <u>denkt</u> zuerst, das ist die übliche Geschichte" (HK, LQ1-3, 0:07)
Features	2H, HS: open, Orient: PTB, Loc: head.
References	Called a *metaphor of mental states* by McNeill (1992: 158)
Similar	Emblem.Despair
LitQua	MRR: 1 (0.1%), HK: 4 (1.4%)

Meta.Bridge

Description	The forefinger traces an arc, moving to the side, either outward or inward.
Speech Sample	"... wo ein Mann, <u>nach</u> dem Tod seiner Frau,..." (HK, LQ1-1, 1:21)
Features	HS: forefinger, Loc: center → side, Move: arc.
References	An *ideograph* that is "tracing the direction of thought" (Poyatos, 1975: 219). Morris (1994: 84) calls it *forefinger hop*, decoded as "tomorrow".
Similar	Meta.Progress
LitQua	MRR: 2 (0.3%), HK: 14 (4.7%)

Meta.Chop

Description	Open, tense hand cuts downward in an abrupt motion.
Speech Sample	"... wo ein Mann, <u>nach</u> dem Tod seiner Frau,..." (HK, LQ1-1, 1:21)
Features	HS: open/tense
References	Weinrich (1992: 115) calls it *chopping hand*. Webb (1997: 97) calls it *chop*. Morris (1994: 103) calls a similar gesture *hand chop*, decoded as "I cut through the argument".
Similar	Beat
LitQua	MRR: 19, HK: 5

Meta.Clockwork

Description	The forefinger of the hand performs a circular movement near the temple of the speaker
Speech Sample	"... worüber <u>er sehr verstört</u> ist" (HK, LQ2-6, 0:14)
Features	HS: forefinger, Orient: pointing at temple, Loc: head, Move: circular.
References	Saitz and Cervenka (1972) call it *insanity* (finger circles) or *intelligence* (finger taps temple). Efron (1941) calls it *crazy* (Italian gesture, circling). Payrató (1993) calls it *mad, madness*. Subsumed by *mental* found by Webb (1997: 100). Morris (1994: 202) calls it *temple circle*, decoded as "crazy!".
Similar	—
LitQua	HK: 2 (0.7%)

Meta.Cup

Description	Open, cup-shaped hand, palm up, is held in front of the speaker at stomach height.
Speech Sample	"was <u>ist das für ein Mann?</u>" (MRR, LQ1-6, 0:34)
Features	HS: open, Orient: PU, Loc: stomach.
References	McNeill (1992: 147ff.) subsumes it under *conduit* metaphorics. Saitz and Cervenka (1972) call it *what happened?* (Colombian gesture). Efron (1941) calls it *don't you see?* (Italian gesture). Webb (1997: 98) calls it *idea on palm*. Morris (1994: 196) calls it *palms up*, decoded as "I implore you".
Similar	—
LitQua	MRR: 21 (2.7%), HK: 15 (5.1%)

Meta.Cup-Flip

Description	Open, cup-shaped hand is brought into palm-up position in a small arc.
Speech Sample	"jedoch: wir wissen, er wurde aus dem Japanischen ins Englische übersetzt" (MRR, LQ2-5, 0:55)
Features	HS: open, Orient: PU, Loc: stomach, Move: small arc (movement from the wrist).
References	Weinrich (1992: 109) calls it *rolling hands*. See also references of Meta.Cup. Webb (1997: 97) subsumes it under *contrast*, it also matches with her *new idea*.
Similar	Beat
LitQua	MRR: 17 (2.2%), HK: 34 (11.5%)

Meta.Dome

Description	Open hand, palm down, traces the surface of a dome or sphere in front of the speaker at stomach height.
Speech Sample	"...oder ein Studio, durch das man geführt wird" (HK, LQ1-5, 1:00)
Features	HS: open, Orient: PD, Loc: stomach, Move: tracing dome.
References	—
Similar	Meta.Umbrella
LitQua	MRR: 21 (2.7%), HK: 6 (2.0%)

Meta.Emerge

Description	Hands rise from stomach level upward and slightly outward.
Speech Sample	"das heißt, <u>dass der Text etwas</u> weckt beim Leser, was gar nicht expressis verbis gesagt wurde" (MRR, LQ3-5, 1:45)
Features	2H, Orient: PI → PU, Loc: stomach → head, Move: slight arc outward.
References	Weinrich (1992: 116) calls it *upward hand*. Both *revelation* and *alot* found by Webb (1997: 101, 96) could apply.
Similar	Iconic.Explode
LitQua	MRR: 5 (0.6%), HK: 6 (2.0%)

Meta.Fling-Down

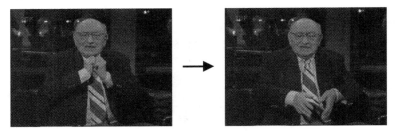

Description	Hands act as if holding something, then throwing it to the ground.
Speech Sample	"also fleißig ist er, fleißig und eitel und <u>ab</u>stoßend wie Richard Wagner" (MRR, LQ1-6, 0:59)
Features	2H, HS: → open, Orient: PI → PD, Loc: stomach, Move: straight down.
References	McNeill (1992: 147ff.) calls it *conduit* metaphoric.
Similar	Meta.Frame, Emblem.Dismiss
LitQua	MRR: 48 (6.2%)

Meta.Frame

Description	Both hands are held some inches apart, palms facing each other, as if holding something.
Speech Sample	"diese <u>Talkshow</u> ist die beste Satire auf eine Talkshow" (HK, LQ1-5, 0:41)
Features	2H, HS: open, Orient: PI, Loc: stomach or chest.
References	McNeill (1992: 147ff.) calls it *conduit* metaphoric. Weinrich (1992: 111) calls it *frame hands*.
Similar	—
LitQua	MRR: 35 (4.5%), HK: 20 (6.8%)

Meta.Heart

Description	Claw-shaped hand, palm facing the speaker's body, is held at chest level, either coming forward in an arc or staying there.
Speech Sample	"<u>wie seine Leiden</u> dargestellt werden, das steht alles zwischen den Zeilen" (MRR, LQ3-10, 1:56)
Features	HS: claw, Orient: PTB → PU, Loc: chest, Move: TS/arc.
References	—
Similar	Meta.Progress, Deictic.Self
LitQua	MRR: 18 (2.3%), HK: 2 (0.7%)

Meta.Idea

Description	Hand starts near the head, usually at the temple, and moves away from there.
Speech Sample	"diese Prosa hat etwas ungeheuer Befreiendes, weil sie in der Phantasie des Lebens etwas freisetzt" (HK, LQ3-8, 0:57)
Features	HS: open or forefinger, Orient: PTB → PI, Loc: head, Move: AB.
References	Payrató (1993) calls it *to remember, idea*. Subsumed by *mental* found by Webb (1997: 100). Morris (1994: 205) calls it *temple touch*, decoded as "I have an idea!".
Similar	Meta.Clockwork
LitQua	MRR: 5 (0.6%), HK: 4 (1.4%)

Meta.Open

Description	Closed hand opens abruptly.
Speech Sample	"eine deutliche Intelligenz des Autors" (MRR, LQ3-4, 0:56)
Features	HS: closed → open.
References	Kendon (1995) refers to it as the *transformation from finger bunch to open hand*.
Similar	—
LitQua	MRR: 3 (0.4%)

Meta.Progress

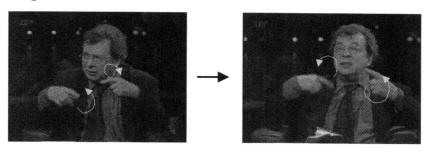

Description	Hand moves in circles where in the upper arc the hand moves away from the body (progressive direction according to Calbris, 1990: 92).
Speech Sample	"was der Romancier mit den Worten, die er schreibt, <u>anregt</u> in der Phantasie des Lesers" (MRR, LQ3-5, 1:17)
Features	Move: progressive circle.
References	Saitz and Cervenka (1972) call it *complication* (Colombian gesture). McNeill (1992: 159) calls it a *metaphor of change*, more specifically of *transition*. Payrató (1993) calls it *continuity, repetition*. Calbris (1990: 69, 92) takes it as a gesture of *development, unfolding, repetition, evolution*. Webb (1997: 101) calls it *process* (maybe her *repeated* applies, too).
Similar	Meta.Clockwork
LitQua	MRR: 9 (1.2%), HK: 3 (1.0%)

Meta.Regress

Description	Hand moves in circles where in the upper arc the hand moves toward the body (regressive direction according to Calbris, 1990: 92).
Speech Sample	"wir wissen, er wurde aus dem Japanischen ins Englische übersetzt [...] und nun aus'm Englischen ins Deutsche" (MRR, LQ2-5, 0:56)
Features	Move: regressive circle.
References	Calbris (1990: 92) takes it as a gesture of *starting over, anteriority, origin.*
Similar	—
LitQua	MRR: 2 (0.3%), HK: 1 (0.3%)

Meta.Snatch

Description	Hand, in a movement toward the body, suddenly closes as if catching something mid-air.
Speech Sample	"sehr zum Unwillen von Frau Löffler" (MRR, LQ3-5, 0:22)
Features	HS: open → fist, Orient: → PTB, Move: TB.
References	Weinrich (1992: 117) calls it *catch hand.*
Similar	—
LitQua	MRR: 12 (1.6%)

Meta.Thought-Grip

Description	Open hand is held near the forehead, palm toward head.
Speech Sample	"...dass Thomas Bernhard solche Verhältnisse in eine Dämonie treiben kann, wo kein Ausweg mehr bleibt" (HK, LQ1-5, 0:27)
Features	HS: open, Orient: PTB, Loc: forehead.
References	Called a metaphoric of mental states by McNeill (1992: 158)
Similar	Meta.Aura
LitQua	MRR: 6 (0.8%), HK: 3 (1.0%)

Meta.Umbrella

Description	Hand is held in front of speaker, palm down, as if touching a spherical object from above.
Speech Sample	"und der neue Roman [...] zeigt im Mittelpunkt einen Juden" (MRR, LQ3-4, 1:27)
Features	HS: open, Orient: PD, Move: down.
References	Kendon (1980: 213) calls it *umbrella gesture*.
Similar	Meta.Dome
LitQua	MRR: 14 (1.8%), HK: 1 (0.3%)

Meta.Walls

Description	Both hands, palms facing each other, are held side by side, as if framing something. Hands are flat open, almost stiff.
Speech Sample	"mich hat <u>eine Sache</u> an dem Roman gestört: die Oper, die er [äh] da schreiben will" (HK, LQ1-3, 0:49)
Features	HS: flat open, Orient: PI, Loc: stomach or chest.
References	Weinrich (1992: 108) calls it *wall hands*.
Similar	Meta.Frame
LitQua	MRR: 1 (0.1%), HK: 10 (3.4%)

B.6 Beats

Description	A quick, short stroke downwards with an open hand. Usually performed in a series of strokes. Hand shape and location can vary, though usually the hand is open, the location is somewhere in center space.
References	Weinrich (1992: 114) calls it *tact hand* or *chopping hand*.
LitQua	MRR: 49 (6.3%), HK: 42 (14.2%)

www.ingramcontent.com/pod-product-compliance
Lightning Source LLC
Chambersburg PA
CBHW060527060326
40690CB00017B/3412